DOMESTIC INJUNCTIONS

by

Margaret de Haas
Christine Bispham

LONDON
SWEET & MAXWELL LTD
1998

Published in 1998 by
Sweet & Maxwell Limited of
100 Avenue Road
Swiss Cottage
London NW3 3PF
http://www.smlawpub.co.uk

Phototypeset by LBJ Typesetting Ltd
of Kingsclere
Printed and bound in Great Britain by
MPG Books Ltd, Bodmin, Cornwall

A CIP Catalogue record for this book
is available from The British Library

ISBN 0421 49860 9

DOMESTIC INJUNCTIONS

AUSTRALIA
LBC Information Services
Sydney

CANADA AND USA
Carswell
Toronto

NEW ZEALAND
Brooker's
Auckland

SINGAPORE and MALAYSIA
Thomson Information (S.E. Asia)
Singapore

FOREWORD

It is always a pleasure to write a foreword to any work whose purpose is to assist busy practitioners to discharge their duties of sound advice and effective representation to clients who are consulting them in moments of deep personal need and crisis. The pleasure is the greater where, as here, the authors themselves know and experience the pressure of those duties and therefore know well what is needed.

Part IV of the Family Law Act 1996 radically overhauls the law on domestic violence and the family home. Whilst many cases decided under the old law would have a similar outcome under the new, there have been significant changes in the range of potential applicants and respondents as well as important changes to the procedural and substantive law. Practitioners will be grateful for access to an informed and easy to use guide to that new law and procedure; they will discover that in this book the authors have done them a valuable service.

Those familiar with the earlier edition of this work will, no doubt, be waiting expectantly for this. There will, however, be others who will also discover here a valuable tool in carrying out what those of us involved know to be a stressful area of practice. The late (and sadly missed) Judge Nance said in the original foreword that he foresaw the book as a valuable judicial aid as well; the same will, I expect, be true of the new edition.

JUDGE MARK HEDLEY

PREFACE

The Family Law Act 1996 is to be welcomed, as it removes the gaps, anomalies and inconsistencies in previous statutory remedies and/or common law remedies. It simplifies the law relating to domestic injunctions and accordingly makes the task for both the Court and the Practitioner easier.

At the same time, the level of of protection previously available has been maintained and hopefully improved.

This book clearly and concisely sets out the following:—

(a) the principles under-pinning the law as it now stands;
(b) a questionnaire to be completed by clients so that the relevant paper work can be submitted quickly and accurately;
(c) a clear outline as to how to obtain an injunction against molestation with concise explanations as to the key definitions under the Act;
(d) a clear explanation as to how to obtain an Occupation Order with full explanation as to the new terms under the Act and the range of orders available and the tests to be applied.

This book concentrates on practice and procedure so that the Practitioner is left in no doubt as to what to do, how to do it and the traps to avoid.

The current law relating to enforcement of orders and, in particular, the enforcement of undertakings is dealt with in detail together with the important aspect of injunctions and children.

No book on injunctions would be complete without a detailed chapter on the law relating to committals and the traps which seek to ensnare the Practitioner in such applications.

Tortious injunctions are again not forgotten as they represent a distinct area—unconnected to the new Act. Similarly, injunctions to preserve property are also covered.

This book, as in the first edition, has a handy case file together with other appendices covering useful High Court rules and/or County Court rules together with the relevant practice directions and statutory provisions.

We have tried to cater for the busy Practitioner who needs a ready reference covering anything and everything which may crop up in daily practice.

We could not have written this book without the considerable assistance from the publishers, Sweet & Maxwell.

Our work is in no small measure due to the considerable patience and diligence of our typists, Jeanette Woodrow, Alex Morris, Amanda McEwan and Christine Fletcher.

The assistance we have received does not excuse any errors which may be found. For such errors, we crave forgiveness and understanding in this new and very exciting development of the law.

MARGARET R. DE HAAS

CHRISTINE BISPHAM

September 1997

CONTENTS

Chapter One—INTRODUCTION

Chapter Two—PRINCIPLES

Chapter Three—PRACTICE AND PROCEDURE

Chapter Four—TORTIOUS INJUNCTIONS

Chapter Five—COMMITTAL

Chapter Six—INJUNCTIONS TO PRESERVE PROPERTY

APPENDICES

ABBREVIATIONS

AJA	Administration of Justice Act 1960
AC	Appeal Cases
All ER	All England Reports
CCA 1984	County Courts Act 1984
CA 1989	Children Act 1989
CJA 1982	Criminal Justice Act 1982
CJA 1991	Criminal Justice Act 1991
CCA 1981	Contempt of Court Act 1981
CMLR	Common Market Law Reports
CCR	County Court Rules
CR	Chancery Reports
CL	Current Law
CAT	Court of Appeal Transcript
CLSA 1990	Courts and Legal Services Act 1990
CLY	Current Law Year Book
Cr.App.R(s)	Criminal Appeal Reports (sentencing)
DVMPA 1976	Domestic Violence and Matrimonial Proceedings Act 1976
DC	Divisional Court
DPMCA 1978	Domestic Proceedings and Magistrates' Courts Act 1978
ECJ	European Court of Justice
ECR	European Court Reports
EPO	Emergency Protection Order
FLR	Family Law Reports
FLA 1996	Family Law Act 1996
FPC(CA 1989) Rules 1991	Family Proceedings Courts (Children Act 1989) Rules 1991

FCR	Family Court Reports
FPR 1991	Family Proceedings Rules 1991
GMA 1971	Guardianship of Minors Act 1971
HLR	Housing Law Reports
ICO	Interim Care order
KB	Kings Bench Reports
Law Com	Law Commission
LR (H & W a 1962	Law Reform (Husband and Wife) Act 1962
LS Gaz.	Law Society Gazette
LT Jo	Law Times Journal
New LJ	New Law Journal
MHA 1983	Matrimonial Homes Act 1983
MCA 1980	Magistrates' Courts Act 1980
MCA 1973	Matrimonial Causes Act 1973
PHA 1997	Protection from Harassment Act 1997
P	Probate Reports
QBD	Queens Bench Division
QB	Queens Bench Reports
RPC	Restrictive Practices Court
RSC	Rules of the Supreme Court
SCA 1981	Supreme Court Act 1981
SCP	Supreme Court Practice
SJ Sol. Jo. }	Solicitors Journal
WLR	Weekly Law Reports

TABLE OF CASES

TABLE OF PRACTICE DIRECTIONS

TABLE OF STATUTES

TABLE OF RULES

Family Proceedings Rules 1991

COUNTY COURT RULES

Rules of the Supreme Court

CHAPTER ONE

Introduction

1. Origins of the Family Law Act 1996

- 1989—Law Commission publish consultation paper: *Domestic Violence and* 1–01
  Occupation of the Family Home (Law Com. working paper No. 113 HMSO).
- May 1992—Law Commission publish Report of the same title (Law Com. No.
  207)—contains recommendations for reform of family law remedies available
  for the "two distinct but inseparable problems" of:

  (a) providing protection for one member of a family against molestation or
      violence by another; and
  (b) regulating occupation of the family home on relationship breakdown
      (temporary or permanent).

- 1995—Family Homes and Domestic Violence Bill gives effect to almost all of 1–02
  the recommendations; is considered to be one of the less contentious areas of
  law reform, but fails to get through the Commons and is withdrawn in
  November 1995.
- 1996—reform proposals re-emerge (with some amendments and additions) in
  the Family Law Bill, Pt 3.
- July 4, 1996—Family Law Bill (as further amended) given Royal Assent; the
  law relating to domestic violence and family homes is enacted in the Family
  Law Act 1996, Pt 4.

2. Previous Civil Remedies

Need for Reform

The previous civil law relating to domestic violence and occupation of the family 1–03
home was described by Lord Scarman in *Richards v. Richards* [1984] A.C. 174, HL as

"a hotchpot of enactments of limited scope passed into law to meet specific situations or to strengthen the powers of specified Courts. The sooner the range, scope and effect of these powers are rationalised into a coherent and comprehensive body of statute law, the better."

Previous Sources of Jurisdiction

1–04   The Courts powers to grant ouster and/or non-molestation orders were derived from a number of sources, each with its own criteria:

— DVMPA 1976 (County Courts)
— DPMCA 1978 (Magistrates Courts)
— MHA 1983 (High Court and County Courts)
— Matrimonial suits (High Court and County Courts)
— Tort actions (High Court and County Courts)
— Wardship (High Court).

Anomalies in Available Remedies

1–05 (a)   Remedies under DVMPA 1976 were available to spouses and to men and women living together as husband and wife. The DPMCA 1978 and MHA 1983 only applied to spouses.

(b)   Power of arrest was available under DVMPA 1976 and DPMCA 1978—not under MHA 1983 or in tort.

(c)   Under MHA 1983 Court could make ancillary orders re discharge of outgoings or payments for occupation—no such power existed under DVMPA or DPMCA.

(d)   Under DVMPA 1976 there was provision to allow the exclusion of the respondent from an area around the family home—not possible under DPMCA 1978 or MHA 1983, and was not ordinarily available in tort.

(e)   Non-molestation injunctions were available under DVMPA 1976—not under DPMCA 1978 or MHA 1983.

(f)   The DVMPA 1976 did not specify the criteria applicable in ouster applications for the exercise of the Courts discretion. These were laid down by the Courts in exercising their own discretion. These criteria were not, however, applied in applications for exclusion orders under DPMCA 1978—the Act had its own criteria mainly based on the use or threat of violence and danger of injury.

Problems in Practice

1–06 (a)   Under DVMPA 1976 the Court could attach a power of arrest to injunctions restraining violence, but not to non-molestation orders or orders restraining threats of violence.

(b) Exclusion orders under DVMPA 1976 related to the "matrimonial home" (or cohabitees equivalent)—no exclusion zone available where applicant has fled, *e.g.* to mother's/friend's home and respondent comes round to harass her.

(c) Under DVMPA 1976 jurisdiction problems arose, *e.g.* where:

(i) spouses were divorced and not living together;

(ii) cohabitees no longer lived together, and the violence upon which the applicant relied did not happen when they were cohabiting.

(*e.g.*: *Pidduck v. Molloy*, *The Times*, March 9, 1992, CA; *Duo v. Duo* [1992] 1 W.L.R. 611, CA).

(d) Where DVMPA 1976 did not apply to the parties' relationship, the alternative was to proceed in tort, with a more cumbersome procedure—difficulties arose over the precise scope of the protection available against molestation.

(e) There were a number of apparently conflicting decisions on the question of whether County Courts had a general inherent power to protect the interests of children where the case fell outside DVMPA 1976.
(See *Quinn* [1983] 4 FLR 394; *Webb* [1986] 1 FLR 541; *Wilde* [1988] 2 FLR 83; *Ainsbury v. Millington* [1986] 1 FLR 331; *P v. P* (ouster) [1993] Fam. Law 283).

(f) Under MHA 1983 the Court could regulate the rights of spouses to occupy the matrimonial home, but difficulties arose where other family members had rights to occupy the home: *e.g. Kalsi v. Kalsi* (1992) Fam. Law 333, CA.

Previous Law—the result

". . . different remedies . . . available to different applicants on different criteria 1–07 in different Courts with different enforcement procedures [resulting] in a vastly complicated system, made even more confusing by the complex inter-relationship between the statutory remedies and the general principles of property and tort law." (Law Com. 207 para 2.24).
Further, the law provided "no protection for a number of people who [had] the misfortune to fall outside the specific categories of people covered by the different Acts, but may nevertheless have a clear need for such protection" (*ibid.* para. 2.28).

3. Family Law Act 1996

The Law Commission's aims

(a) Remove the gaps, anomalies and inconsistencies in the previous remedies, 1–08 with a view to synthesising them, so far as possible, into a clear, simple and comprehensive code;

(b) Maintain (and hopefully improve) the level of protection previously available;

(c) Avoid increasing hostilities between the adults involved, so far as that is compatible with providing proper and effective protection both for adults and for children.

(d) Remove unnecessary distinctions between different Courts and where possible give them uniform powers within a unified jurisdiction.

The new legislation—effect (Law Com. para. 1.5)

1–09 (a) Provides a "unified body of law" with a single consistent set of remedies available in all Courts having jurisdiction in family matters (with some specific limitations on Magistrates Courts' powers);

(b) Repeals DVMPA 1976 and DPMCA 1978, ss. 16–18
Repeals (but substantially re-enacts) MHA 1983
Amends Children Act 1989;

(c) Recognises that domestic violence is not limited to violence between spouses and cohabiting partners, but is present in many other forms of relationship—widens range of persons who are eligible to apply for statutory protection;

(d) Simplifies the law and reduces the need to seek injunctive relief under the Courts inherent jurisdiction, as orders ancillary to matrimonial proceedings or actions in tort. The right to seek such orders is not restricted, and will doubtless form a "safety-net" for those applicants who are not caught by the new legislation;

(e) Provides for a flexible new scheme with "two distinct kinds of remedy, a non-molestation order and an occupation order, each with its own criteria and incidents but capable of combination with one another and with other family law remedies in an appropriate case" (Law Com. para. 2.48).

CHAPTER TWO

Principles

A. Domestic Injunction Questionnaire

The following questionnaire is designed to cover those instructions usually required 2–01
in injunction proceedings. Attention is particularly drawn to part C of the first
section where contact with children is possible despite an injunction (sight should
not, however, be lost of the fact that emergency Legal Aid will be required in many
cases).

Background

A. In respect of the proposed parties:

— Full names/ages   2–02
— Present addresses
— Nature of parties' relationship *e.g.*:

- Present/former spouses/cohabitants: Address of last place of cohabitation.
  Date of marriage/divorce; when cohabitation commenced/ended.
- Share/have shared same household: Date when sharing commenced/ended;
  particulars of domestic arrangements; check legal relationship: is one party
  "merely" the other's employee, tenant, lodger or boarder?
- Relatives; do parties fall within FLA 1996, s.63(1)?
- Agreed to marry: when? any evidence in writing/by engagement ring/
  witnessed ceremony? Has agreement terminated? If so, when and in what
  circumstances?

B. In respect of any children:

— Full name(s)   2–03
— Date(s) of birth

— With whom they are presently living
— In respect of each child—full names of the parents
— In respect of each child—who has/has had parental responsibility in respect of the child.

C. In respect of any other proceedings:

2–04 — Are you and respondent parties in any other proceedings?
— If YES—what do they relate to? (Children, finance, property etc)
— Are there any other parties? In which Court?—give dates and details of any orders made so far/future hearings.

D. In relation to residence/contact:

2–05 — Do you have residence of the children?
If YES—give dates of order and Court
If NO —

(i) Who does? Under a Court Order?
(ii) Is it your present intention to apply for residence?

— If you intend to apply for residence:
• Are you at home full time?
• If NO—who will look after the children when you are away from home?
• Have you any proposals for contact?
If NO—why not?
If YES—please answer questions below.
— With regard to contact arrangements (in the event that you have/get/keep residence):
• At what precise address do you wish contact to take place?
• If that is not your home—how are the children to get to that address?
• If it will cost money for the transport of the children to that address—who do you propose should pay, and why do you so propose?
• Between what precise times do you wish contact to be exercised, on what days of the week, and with what degree of frequency/regularity (including reference to staying contact).
• If not applying for residence, what are your proposals for contact?

Orders sought

1. Orders to be applied for

2–06 — FLA 1996: If the application for an injunction is under the FLA 1996, specify which of the following orders you seek:

(a) Non Molestation Orders

— A provision restraining the other party from molesting you

6

— A provision restraining the other party from molesting a "relevant child" *e.g.* a child living with you (if not all the children—which child?)
— Power of Arrest
— Penal clause
— Costs

(b) Occupation Orders

— A provision excluding the other party from the home or part of the home or 2–07 from a specified area in which the home is included
— A provision requiring the other party to permit you to enter and remain in the home or part of the home
— Declaring rights of occupation
— Enforcing rights of occupation
— Regulating rights of occupation
— Prohibiting, suspending, restricting or terminating rights of occupation
— Extending rights of occupation beyond death/divorce
— Power of Arrest
— Penal clause
— Costs

Sight should not be lost of the fact that the applicant must be eligible for the particular orders sought *i.e.*

(a) Non-molestation orders—the applicant must be "associated" with the other party

(b) Occupation orders—applicant must have pre-existing right to occupy the property, or be a present/former spouse/cohabitant: precise terms and duration of occupation orders available is determined by which of these categories the applicant falls into.

2. Alternative accommodation

— What other accommodation is available: 2–08

    To you
    To the other party

— Particulars of such accommodation must include:
• Address
• Number of rooms
• Number of persons presently in occupation
• In respect of persons presently in that accommodation, who, age, relationships to each other, etc.

3. Merits of the injunction application

— Why do you want it? Give particulars, etc:
• Of conduct: has the other party used or threatened violence against you/child?

7

- Of such matters you think indicate that without an injunction, the other party will continue to misbehave. In relation to such conduct, etc.—specify precisely what behaviour took place during any cohabitation
— Have you had an injunction before?
  If NO, proceed to next point
  If YES:
- How many previous injunction orders have there been (identifying them particularly)?
- Which Solicitor(s) did you consult, giving names and addresses?
- Were you legally aided?
- What has become of your previous orders (discharged? lapsed? committal proceedings? etc.)
— If you get an "ouster" type injunction, do you realise that without leave of the Court the other party cannot return, even at your invitation?
— Being frank, is "conduct" all one-sided; or have you also played a part in the deterioration of the relationship? If you are not free from responsibility, what have you done?

4. The other party's reaction to an injunction application

2–09 — Does the other party know of your wish to launch injunction proceedings?
— If YES—what is the reaction (if negative—is that because the other party does not realise that he or she has a right to contact to any children)
— Has the other party instructed Solicitors, giving names and addresses.

5. As to the children:

2–10 — Before the breakdown of the relationship, how were they, and how was their school work?
— How are they now—and what is their school work like (please produce reports, *e.g.* from teacher, doctor, social worker, etc.)
— If they have put up with a bad domestic relationship for some time, could they not soldier on for a little longer?

6. Earnings and earning capacity

2–11 — In relation to each party:

- Qualifications for work?
- Present income (net and gross)
- Present employment—work prospects
- What other financial resources are available?
- If in receipt of welfare benefits, list the benefit received, at which office the client claims, and the client's reference number.

— Particulars of weekly ongoings/financial obligations (including any to the other party/any children).

7. The property

— Is the property which is the subject matter of the application occupied under 2–12 the terms of a tenancy/lease?
  If YES—name and address of the landlord.
— Is title to the land registered or unregistered? If registered, what is the Land Registry number? (If necessary obtain another authority to inspect the Register).
— Is the land subject to any mortgage and/or charge?
  If YES —

  ● Give full particulars of the mortgage and in whose favour it is made.
  ● Give similar particulars, as to the charge.

— In whose name(s) is the property?
— Is the property the parties' home? If not, was it at any time intended to be such a home?

B. Injunctions against Molestation.

Sources of jurisdiction

1. Family Law Act 1996, s.42

This section enables persons "associated" with the respondent to apply for their 2–13 own protection, or for the protection of a "relevant child" (section 42(1)) without the necessity of launching any other family proceedings (section 42(2)). Further, the Court may make a non-molestation order either on application, or of its own motion in any "family proceedings" to which the respondent is a party, for the benefit of any other party to the proceedings or any relevant child (sections 42(2) and (3)): But note that such orders made in family proceedings will cease to have effect if those proceedings are withdrawn or dismissed (Section 42(8)).

A non-molestation order may restrain molestation in general, or particular acts of molestation, or both (section 42(6)). The "Court" means the High Court, a County Court or a Magistrates Court (section 57(1)).

2. Matrimonial suits

The High Court and County Courts retain their powers under SCA 1981, s.37 2–14 and CCA 1984, s.38 to grant non-molestation injunctions ancillary to divorce and judicial separation proceedings for the protection of a party to those proceedings. The FLA 1996 does not purport to restrict these powers. In practice, however, the remedies provided under the FLA 1996 and their availability in any family proceedings "should eliminate the need for orders to be made under the inherent jurisdiction unless there is a particular reason for this being more appropriate" (Law Com. para. 1.6).

What is molestation?

1. Meaning

2–15   Molestation is an umbrella term which covers a wide range of behaviour. It has been judicially defined and includes, but is wider than, violence. There is no statutory definition of molestation in FLA 1996, as that might operate to reduce the current level of protection. Molestation encompasses any form of serious pestering or harassment:

(a)   *Vaughan* (1973) (below case 28) The Court considered the definition of molestation in the *Shorter Oxford Dictionary*, namely "to cause trouble; to vex; to annoy; to put to inconvenience". Stephenson L.J. considered that "molest" was a "wide, plain word" which was synonymous with "pester". The Court found that the husband who had persistently called at his wife's home and place of work and was "making a perfect nuisance of himself to her the whole time" was guilty of molestation.

(b)   *Davis v. Johnson* [1979] A.C. 264 at 334 *per* Viscount Dilhorne:

"violence is a form of molestation but molestation may take place without the threat or use of violence and still be serious and inimical to mental and physical health".

(c)   *Horner* (1982) (below case 1) *Held*: "molesting" included conduct which did not amount to violent behaviour, or threats of violence.

"It applies to any conduct which can properly be regarded as such a degree of harassment as to call for the intervention of the Court" (*per* Ormrod L.J.).

(d)   *Johnson v. Walton* (1990) (below case 2). It was held that sending partially nude photographs of the plaintiff to a national newspaper for publication with the intent of causing her distress was within a prohibition against molestation.

(e)   *Smith v. Smith* (1988) (below case 3) P complained of "various untoward occurrences" including her car locks being filled with superglue, receiving unpleasant anonymous letter in D's handwriting, and seeing the D drunk, pressing his face against her window and waving pieces of paper at her. All capable of amounting to molestation, if proved.

Questions for the court

1. Conditions precedent—general

2–16   The Court must be satisfied that:

(a)   Molestation has occurred on a balance of probabilities. *In Spindlow v. Spindlow* [1979] Fam. 52, the respondent was found not to be guilty of any violence or adverse conduct. Whilst an order was made excluding him from the house, the non-molestation injunction against him was discharged on appeal.

(b)   An order is necessary to protect the applicant and/or a relevant child.

(c)   The behaviour complained of warrants the intervention of the Court. The Courts are not concerned with trivia. In assessing the degree of seriousness of the case, the following questions may assist:

— What is the nature of the conduct complained of?
— Does it form part of a pattern of behaviour?
— What is the effect on the applicant or relevant child?

2. Criteria—Family Law Act 1996

In deciding whether (and if so, how) to exercise its powers under section 42, the **2–17** Court must have regard to all the circumstances of the case, including the need to secure the health, safety and well-being of the person in whose favour the order would be made, and of any relevant child (section 42(5)).

3. Aims of statutory criteria

— Flexible response to applications
— Consistency of approach
— Help and guidance for Magistrates in exercising their powers
— Focus attention on *effect* of respondent's conduct on health, safety and well-being of the applicant or relevant child—consider their need for protection, rather than the *nature* of that conduct (Law Com. para. 3.6).

C. Key Definitions under FLA 1996

"Associated persons"

1. Relevant sections:

(a)   Section 33 (eligible applicants seeking occupation orders)   **2–18**

(b)   Section 42 (non-molestation orders).
    Under these sections, an applicant may seek orders against another person with whom he is associated.

2. Meaning

A person is associated with another where their relationship falls within section 62(3), and (4) *i.e.*:

(a)   They are or have been married to each other [note section 63(5)—polygamous marriages are within FLA 1996, Pt 4].

(b)   They are cohabitants or former cohabitants [as defined in section 62(1)]

(c)   They live or have lived in the same household, otherwise than merely by reason of one of them being the other's employee, tenant, lodger or boarder.

(d)   They are relatives [widely defined in section 63(1)].

(e)   They have agreed to marry one another (whether or not that agreement has been terminated) [For proof of agreement, see section 44. Also note time limit for applications imposed by sections 33(2) and 42(4)].

(f)   In relation to any child, they are both parents of the child *or* have or have had parental responsibility for the child [note that they need not marry or live together under this category. For parental responsibility provisions under CA 1989, see Appendix D below]

(g)   They are parties to the same family proceedings (other than proceedings under FLA 1996, Pt IV) [Family proceedings defined in section 63(2)—but note the Pt 4 exception here].

3. Adoption

2–19   Under section 63(5), where a child has been adopted or freed for adoption, two persons are associated with each other if:

(a)   One is a natural parent or grandparent of the child; and
(b)   The other is the child or any person —

(i) who has become a parent of the child by virtue of an Adoption Order or has applied for an Adoption Order, or
(ii) with whom the child has at any time been placed for adoption.

This would provide protection in the extreme example posed by the Law Commission where a child is adopted after father has killed mother. If father discovers the child's whereabouts after his release from prison, the new carers may wish to seek protection against molestation, particularly in view of the father's history of violence (Law Com. para. 3.25).

4. The statutory formulation—effect

2–20   The FLA 1996 significantly widens the range of people who are entitled to apply to the Courts for protection from molestation: the emphasis is now more on "family violence" than "domestic violence".

(a) Protected Parties

Examples will include:

—   a wife seeking protection from her husband
—   a divorced woman seeking protection from her ex-husband with whom she no longer lives
—   an unmarried woman seeking protection from her cohabitee with whom she is living (or has been living) as husband and wife
—   parents seeking protection from their violent child or children
—   elderly people seeking protection from members of their family with whom they are living
—   a parent seeking protection from his/her child's cohabitee

— a child seeking protection from his/her mother's new boyfriend
— a child seeking protection from his/her relative(s)
— homosexuals living together in the same household would be associated persons
— the mother of a child seeking protection from the child's father where they have never lived together
— the adoptive parents of a child seeking protection from the child's natural parents
— a man/woman seeking protection from his/her fiance(e) where they have never lived together and there are no children of the relationship.

(b) Excluded Relationships

Examples include: 2–21

— neighbour disputes
— harassment in the workplace
— landlord and tenant disputes
— a student renting the spare room in a house
— a live-in Nanny employed to care for children/housekeeper
— a person who takes the tenancy of a property and sublets rooms to their friends
— boyfriends and girlfriends who have never lived with each other, where there are no children and where they have never agreed to marry one another
— a person harassed by a stranger or mere acquaintance who displays obsessional behaviour
— a man and/or his new girlfriend harassed by an obsessive discarded girlfriend (where there was no agreement to marry one another).

Such excluded parties must resort to tortious remedies, remedies available under the law of property, landlord and tenant, or employment law, or seek redress under the criminal law as appropriate.

The statutory definition of cohabitation

1. Definition

Cohabitants are a man and woman who, although not married to each other, are 2–22 living together as husband and wife (section 62(1)). Former cohabitants is to be read accordingly, but does not include cohabitants who have subsequently married each other.

2. Meaning

The phrase "living together as husband and wife" has been judicially considered in matrimonial proceedings:

(a) *Santos v. Santos* [1972] 2 All E.R. 246, CA. Parties may continue to live together as husband and wife, even though they are living in different places; it is important to consider the state of mind of the parties. Do they both recognise the relationship of living together as husband and wife as subsisting, or has one of the parties determined that it has come to an end? Sachs L.J. considered that "physical separation . . . does not of itself preclude the parties being in a state of 'living together'".

(b) *Fuller v. Fuller* [1973] 2 All E.R. 650, CA:W was living with another man in the same household and her husband was living in the other man's house as a lodger due to ill health. *Held* H and W were not "living together as husband and wife", which connotes "something more than living in the same household" (*per* Stamp L.J. at p.652j).

Accordingly, where a couple cannot be said to be living together as husband and wife (and therefore do not fall within section 62(3)(b)), they may nonetheless be living in the same household under section 62(3)(c).

Living in the same household

(a) Meaning

2–23 Section 62(3)(c) is intended to include people who live "in the same household" other than on a purely commercial basis. This phrase is not defined in FLA 1996 and may be expected to retain the usual meaning which it has acquired in matrimonial proceedings. It is possible, therefore, for people to live in separate households, even though they are living in the same house.

(b) The Two-Household Test

The Law Commission considered that the crucial test was the degree of community life which goes on (Law Com. para. 3.21). If the parties shut themselves up in separate rooms and cease to have anything to do with each other, they live in separate households. If, however, they share domestic chores and shopping, eat meals together and share the same living room, they are living in the same household, however strained their relationship may be.

(c) A Practical Approach

2–24 In the case of *Adeoso* [1981] 1 W.L.R. 1535, the Court of Appeal (in considering the phrase "living with each other *in the same household* as husband and wife" under DVMPA 1976, s.1(2)) had regard to the size and practicalities of the accommodation in deciding whether it was realistic to find that separate households existed. The parties were living in a Council flat which consisted of one bedroom, a sitting room, kitchen and bathroom. The applicant contended that the parties no longer had sexual intercourse and that they slept in separate bedrooms. She further added that she no longer cooked or washed for the respondent. They communicated by notes. As Ormrod L.J. described it at p.1537:

> "In other words, in ordinary human terms, the relationship is exactly comparable to a marriage which is in the last stages of breaking up".

In answering the question as to whether they were living in the same household, he said at p.1539:

"In practical terms one cannot live in a two-roomed flat with another person without living in the same household. One has to share the lavatory, share the kitchen, share the bathroom and take great care not to fall over one another; and it would be quite artificial to suggest, that two people living at arm's length in such a situation, from which they cannot escape by reason of the housing difficulties, are to be said to be living in two different households. Of course, if this were a large household and they were middle class persons, no doubt one could live upstairs and the other could live downstairs, one of them could improvise some cooking facilities and one use the kitchen, and so on. There would of course, then come a stage when one could say: 'Well, they really have separated their households.' But, on the facts of this case, it would be totally artificial, in my judgement, to say that they succeeded in separating themselves into two individual households. They obviously have not."

In deciding whether the parties live together in the same household, previous 2–25 decisions relating to the divorce jurisdiction under sections 1(2)(d) and (e) of the MCA 1973 (and previous Acts) have no application. In *Adeoso* (above) Ormrod L.J. said at p. 1537:

"The Judge, I think, attached, with respect, too much importance to the old cases about desertion and was thinking in terms of those old cases, which held that it was possible for a spouse to desert the other while living in the closest possible contiguity in the same house, if they succeeded in severing the cooking and washing arrangements and so on. I do not, for my part, think that those cases have any application to the present situation. They were invented by a succession of judges to get over the impossible position where a couple had ceased to communicate altogether but neither could leave because they had no alternative accommodation; and so a certain amount of stretching of the law had to be done. I see no useful purpose in reviving those cases and that doctrine in this present position."

"Relevant child"

1. Meaning

A relevant child is defined in section 62(2) as: 2–26

(a) any child who is living with or might reasonably be expected to live with either party to proceedings;

(b) any child in relation to whom an order under the Adoption Act 1976 or the Children Act 1989 is in question in the proceedings;

(c) any other child whose interests the Court consider relevant.

2. The position of the relevant child

The Court must consider the health, safety and well-being of any relevant child when deciding whether (and if so, how) to exercise its powers:

(a) to make occupation orders under section 33, 35, 36, 37 and 38;

(b)   to make non-molestation orders under section 42.

Further, the interests of a relevant child fall to be considered where appropriate under section 45 (*ex parte* orders) and section 47 (power of arrest).

3. Powers of the court

2–27   Under FLA 1996 the Court has wide powers to protect a broad range of children from molestation whenever necessary and appropriate by the interaction of:

(a)   its wide inclusionary discretion under section 62(2) (c)
(b)   its power to make orders of its own motion in any family proceedings for the benefit (*inter alia*) of any relevant child
(c)   a child's ability to apply for a non molestation order in his/her own right, for example as against a relative (under section 62(3) (d)).

"Family proceedings"

1. Meaning

2–28   Family proceedings means any proceedings under:

(a)   the inherent jurisdiction of the High Court in relation to children;
(b)   Pt 2 of the FLA 1996 (divorce and separation);
(c)   Pt 4 of the FLA 1996 (family homes and domestic violence);
(d)   the Matrimonial Causes Act 1973;
(e)   the Adoption Act 1976;
(f)   the DPMCA 1978;
(g)   Pt 3 of the Matrimonial and Family Proceedings Act 1984;
(h)   Pts 1, 2 and 4 of the Children Act 1989;
(i)   section 30 of the Human Fertilisation and Embryology Act 1990.

See sections 63(1), (2).

2. Powers of the courts

2–29   The breadth of proceedings within which non-molestation orders may be made, together with the power of the Court to make orders of its own motion in family proceedings, should ensure that appropriate orders can be made whenever they are necessary and appropriate. For example in Children Act 1989 proceedings, where the Court makes an order that the child reside with one party, it may make an order restraining the other party from assaulting, molesting or otherwise interfering with the other party or child (as was often achieved under the GMA 1971—see *Re W* (a minor) [1981] 3 All E.R. 401).

D. Occupation Orders under FLA 1996

Jurisdiction under FLA 1996

1. Repeals

2–30   The following provisions are repealed:

(a)   DVMPA 1976 (the whole Act)
(b)   DPMCA 1978 (ss. 16–18)
(c)   MHA 1983 (whole Act repealed, but substantially re-enacted in FLA 1996, ss. 30–32 and Sched. 4).

2. Jurisdiction—its extent

The Court's powers are wide. It may make occupation orders with a variety of possible terms, depending on the circumstances of the case. Those terms can either be:

(a)   "declaratory", which declare, confer or extend occupation rights
      or
(b)   "regulatory", which control the exercise of existing rights.

3. Declaratory orders—scope

Declaratory orders are those which: 2–31
(a)   Declare pre-existing occupation rights in the home (s. 33(4));
(b)   Extend statutory occupation rights beyond the termination of the marriage on divorce or death (s. 33(5));
(c)   Grant occupation rights in the home to non-entitled applicants—"an occupational rights order" (ss. 35(3)(4) and 36(3)(4)).

4. Regulatory Orders—court powers

The full range of regulatory orders allows the Court to: 2–32

(a)   Require the respondent to leave the dwellinghouse or part of it;
(b)   Suspend, prohibit or restrict the respondent's right to occupy the dwellinghouse;
(c)   Require the respondent to allow the applicant to enter and/or remain in the dwelling or part of it;
(d)   Regulate the occupation of the dwelling by either or both parties;
(e)   Terminate or restrict matrimonial home rights;
(f)   Exclude the respondent from a defined area around the dwelling;
(g)   Enforce the applicant's occupation rights against the respondent.

See section 33(3)(a)–(g), section 35(5)(a)–(d), section 36(5)(a)–(d), section 37(3)(a)–(d), and section 38(3)(a)–(d).

5. Status of applicant—Relevance

The range of persons who may apply for occupation orders is narrower than for 2–33 non-molestation orders. To be eligible to apply, the applicant must either:

(a)   have a pre-existing right of occupation in the property; or
(b)   be a present or former spouse or cohabitant.

The range of declaratory or regulatory orders available to the Court in any given case is determined by the status of the applicant—*i.e.* whether the applicant is *"entitled"* or *"non-entitled"* (see below). In some circumstances, the status of the respondent is also relevant (sections 37, 38).

6. Applications

2–34 An application for an occupation order may be free-standing, without the necessity of launching other (*e.g.* divorce) proceedings; or, the application may be made in other family proceedings (section 39(2)). Where the Court has no power to make an occupation order under the section relied upon by the applicant, but does have such power under another section, the Court may make an order under that section (section 39(3)).

7. Timing of applications

2–35 Where an ouster order is sought due to the respondent's violent conduct, it is considered that such application may be made whether

(a) the violence has caused the parties' separation (maintaining pre–FLA 1996 protection);

(b) the violence occurs after the parties' separation. It should be noted that:

— the FLA 1996 does not purport to restrict such an application
— the occupation order provisions apply to present or former spouses/cohabitants
— the court is directed to consider, in certain circumstances, the length of time that has elapsed since the parties ceased to live together. See sections 35(6)(e) and 36(6)(h).

8. Definitions

2–36 (a) "Family proceedings"—see section 63(1), (2);

(b) "Dwellinghouse" includes any building (or part thereof), caravan, house boat or structure which is occupied as a dwelling and any yard, garden, garage or outhouse belonging to it and occupied with it (section 63(1)—but note the restriction in section 63(4));

(c) "Spouse": Polygamous marriages are within the FLA 1996: section 63(5). In *Seray-Wurie* [1987] Fam. Law 124, CA, it was held that when the validity of a marriage was in dispute the judge could, for the purposes of an application for interlocutory relief, treat the marriage as binding until the issue could be properly determined.

9. Forum

Under section 57(1) "the Court" means the High Court, a County Court or a Magistrates' Court. The jurisdiction of a Magistrates' Court is restricted where there is a material dispute over occupation rights; further a Magistrates' Court may decline jurisdiction where the case would be more conveniently dealt with by another Court: section 59(1),(2).

Potential applicants under FLA 1996

1. Scheme of the act

The potential applicants for occupation orders fall into two main categories: 2–37

(a)   entitled applicants: those who are entitled to occupy the home by virtue of a legal or beneficial estate or interest or a contractual or statutory right (FLA 1996, s.33) *or* have "matrimonial home rights" of occupation (previously granted to spouses by MHA 1983, and now re-enacted in FLA 1996, section 30);

(b)   non-entitled applicants: those who do not have an existing entitlement to occupy the property arising either out of a proprietary interest or out of their rights as a spouse.

2. Categories of non-entitled applicants

Potential applicants who are *not* entitled to occupy the home fall into four 2–38 categories:

(a)   where applicant is a former spouse, and the respondent (the other former spouse) has existing occupation rights: see section 35;

(b)   where applicant is a cohabitant or former cohabitant, and the respondent (the other cohabitant or former cohabitant) has existing occupation rights: see section 36;

(c)   where applicant is a spouse or former spouse and the respondent (the other spouse or former spouse) has no rights of occupation either: see section 37;

(d)   where applicant is a cohabitant or former cohabitant and the respondent (the other cohabitant or former cohabitant) has no rights of occupation either: see section 38.

3. Status of applicant—relevance

The question of whether the applicant is entitled or not has a bearing on: 2–39

(a)   the range of orders available;

(b)   the range of persons against whom an order may be sought;

(c)   the factors that the Court must consider in exercising its discretionary powers;

(d)   the duration of any order obtained.

Occupation orders where applicant is "entitled".

1. Range of respondents

If the applicant is a "person entitled" under section 33, he or she can apply for an 2–40 occupation order as against another person with whom he is associated; *i.e.* they fall into any of the categories of relationship set out in sections 62(3), (4) or (5). The respondent may or may not be entitled to occupy the property.

2. The dwellinghouse

The Court has power to make an occupation order in respect of any dwelling-house which is, was, or was intended to be the joint home of the parties (section 33(1)(b)).

3. Range of orders available

2–41 The entitled applicant may seek any of the following orders:

(a) order declaring the applicant's pre-existing occupation rights in the home: section 33(4);

(b) order extending any matrimonial home rights (where the respondent is the other spouse) beyond the termination of the marriage by death or otherwise (section 33(5)) where the Court considers it just and reasonable to do so in all the circumstances (section 33(8));

(c) *any* of the full range of regulatory orders set out in section 33(3).

4. Factors for the Court

2–42 In exercising its discretionary powers, the Court "shall have regard to all the circumstances" including:

(a) the respective housing needs and resources of the parties and of any relevant child;

(b) the respective financial resources of the parties;

(c) the likely effect of any order or of any decision by the Court not to exercise its powers under section 33(3) [the regulatory orders] on the health, safety or well-being of the parties and of any relevant child;

(d) the conduct of the parties in relation to each other and otherwise.

See section 33(3)(6) but note sub-section (7) below.

5. The balance of harm test

2–43 Section 33(7) provides:

"If it appears to the Court that the applicant or any relevant child is likely to suffer significant harm attributable to conduct of the respondent if an order under this section containing one or more of the provisions mentioned in sub-section (3) is not made, the Court shall make the order unless it appears to it that: —

(a) the respondent or any relevant child is likely to suffer significant harm if the order is made; and

(b) the harm likely to be suffered by the respondent or child in that event is as great as, or greater than, the harm attributable to conduct of the respondent which is likely to be suffered by the applicant or child if the order is not made".

It should be noted that the Court has a duty to make an order if it appears likely that the applicant or any relevant child will suffer significant harm attributable to the respondent's conduct if an order is not made and that such harm will be greater than the harm which the respondent or any relevant child will suffer if the order is made.

6. Balance of harm—four examples

(a)	Question of significant harm does not arise	Court has *power* to make order taking into account factors in s. 33(6); may make or refuse order	2–44
(b)	Applicant/relevant child likely to suffer greater harm if order not made	Court is under a *duty* to make order. Note: that the harm must be attributable to R's conduct	
(c)	Respondent/relevant child likely to suffer greater harm if order is made	Court has *power* to make order; no duty to do so	
(d)	Balance of harm equal	Court has *power* to make order; no duty to do so	

7. "Harm"—meaning

Harm has a narrower meaning than hardship. It is defined in section 63(1) as ill- 2–45 treatment 'including non-physical ill-treatment' or the impairment of physical or mental health. In relation to children, it is defined as ill-treatment (including sexual abuse and non-physical ill-treatment), or the impairment of (physical or mental) health or development.

8. "Harm"—narrower than "Hardship"

The Law Commission gave the following example of how the balance of harm 2–46 may operate:

> "It is likely that a respondent threatened with ouster on account of his violence would be able to establish a degree of hardship (perhaps in terms of difficulty in finding or unsuitability of alternative accommodation or problems in getting to work). But he is unlikely to suffer significant harm, whereas his wife and children who are being subjected to his violence or abuse may very easily suffer harm if he remains in the house. In this way the Court will be treating violence or other forms of abuse as deserving immediate relief, and will be directed to make an order where a risk of significant harm exists"

(Law Com. No. 207 para. 4.34)

9. Duration of Orders

Under section 33(10) an order may be made for a specified period, until the 2–47 occurrence of a specified event, or until further order.

10. Entitled applicants—purpose of order

The Law Commission anticipated that "in the case of entitled applicants, particularly where the respondent is also entitled, an occupation order has a purpose beyond short term protection, namely to regulate the occupation of the home until its medium or long term destiny has been decided (in divorce or judicial separation proceedings . . .), or in some cases, indefinitely (for example, where a married couple separate and there is no need to sell the home") (Law Com. No. 207, para. 4.7).

Non-entitled Former Spouse v. Entitled Respondent

1. Appropriate respondent

2–48   If the applicant is a former spouse with no existing occupation rights (*i.e.* where "matrimonial home rights" have not been extended beyond decree absolute) he or she can apply for an occupation order under section 35 as against the other former spouse who has such rights of occupation.

2. The Dwellinghouse

The Court has power to make an occupation order in respect of a dwellinghouse which at any time was, or was intended to be the parties' matrimonial home (section 35(1)(c)).

3. Mandatory Provisions/Occupation Rights Order

2–49   If the Court makes an occupation order under section 35, it must give the applicant (if in occupation) the right not to be excluded or evicted from the home or part of it by the respondent for a specified period. If the applicant is not in occupation, the order must give him/her the right to enter into and occupy the home for a specified period; the respondent must permit the exercise of such right (section 35(3), (4)).

4. Regulatory Orders available

2–50   The Court may also include provisions which:

(a)   regulate the occupation of the home by either or both parties;
(b)   prohibit, suspend or restrict the respondent's right to occupy the home;
(c)   require the respondent to leave the home or part of it; or
(d)   exclude the respondent from a defined area around the home (section 35(5)).

5. Criteria to consider—Stage 1

2–51   The Court should first decide whether an occupation rights order should be granted and in what manner, having regard to all the circumstances, including:

(a) the respective housing needs and resources of the parties and of any relevant child;

(b) the respective financial resources of the parties;

(c) the likely effect of any order, or of any decision by the Court not to exercise its powers under subsection (3) or (4) on the health, safety or well-being of the parties and of any relevant child;

(d) the conduct of the parties in relation to each other and otherwise;

(e) the length of time that has elapsed since the parties ceased to live together;

(f) the length of time that has elapsed since the marriage was dissolved or annulled;

(g) the existence of specified pending proceedings between the parties for financial provision or relating to the legal or beneficial ownership of the dwellinghouse (section 35(6) (a)—(g)).

6. Criteria to consider—Stage II

If the Court decides to grant an occupation order, it should then go on to decide **2–52** whether one or more of the regulatory orders in subsection (5) should be included, having regard to all the circumstances including the factors set out in sections 35(6) (a)—(e) above. It should be noted that in so deciding, the balance of harm provisions apply; section 35(8) puts the Court under a duty to make such order if it appears likely that the applicant or any relevant child will suffer significant harm due to the respondent's conduct if such order is *not* made and that the harm will be greater than the harm which the respondent or relevant child will suffer if the order *is* made.

7. Duration of Orders

Under section 35(10) an order must be limited up to six months in the first **2–53** instance with the possibility of one or more renewals for up to six months at a time.

8. Nature and effect of Order

While any occupation order made under section 35 remains in force, the non-entitled applicant will be afforded the same protection and security under section 30(3)—(6) (against Landlords, mortgagees and trustees) as is available to a spouse with matrimonial home rights. However it should be noted that:—

(a) a spouse's matrimonial home rights can be registered as a charge on the dwellinghouse (see FLA 1996, ss.31 & 34) as protection against subsequent sale or mortgage of the property; whereas

(b) a non-entitled applicant's occupation rights are personal rights only, and cannot be registered as a charge against the property and are not valid against the purchaser.

9. Purpose of the Order

The Law Commission anticipated "in the case of non-entitled applicants, an **2–54** occupation order is essentially a short term measure of protection intended to give them time to find alternative accommodation, or, at most, to await the outcome of an application for a property law remedy" (Law Com. No. 207, para. 4.7)

Non-entitled Cohabitant/Former Cohabitant v. Entitled Respondent

1. Jurisdiction

2–55   If the applicant is a cohabitant or former cohabitant with no existing occupation rights, he or she can apply for an occupation order under section 36 as against the other cohabitant or former cohabitant who has such rights of occupation.

2. The dwellinghouse

The Court has power to make an occupation order in respect of a dwellinghouse which is, was or was intended to be, the home in which they live together as husband and wife (section 36(1)(c)).

3. Occupation Rights Order

2–56   Any occupation order made under section 36 must give the applicant the right not to be excluded/evicted from the home or part of it by the respondent, or the right to enter into/occupy the home, for a specified period (sections 36(3), (4)).

4. Regulatory Orders

Under section 36(5) the Court may also include provisions which:

(a)   regulate the occupation of the home by either or both parties;
(b)   prohibit, suspend or restrict the respondent's right to occupy the home;
(c)   require the respondent to leave the home or part of it; or
(d)   exclude the respondent from a defined area around the home.

5. Criteria to consider—Stage I

2–57   The Court should first decide whether an occupation rights order should be granted and in what manner, having regard to all the circumstances, including:

(a)   the respective housing needs and resources of the parties and any relevant child;
(b)   the respective financial resources of the parties;
(c)   the likely effect of any order, or of any decision by the Court not to exercise its powers under subsection (3) or (4), on the health, safety or well-being of the parties and of any relevant child;
(d)   the conduct of the parties in relation to each other and otherwise;
(e)   the nature of the parties' relationship (but see additional consideration in section 41);
(f)   the length of time during which they had lived together as husband and wife;
(g)   whether there are/have been any children of both parties, or for whom they have shared parental responsibility;
(h)   the length of time that has elapsed since the parties ceased to live together;

(i)   the existence of any specified pending proceedings between the parties for financial relief or relating to the legal or beneficial ownership of the home (section 36(6)(a)—(i)).

6. Criteria to consider—Stage II

If the Court decides to grant an occupation order, it should then go on to decide 2–58 whether one or more of the regulatory orders in subsection (5) should be included, having regard to all the circumstances including:

(a)   the factors set out in subsection (6) (a) to (d) above; and

(b)   the "balance of harm" provisions: See section 36(8).

It should be noted that in relation to non-entitled cohabitants/former cohabitants the Court is *not* under a *duty* to make an order where the balance of harm comes out in favour of the applicant or any relevant child. The balance of harm is one of the circumstances the Court must "have regard to" when deciding how to exercise its discretionary powers (contrast non-entitled former spouses above).

7. Duration of Orders

Under section 36(10) an order must be limited up to six months in the first 2–59 instance with the possibility of one extension for up to six months.

8. Nature and effect of Order

As for non-entitled former spouses, occupation rights are personal rights only, and the protection afforded by section 30(3)—(6) will apply for the duration of the occupation order (see section 36(11), (13)).

9. Frustrating the "ouster" Order

Where the Court makes an occupation order *e.g.* requiring the respondent to 2–60 leave the dwellinghouse, it is giving priority to the non-entitled applicant's need for short term protection/accommodation over the respondent's rights to occupy the home. However, Lord Salmon in *Davis v. Johnson* [1979] A.C. 264 at 343 explained how an excluded party could frustrate the purpose of an ouster order:

> "The former mistress acquires no proprietary right in the premises in question and there is nothing to prevent the man from selling or letting his own property whenever he likes".

For an example of a case where an order *prohibiting* ouster was "frustrated", See *Harrow L.B.C. v. Johnstone* (1997) (below case 4).

Occupation Orders where neither Party Entitled

1. Jurisdiction

Under section 37 the Court may make an occupation order where neither spouse 2–61 or former spouse is entitled to occupy the dwellinghouse which is or was the matrimonial home (*e.g.* they are trespassers or bare licensees). Section 38 applies where neither cohabitant or former cohabitant is entitled to occupy the home in which they live or lived as husband and wife. In each case, either party may apply for an order against the other.

2. Range of orders available

2–62   Under each section an Order may:

(a)   require the respondent to permit the applicant to enter and remain in the home or part of it;
(b)   regulate the occupation of the home by either or both parties;
(c)   require the respondent to leave the home or part of it;
(d)   exclude the respondent from a defined area around the home (section 37(3), 38(3)).

3. Criteria

2–63   In exercising its powers the Court shall have regard to all the circumstances including:

(a)   the respective housing needs and resources of the parties and any relevant child;
(b)   the respective financial resources of the parties;
(c)   the likely effect of any order, or of any decision by the Court not to exercise its powers on the health, safety or well-being of the parties and of any relevant child;
(d)   the conduct of the parties in relation to each other and otherwise;
(e)   the balance of harm provisions.

It should be noted that where the applicant is a non-entitled spouse or former spouse, the Court is under a duty to make an order if the balance of harm is determined in favour of the applicant or any relevant child: sections 37(4) and 33(7). In cases involving non-entitled cohabitants or former cohabitants the Court has the power to make an order but would have no duty to do so and would still be able to reach the right result.

4. Duration of order

2–64   An Order must be limited up to six months in the first instance. Non-entitled spouses or former spouses may seek one or more extensions for up to six months at a time. Non-entitled cohabitants or former cohabitants may seek one such extension: sections 37(5) and 38(6).

5. Effect of Order

The order regulates occupation of the property as between the parties; the order cannot bind third parties who have a proprietary interest in the property, who may choose to eject both parties by means of available property law remedies.

Rights relating to the matrimonial home where one spouse has no estate.

1. Matrimonial Home rights

FLA 1996, s.30(1) re-enacts the rights of occupation provisions formerly found in 2–65 MHA section 1(1) (now repealed). The effect of this provision is that the majority of spouses who are neither co-owners nor joint tenants of the home will be "entitled" applicants under section 33 when seeking occupation orders, (it should be noted that no statutory right of occupation is conferred where neither spouse is entitled to occupy).

2. Protecting the wife against a Landlord, etc

Section 30(3) (formerly MHA, s.1(5)) prevents a landlord or mortgagee from 2–66 refusing to accept payment from a deserted wife and using non-payment by the husband as grounds for bringing possession proceedings. It is only necessary to rely on this provision where the wife is not herself a tenant or owner with a right to tender payment.

3. The problem of tenure being dependant upon possession

Section 30(4) (formerly MHA, s.1(6)) covers the case where a tenant's security of 2–67 tenure is dependant upon his remaining in possession or occupation. This provision preserves the tenant's security in order to protect the wife.

4. "Contributions" to purchase price etc

A contribution to the mortgage payment will frequently give the wife a claim to an interest in the home by virtue of her contribution to the purchase; section 30(5) (formerly MHA, s.1(7)) preserves that interest.

5. Interest under a Trust

Section 30(6) (formerly MHA, s.1(8)) protects the wife's position where the house 2–68 is owned, for example, by a family trust, rather than by her husband.

6. The "matrimonial" home

The section 30 provisions only apply to a dwellinghouse which has been, or was intended by the spouses to be their matrimonial home. This will be a question of fact: *Collins v. Collins* (1973) 4 Fam. Law 133, *Kinzler v. Kinzler* (1985) Fam. Law 26, CA (below case 5). The provisions do not apply if the parties occupy property as trespassers.

6. Duration of matrimonial home rights

Under section 30(8) "A spouse's matrimonial home rights shall continue:— 2–69

(a)   only so long as the marriage subsists, except to the extent that an order under section 31(8) of this Act otherwise provides, and

(b)   only so long as the other spouse is entitled as mentioned in subsection (1) to occupy the dwellinghouse, except where provision is made by section 31 for those rights to be a charge on an estate or interest in the dwellinghouse".

8. The problem of contributions

2–70   A spouse may acquire an equitable interest in a dwellinghouse through his/her contributions to the purchase, and may have a right of occupation by reason of that equitable interest. Notwithstanding that, section 30(9) declares that such a spouse shall have matrimonial home rights in relation to the dwellinghouse (formerly MHA, s.1(11)).

9. Nature of rights

Matrimonial home rights can be registered as a charge on the dwellinghouse, as protection against subsequent sale or mortgage of the property (see sections 31 and 34 and Sched. 4).

Orders Ancillary to occupation.

1. Jurisdiction

2–71   When the Court makes an occupation order under section 33, 35 or 36, or at any time after, the Court has power to make the following ancillary orders where it is just and reasonable so to do:

(a)   to impose on either party obligations regarding the discharge of rent, mortgage instalments and other outgoings;

(b)   to impose on either party obligations as to repair and maintenance of the home;

(c)   to order payments by the occupying party to an entitled non-occupier for that occupation;

(d)   to grant one party possession or use of furniture or other belongings;

(e)   to order either party to take reasonable care of furniture or other belongings and/or take reasonable steps to keep them secure, (section 40(1)).

2. Criteria

2–72   In deciding whether an order is just and reasonable, the Court must have regard to all the circumstances of the case, including the parties' financial needs and resources and any financial obligations which they have or are likely to have in the foreseeable future, including financial obligations to each other and to any relevant child (section 40(2)).

3. Duration of Order

Any ancillary order made will cease to have effect when the occupation order to which it relates ceases to have effect: section 40(3).

4. Purpose of ancillary orders

(a) clarify the parties' financial responsibilities in the interim; 2–73
(b) achieve fair outcome as between the parties, *e.g.* where a long term occupation order has been made;
(c) any dispute over ancillary orders should not be allowed to delay the making of occupation orders;
(d) ancillary orders should not be used as "back door" maintenance claims.

E. Other sources of jurisdiction for "ouster"

Inherent Jurisdiction: Pre-FLA 1996

1. Scope of power

Since *Richards v. Richards* [1984] 1 A.C. 174, HL, there have been a number of 2–74
Court of Appeal authorities reported addressing the question whether the Court has inherent powers to make ouster orders where the parties' relationship has broken down and they were not living together; these authorities "are not easy to reconcile" (*Pearson v. Franklin* (parental home: ouster) [1994] 1 F.L.R. 246 at 250 *per* Thorpe J.).

2. Basis of the power

In *Pearson* (above), Thorpe J. considered that the foundation of the inherent 2–75
jurisdiction to make an ouster order is the protection of the interests of children, but that the powers of the Court in this respect may be different where the children's parents have been divorced than in a case where the parents have ceased to cohabit. In the case of former spouses an ouster order could be made under the inherent jurisdiction (see *Webb* (1986), *Wilde* (1988), *Lucas* (1992), *Hennie* (1993) and *Quinn* (1983)); in the case of former cohabitants, there was no such power: *Ainsbury v. Millington* (1986)—an injunction could only be made in support of a legal right requiring protection.

3. A satisfactory analysis?

Although Thorpe J. considered this to be a "rational reconciliation" of the 2–76
authorities, he also felt that it seemed "questionable". The distinction drawn between former spouses and former cohabitants "may not, on a long view, be satisfactorily explicable" (*ibid.*, *per* Nourse L.J. at p.249).

4. Modern application of inherent jurisdiction

In *C v. K* (inherent powers; exclusion order) [1996] 2 F.L.R. 506, C and K 2–77
occupied a council property as joint tenants, though they were neither spouses, nor former spouses, and were no longer living together as husband and wife. C began to

care for her grandson, J, in August 1995. K resented the child's presence in the house, and was abusive of C and J in the presence of the child; C sought, and obtained, a residence order in respect of J, and she also sought an injunction excluding K from the property. The primary issue in the case was whether or not the court had the power, exercising its inherent jurisdiction, to exclude a person from occupation of property of which he is a joint tenant:

(1)   where the order is said to be required:—

(a)   to protect a child living in the same property from harm; and/or
(b)   to prevent interference by the joint tenant, whom it is sought to exclude, with the proper exercise of parental responsibility under a residence order in relation to the child held by the other joint tenant; and

(2)   Where the joint tenants are neither spouses nor former spouses and are not living together as husband and wife; and
(3)   Where the person sought to be excluded is not the parent of the child concerned.

2–78   Wall J. reviewed a "plethora of authority on the point", observing that "there remains in my judgment a substantial degree of confusion, both about the nature of the inherent jurisdiction and the extent of the powers exercisable under it. I also confess that I do not find the authorities easy to reconcile" (at p.511). Notwithstanding this, Wall J. derived the following propositions (at p.523–4);

2–79   (1) Where judicial interference with the rights of occupation of property, as between spouses, cohabitees or former cohabitees, is specifically governed by statute, the relevant statutory provisions apply.

(2) Leaving on one side the *parens patriae* jurisdiction of the High Court over children who are specifically its wards, there exists an inherent jurisdiction in both the High Court and the county court to protect children from harm which is exercisable irrespective of the proceedings in which the issue of the need to protect the children arises.

(3) There is a co-existing jurisdiction given in the High Court by section 37 of the Supreme Court Act and in the county court by section 38 of the County Courts Act to grant injunctive relief in support of legal and equitable rights.

(4) The powers exercisable under sections 37 and 38 of the respective statutes may be invoked in support of the rights and duties conferred on a person by a residence order. Thus, in cases where neither the [Matrimonial Homes Act 1983 nor the Domestic Violence and Matrimonial Proceedings Act 1976] applies, a non-residential parent may be restrained from interfering with the residential parent's exercise of parental responsibility. The powers of the court in this context extend to orders against molestation and to ouster injunctions.

2–80   (5) The powers exercisable by the court under sections 37 and 38 extend to the grant of injunctions against third parties. Thus, a person who is not a parent of the child may be restrained from interfering with the exercise of parental responsibility by a person who has a residence order in relation to the child. The powers of the court to grant injunctive relief to include the power to exclude the stranger from property in which he has a beneficial interest.

(6) There is no reported case in which the inherent jurisdiction, unaffected by sections 37 and 38, has been used to exclude anybody who is not a parent from the occupation of property in which he has a proprietary interest. Whilst the power to make such an order may exist, the better course, in my judgment, is to invoke the jurisdiction under sections 37 and 38, since the need to protect the child is then bolstered by the need to protect the rights of the party with parental responsibility to exercise that parental responsibility appropriately.

(7) The powers of the court to exclude a person from property in which he has a 2–81 proprietary interest should be exercised with extreme caution. By analogy with section 100(4) of the Children Act the jurisdiction is likely only to be exercised where the court is satisfied that if the jurisdiction is not exercised the child is likely to suffer significant harm. In reaching any conclusion the court must look at all the circumstances of the case, including of course the circumstances of each of the parties and the conduct of the parties towards each other and the child. The court must make findings of fact upon which the assessment of likely future harm can be made.

(8) Whilst the jurisdiction exists to make a final order excluding a person from occupation of property in which he has a proprietary interest, without limitation of time, the court cannot by these means vary proprietary interests and must in every such case consider whether an indefinite order is required in order to protect the child from the likelihood of significant harm, and to achieve a result which is just.

The court adjourned C's ouster application for three months and made interim non molestation injunctions.

5. Impact of FLA 1996

The FLA 1996 does not purport to restrict any powers of the higher Courts to 2–82 make ouster orders under the inherent jurisdiction. However, occupation orders may now be sought by applicants who are spouses, former spouses, cohabitants or former cohabitants, thus "side-stepping" the need to further rationalise the various decisions concerning the existence and/or scope of the Court's general inherent power to make ouster orders in family cases; interference with rights of occupation of property between such parties is now "specifically governed by statute."

Children Act 1989 Cases

1. Cannot use section 8 powers to "oust"

The Court cannot oust a parent from the family home by making a specific issue 2–83 order as to where a child should live under CA 1989, s.8; there is no jurisdiction to make such an order where it would interfere with occupation rights: *Pearson v. Franklin* (parental home: ouster) [1994] 1 F.L.R. 246, CA. Further, it is "very doubtful indeed whether a prohibited steps order could in any circumstances be used to oust a father from a matrimonial home" (*Nottinghamshire C.C. v. P* [1993] 2 F.L.R. 134, CA *per* Sir Stephen Brown at p.144c). The Court has no jurisdiction to make a prohibited steps order preventing a husband from staying overnight at the former matrimonial home: *D v. D* (ouster order) [1996] 2 F.C.R. 496, CA.

Nor can a Court make an exclusion order under the guise of a conditional residence order: see *Re D* (Minors) (residence: imposition of condition) (1996–below Case 6).

2. *Ouster via property transfer*

2–84 In *Pearson v. Franklin*, where the parties were unmarried parents with a tenancy in joint names, the Court considered the appropriate remedy for the applicant mother was an application under CA 1989, s.15 and Sched. 1, paras (1) to (4), for an order requiring the father to transfer to her, for the benefit of the children, his interest in the joint tenancy of the home, thus giving her (as against him) an exclusive right to occupy the home. See also *K v. K* (Minors: property transfer) [1992] 1 W.L.R. 530 and *J v. J* (A minor) (property transfer) [1993] 2 F.L.R. 56 (below case 7).

(Note: The FLA 1996 provisions relating to transfers of tenancies are set out in Sched. 7).

3. *Local Authorities seeking ousters*

2–85 A Local Authority cannot apply for CA 1989, s.8 private law orders: *F v. Cambridgeshire C.C.* [1995] 1 F.L.R. 516 (see below case 8). In the circumstances in *Re S* (Minors) [1994] 1 F.L.R. 632, a Local Authority successfully invoked the inherent jurisdiction of the High Court to obtain an order ousting a father from the family home (see below case 9). The County Court, however, does not possess an inherent jurisdiction to order injunctions to protect children: *D v. D* (County Court: jurisdiction: injunctions) [1993] 2 F.L.R. 802, CA; *Re S and D* (Children: Powers of Court) [1995] 2 F.L.R. 456 at 463 *per* Balcombe L.J.; *Re B* (A Minor) (supervision order: parental undertaking) *The Times*, January 12, 1996 CA.

However by virtue of the new powers set out in FLA 1996, Sched. 5, the Courts have express statutory powers to oust alleged abusers from the family home upon making an emergency protection order or an interim care order (These provisions are considered in Chapter 3).

CHAPTER THREE

Practice and Procedure

A. *Ex Parte* Orders

Introduction

1. *Conditions precedent*

Ex parte applications, by definition, offend the rules of natural justice, and should **3–01** not be granted unless:

(a)   the application is made promptly;

(b)   there are sufficiently strong grounds to justify the order being made *ex parte*; and

(c)   the Court is satisfied that the interests of justice or the protection of the applicant or relevant child clearly demands immediate intervention by the Court.

2. *Forum*

In the High Court and County Court, applications are generally heard in **3–02** Chambers unless the Court in its discretion directs the matter to be heard in open Court. For sittings of Magistrates' Courts in "family proceedings" (which includes proceedings under FLA 1996, Pt 4) see MCA 1980, s.65(1), 69.

3. *Arranging a hearing*

Where the application is urgent, a hearing can be arranged with the relevant officials at the Court.

4. *Power of arrest*

The Court may in its discretion attach a power of arrest to one or more provisions **3–03** of an *ex parte* order if it appears that the respondent has used or threatened violence against the applicant or a relevant child, and that there is a risk of significant harm to the applicant or child due to the respondent's conduct if the power of arrest is not made *ex parte* (section 47 (3)).

5. Full disclosure required

3–04   In the interests of justice an applicant seeking an *ex parte* injunction must reveal/ disclose *all* material information: *Sal Oppenheim Jr and Lie Kgaa v. Rotherwood (UK) Ltd*, April 19, 1996, CA. Those seeking *ex parte* orders should behave with scrupulous care in relation to the application and to the implementation of any order made: *Re J (Minors) (ex parte orders)* (1997) (below case 10).

Powers of the Court

1. Jurisdiction

3–05   By FLA 1996, s.45(1) the Court has a general power to grant non—molestation and/or occupation orders where the notice prescribed by the rules of the Court has not been given. The Court may make such an order when it would be "just and convenient" to do so.

2. Special factors

3–06   In deciding whether to exercise its discretionary powers the Court is required to have regard to all the circumstances including the following factors:

(a)   any risk of significant harm to the applicant or a relevant child attributable to the respondent's conduct if the order is not made immediately;

(b)   whether it is likely that the applicant will be deterred or prevented from pursuing the application if an order is not made immediately; and

(c)   whether there is reason to believe that the respondent is aware of the proceedings but is deliberately evading service and that the applicant or a relevant child will be seriously prejudiced by the delay involved either in effecting service in Magistrates' Court proceedings or, in any other case, in effecting substituted service.

3. Purpose of statutory criteria

3–07   The Law Commission considered that the standard test and specified factors would:

(a)   promote consistent approach in all Courts dealing with *ex parte* applications;

(b)   provide guidance to Magistrates (who hitherto had no power to make *ex parte* exclusion orders under DPMCA, but could grant expedited personal protection orders.

Further, the factors in section 45(2) are not exclusive, but are cumulative; any one of them may be decisive in a particular case (Law Com. para. 5.7).

Return Date etc.

1. When?

At the *ex parte* hearing the Court is reaching a decision on the basis of the 3–08 applicant's view; any delay may lead to injustice or otherwise prejudice the respondent, particularly where the order is considered to be draconian. Accordingly the Court *must* give the respondent an opportunity to make representations relating to the order at a full hearing (*i.e.* a hearing on notice) as soon as just and convenient: See section 45(3).

2. How?

It is submitted that the requirements of section 45(3) could be achieved either by 3–09 fixing a "return date", or by giving the respondent liberty to apply on short notice.

3. Discharge of Order

If the respondent objects to the *ex parte* order, the proper course is to go back to the judge who made it, rather than appealing: *WEA Records Ltd v. Visions Channel 4 Ltd and others* [1983] 1 W.L.R. 721, CA.

4. Notice period—how long?

The order may provide that the respondent "may apply on 24 hours' notice to 3–10 discharge the injunction": *Ansah v. Ansah* (1977) Fam. 138 *per* Ormrod L.J. In *G v. G* [1990] 1 F.L.R. 395, Lord Donaldson MR considered "there could be no possible justification" for inserting a 48-hour notice provision on an *ex parte* ouster order when all that was required where the applicant husband was represented by a local solicitor, was liberty to either party to apply to discharge or vary the order upon notice, however short, to the applicant's Solicitors. The case should be treated as an emergency: a 48-hour notice provision "would probably give the wrong impression to the County Court office charged with the duty of trying to fit the case in. It does not on a 48-hour return date look to be particularly urgent" (*per* Butler-Sloss L.J. at p.402 D).

5. Exercising liberty to apply

Court officials should never turn away a person seeking to exercise a liberty to 3–11 apply without first obtaining instructions from the Court; such a matter was for a judicial and not administrative decision: *G v. G per* Lord Donaldson M.R. p.400).

6. The importance of speedy service

It is important that an *ex parte* order together with any supporting written evidence should be served on the respondent as soon as possible. This has two advantages:

(a)   to secure compliance by the respondent, and

(b)   until he is told of the order, committal cannot ensue: *Howes v. Howes* (1992) 2 FCR 287, CA.

Principles

1. *Ex parte* relief—when, in principle

3–12   In *Ansah* (1977) (below case 11) the Court of Appeal advanced the following principles relating to the grant of *ex parte* relief:

(a) Necessity/Caution

The power of the Court to intervene immediately and without notice in proper cases is essential to the administration of justice. But this power must be used with great caution and only in circumstances in which it is really necessary to act immediately (*per* Ormrod L.J. at p. 642).

(b) Ex parte relief—should be rare

3–13   Such circumstances do undoubtedly tend to occur more frequently in family disputes than in other types of litigation because the parties are often still in close contact with one another and, particularly when their marriage is breaking up, in a state of high emotional tension; but even in such cases the Court should only act *ex parte* in an emergency, when the interests of justice or the protection of the applicant or child clearly demands immediate intervention by the Court. Such cases should be extremely rare since any urgent application can be heard *inter partes* on short notice to the other side (see the judgment of Ormrod L.J. above).

(c) The need for a strict time limit

3–14   If the order is made *ex parte* it must be strictly limited in time if the risk of causing serious injustice is to be avoided. The time is to be measured in days, *i.e.* the shortest period which must elapse before a hearing *inter partes* can be arranged and the order must specify the date on which it expires; orders expressed to continue "until the further hearing of this application at the time and place to be notified" are unjustifiable and improper (*ibid.*)—also see *Morgan* (1978) (below case 31). If an *ex parte* order is to be made it should be made for the shortest possible time and should be returnable on notice, however short, to the respondent's solicitors and treated as an emergency (*G v. G* (1990) *per* Butler-Sloss L.J. at p. 402); a hearing date of seven weeks was held to be completely unjustifiable.

(d) What if difficulty in service?

3–15   If difficulty in serving the other party is anticipated it may be permissible to fix a longer period and to provide in the order that the other party may have 24 hours notice to discharge the injunction, (*Ansah, per* Ormrod L.J.).

2. *Ex Parte* relief—when, in practice

3–16   The Court must be satisfied that it is "just and convenient" in all the circumstances to make the *ex parte* order sought. Such orders may be considered to be justified in the following categories of case:

(a) Urgent need for protection

e.g. where respondent has used or threatened violence against applicant or a child and there is a real danger that the violence will either recur or occur if an order is not made immediately;

(b) Need to pursue remedy

e.g. where the applicant is so afraid of the respondent that some protection must be provided against a violent response to service of proceedings, so that the applicant may pursue the application;

(c) Impossibility of service

e.g. where the respondent is deliberately evading service and serious prejudice is caused to applicant or a child by the consequent delay, *or* where prior notice cannot be given, for example where one parent has disappeared with the children.
See *Ansah, per* Ormrod L.J., and FLA 1996, s.45(2)), and *Loseby v. Newman* [1995] 2 FLR 754, CA (below case 12).

Ex parte applications for ouster

1. Only in sufficiently exceptional circumstances

Ex parte occupation orders, particularly ouster orders are and should continue to be, rare and made only in the most exceptional circumstances. In *G v. G* the parties' Affidavits indicated a considerable conflict of evidence and the matters raised did not amount to sufficiently exceptional circumstances so as to justify an *ex parte* ouster order (see judgment of Butler-Sloss L.J. at p. 401). The Court should have made an *ex parte* non-molestation order in the widest possible terms which could have been served on the respondent at the same time as notice of an *inter partes* hearing for consideration of an application for an ouster order (see judgment of Lord Donaldson M.R. p. 399). The Court may abridge time and require the respondent to attend on short notice. 3–17

2. Service on the respondent

In *G v. G*, the respondent wife was known to be available for service, but the applicant thought that the service of notice of the application and an *inter partes* hearing would itself precipitate violence or "act as a catalyst". Butler-Sloss L.J. (at p. 402) took the view that this problem would be met by serving the respondent through her Solicitors at very short notice or by giving informal notice to her lawyers that an application would be made the next morning or perhaps the same day. 3–18

3. Trap for solicitors

In *Ansah*, Ormrod L.J. stated that such applications were an abuse of the process of the Court and solicitors promoting such applications "might find themselves liable to pay the costs". In that case, the wife had complained of the husband's 3–19 domineering attitude. Violence was not alleged and there was nothing to justify the ejecting of the husband out of his home without hearing from him. Also see *Masich* (1977) (below case 30).

4. Effect on final order

3–20   If the Court makes a full occupation order at the *inter partes* hearing, the *ex parte* order is to be taken into account when calculating the duration of the final order: section 45(4).

B. Duration of orders

How long may an injunction last?

1. Non-molestation orders

3–21   The Court may make a non-molestation order for a specified period or until further order—section 42(7)—the aims of which are:
(a)   allow flexible response to applications,
(b)   provide short, medium or long term protection according to the circumstances of the case, and
(c)   duration is irrespective of the category of applicant.

Where such order is made in other family proceedings, it will cease to have effect if those proceedings are withdrawn or dismissed: section 42(8).

2. Occupation orders

3–22   The maximum duration of such orders, and the number of extensions available is determined by the particular category of applicant:

(a) Entitled applicants

Order may be made for a specified period, until the occurrence of a specified event or until further order (section 33(10)).

(b) Non-entitled spouse/former spouse

Order must not exceed six months duration; order may be extended for up to six months at a time (section 35(10); section 37(5)).

(c) Non-entitled cohabitant/former cohabitant

Order must not exceed six months duration; order may be extended once for up to six months (section 36(10); section 38(6)).

3. Death of the parties

3–23   An occupation order made under section 33, 35 or 36 will cease to have effect on the death of either of the parties (except in the case of an order extending matrimonial home rights under section 33(5)(a)). Further, occupation orders under these sections may not be made if either of the parties has died: sections 33(9), 35(9) and 36(9).

4. Effect of ex parte orders

Where the Court is calculating the maximum duration of a "full" or final 3–24 occupation order, in a case where an *ex parte* occupation order has already been made, the full order is deemed to run from the date on which the *ex parte* order first had effect: section 45(4) (a).

5. Injunctions—never final

Whatever period is granted, it is open to either the applicant or respondent to 3–25 apply under section 49(1) for a variation or discharge of the injunction (*e.g.* on the grounds of reconciliation or other change of circumstance). Where the Court makes a non-molestation injunction of its own motion in family proceedings, the Court may vary or discharge such order of its own motion: section 49(2).

6. Third party variations

Where an occupation order is made against a respondent spouse under section 33 3–26 in favour of a spouse whose matrimonial home rights are a charge on the property, a person deriving title under the respondent and who is affected by the charge may also apply to vary or discharge the occupation order: section 49(3).

7. Policy

The Law Commission considered that earlier guidelines relating to the duration of 3–27 occupation orders should be revised. *Davis v. Johnson* [1979] A.C. 264, had emphasised that a DVMPA ouster was a short term remedy; and a Practice Note [1978] 1 W.L.R. 1123 suggested that in most cases a period of up to three months was "likely to suffice" in the first instance.

The Law Commission did not consider time limits to be appropriate to the regulation of occupation between those who have equal rights to occupy, and felt that all such occupation orders should be capable of being made for any specified period or until further order. It was felt that the six month statutory time limit for occupation orders granted to non-entitled applicants would allow applicants a more realistic period in which to find alternative accommodation, and would render the 1978 Practice Note "largely redundant" (Law Com. No. 207 para. 4.35–37).

Duration/variation of other orders

1. Matrimonial home rights

If the parties are spouses and the applicant has matrimonial home rights, the 3–28 Court may provide that those rights should not be brought to an end by:

(a)   the death of the respondent spouse; or

(b)   the termination (otherwise than by death) of the marriage: section 35(5).

2. Ancillary orders

3–29   Any order made under section 40 (regarding payment of rent, mortgage, possession of furniture, etc.) will cease to have effect when the occupation order to which it relates ceases to have effect: section 40(3).

Examples of Orders made "unlimited in time".

1. Spencer v. Camacho (1983) 4 FLR 662

3–30   This case involved a property in which the unmarried parties had a joint interest. The respondent had been violent with the result that there had been a number of injunctions granted. Eventually, an injunction was granted for six months, although the applicant had applied for the order to be indefinite. On appeal it was held (*per* Sir David Cairns):

> "that having regard to the history of the instant case and the fact that the matter had repeatedly returned to the Court and each time a further extension had been made, and each time the respondent had behaved in such a way as to make it proper for the applicant to come back and ask for a further extension, the appropriate time had arrived to make an injunction until further order".

It was always open to the respondent to apply at an appropriate time for its discharge.

2. Galan v. Galan (1985) (below case 34).

3–31   H was found to be a man of "irrational behaviour" and the Judge concluded that there was a risk of violence if H was at liberty to return to the matrimonial home. He made an exclusion order unlimited in time. The Court of Appeal upheld the order; there had been a number of injunction applications by W and two successful committal applications. Both parties had a legal interest in the property but if H were to exercise his right to return "there was clear evidence which constituted a risk of violence and certain detriment to the family". Moreover, the Judge had found that "it would be intolerable for the elder daughter if the husband were to be allowed back into the house . . ."

3. Summary

3–32   The above cases were decided under DVMPA criteria and should be viewed in light of the changes made by FLA 1996. The Court may make an occupation order "until further order" where the applicant is a "person entitled" under section 33. The matters set out in section 33(6) will be relevant in deciding the duration of any regulatory orders granted. When considering all the circumstances of the case, it is submitted that the following features are also relevant:

(a)   how many previous injunctions and/or committals have been obtained successfully?—and with what degree of frequency?

(b)   what would be the likely result of the respondent returning to the home within a short period of time if the injunction were so limited?

If ouster granted, how long will respondent be given to vacate the home?

1. Criteria

The Court has discretion as to when the order should take effect and should   3–33 weigh the following factors in the balance:

(a)   has the respondent alternative accommodation?

(b)   if not, how soon can the respondent make alternative accommodation arrangements?

(c)   what is the respondent's income?

(d)   what are the applicant's circumstances? To what extent is he or she prejudiced by any delay in the home being vacated?

2. The sooner the better

Where an ouster order is justified, it should take effect within a reasonable time,   3–34 and generally the sooner the better; where an ouster order is made against a spouse, its implementation should not be delayed to allow time for ancillary matters between the parties to be resolved: *Dunsire v. Dunsire* [1991] 2 FLR 314, CA. When an ouster order is made it should, in the normal way, be made to take effect within a week or two: Chadda (1981) (Below case 35); *Burke v. Burke* [1987] 2 FLR 71; *G v. J (ouster order)* [1993] 1 FLR 1008, CA.

C. The Power of Arrest

Introduction

1. Source of jurisdiction

The jurisdiction derives from FLA 1996, s.47(2): where the Court makes an   3–35 occupation order or non-molestation order and it appears to the Court that the respondent has used or threatened violence against the applicant or a relevant child, it must attach a power of arrest to one or more provisions of the order, *unless* it is satisfied that in all the circumstances the applicant or child will be adequately protected without a power of arrest being attached. The presumption, accordingly, appears that the Court should attach a power of arrest in cases where there has been violence.

2. Ex parte orders

In relation to orders made *ex parte*, the Court is not required to attach a power of   3–36 arrest, but *may* do so if it appears that:

(a)   the respondent has used or threatened violence against the applicant or a relevant child; and

(b)   there is a risk of significant harm to the applicant or child, attributable to the respondent's conduct if the power of arrest is not attached immediately to one or more provisions of the order; see section 47(3).

3. Power afforded to the Police

3–37   If a power of arrest is attached to one or more provisions of an order, a constable may arrest a person without warrant whom he has reasonable cause for suspecting to be in breach of any such provision: section 47(6).

4. Obligations upon the police

3–38   If someone is arrested under a power of arrest, he or she is to be brought before the "relevant judicial authority" within a period of 24 hours beginning at the time of his arrest (but no account is taken of Christmas Day, Good Friday or any Sunday) section 47(7). This means that he or she will be brought before a High Court Judge, or any County Court Judge/District Judge, or any Magistrates' Court, depending on the level of court that made the Order: see section 63(1).

5. To which orders can a power of arrest attach?

3–39   Under section 47, the power of arrest is attached to one or more provisions of "a relevant order" *i.e.* an occupation or non-molestation order. It is not confined to provisions restraining violence or creating exclusion zones around property. Accordingly, molestation without violence can trigger the power of arrest; for this reason the Court should clearly specify the particular breach(es) which will lead to the exercise of the power of arrest (Law Com. No. 207, para. 5.14). A power of arrest cannot be attached to an undertaking: section 46(2)—*Carpenter v. Carpenter* [1988] 1 FLR 121, CA.

6. Parties

3–40   The parties to an order to which a power of arrest is attached will be:

(a)   those persons who are eligible to apply for an occupation or non-molestation order, and

(b)   those persons who fall within the appropriate category of respondent.

Warrants for arrest

1. When?

3–41   If the Court has made an occupation order or non-molestation order but either:

(a)   does not attach a power of arrest to any provisions of the order; or

(b)   only attaches a power of arrest to certain (but not all) provisions of the order;

if the applicant considers that the respondent is in breach, he or she may apply to the relevant Court for the issue of a warrant for the respondent's arrest: see section 47(8).

2. Powers of the court

The application is made to the same level of Court that made the occupation 3–42 order or non-molestation order, though it need not be the same judge. A warrant shall not be issued under section 47(8) unless:

(a)   the application is substantiated on Oath; *and*
(b)   the Court has reasonable grounds for believing that the respondent has breached the order.

An application for an arrest warrant should not be made where a power of arrest covers the alleged breach.

Powers of remand following arrest

1. Introduction

The following powers of remand apply in all levels of Court, and apply whether 3–43 the respondent is brought before the Court pursuant to a power of arrest or under an arrest warrant.

2. Remand—pending committal

The Court may remand the arrested person if the matter is not disposed of forthwith: section 47(7)(b), and (10). The arrested person may be remanded in custody or on bail pending hearing of committal proceedings. Magistrates Courts have existing powers of remand in civil cases under MCA 1980, ss.128, 129. The High Court and County Courts now have corresponding powers by virtue of FLA 1996, Sched. 5.

3. Remand on bail

Where the respondent is bailed, the Court may impose "requirements" to ensure 3–44 that he does not interfere with witnesses or otherwise obstruct the course of justice: section 47(12). Further, under Sched. 5, para. 2(3) the Court may direct that his "recognizance be conditioned" for his appearance at specified times.

4. Duration of remand

Under Sched. 5, para. 2(5) the period of remand must not exceed eight clear days 3–45 unless:

(a)   respondent is on bail and parties agree to remand for a longer period,

(b)   the Court adjourns the case for medical examination and report under section 48(1).

At the expiration of the remand period the Court may further remand the respondent: Sched. 5, para. 2(2)—it may do so in his absence if satisfied he is unable to attend Court due to illness or accident: Sched. 5, para. 3.

5. Medical examination and report

3–46   The Court may exercise its powers of remand for the purpose of enabling a medical examination and report to be made where it has reason to consider that a medical report will be required: section 48(1). Where the remand is on bail the adjournment must not be for more than four weeks at a time; where the remand is in custody the adjournment must not exceed three weeks at a time: section 48(2), (3).

6. Report on mental condition

3–47   There is also power to remand an arrested person to a hospital specified by the Court for a report on his mental condition, where there is reason to suspect that he is suffering from "mental illness or severe mental impairment": section 48(4). In this regard the Court has the same power as the Crown Court has in relation to an accused person under Mental Health Act 1983, s.35. It is to be noted that the Court is not required to make any findings of contempt by the arrested person before ordering such a remand.

7. Power of adjournment

3–48   Where it is considered unnecessary to remand the arrested person in custody or on bail, the Court may simply adjourn the case.

Applications for power of arrest *ex parte*.

1. Jurisdiction

3–49   If the applicant can show that violence has been used or threatened, and that there is a risk of significant harm attributable to the respondent's conduct if a power of arrest is not attached immediately, the Court may grant the application but is under no duty to do so.

2. Significant harm and respondent's conduct

3–50   The Court is required to consider whether there is a risk of significant harm; such harm need not be likely under section 47 but must be attributable to the respondent's "conduct"—this is not limited to further violence or threats of violence, although in many cases this will be the nature of the conduct feared if a power of arrest is not attached *ex parte*. The following factors may assist when considering the question of future conduct:

(a) What is the nature of the conduct feared?
(b) How serious is the used or threatened violence?
(c) How long has such conduct or violence persisted?
(d) What is the nature of the parties' relationship?
(e) How long is the relationship?
(f) How long has it been subject to deterioration and why?
(g) Have there been previous injunctions?
(h) Have they been flouted and/or been the subject-matter of committal proceedings? In each case, with what degree of frequency?
(i) Has the respondent a criminal record?
(j) Has the respondent been arrested for the violence or threats in question? Is the respondent on bail subject to any conditions? If yes, what conditions? At what stage are the criminal proceedings?

3. Example—risk of violence on service

If the reasonable inference from the evidence is that the applicant or relevant 3–51
child is at risk of suffering significant harm due to a real risk of violence either upon the occasion of service or during the interval between service of the *ex parte* order and the hearing *inter partes*, this would appear to be appropriate for a power of arrest to be added to the order.

4. Necessity/caution

It is to be borne in mind that in exercising these discretionary powers, the Court 3–52
is granting a power of arrest on the basis of the applicant's view. It is suggested that the principles advanced by the Court of Appeal in *Ansah* (1977) and *G v. G* (1990) (above) should be further considered when deciding whether to attach a power of arrest *ex parte*—in particular:

(a) the need for caution;
(b) the possibility of giving short notice or informal notice to the other side rather than no notice;
(c) the need for strict time limits;
(d) giving the respondent liberty to apply on short notice to discharge the power of arrest provision.

5. Duration and variation

An *ex parte* power of arrest should not be made to continue until further order. 3–53
The Court may provide that the power of arrest is to have effect for a shorter period than the other provisions of the *ex parte* order: section 47(4). The Court may extend this period on an application to vary or discharge the *ex parte* occupation or non-

molestation order: section 47(5). Further the Court may, on application, vary or discharge the power of arrest irrespective of whether any application has been made to vary or discharge any other provisions of the order: section 49(4).

6. Trap for the unwary Solicitor

Service on the police of an order to which a power of arrest has been attached should not be effected until after service on the respondent.

D. Undertakings

Introduction

1. Statutory framework

3–54   Under FLA 1996, s.46(1), where the Court has power to make an occupation order or non-molestation order, it may accept an undertaking from any party to the proceedings.

2. Non-acceptance of undertakings

Section 46(1) must, however, be read subject to section 46(3) which states that the Court "shall not accept" an undertaking "in any case where apart from this section a power of arrest would be attached to the Order".

3. Effect of FLA 1996

3–55   In view of the statutory presumption that a power of arrest will be attached where the respondent has used or threatened violence (section 47(2)), it may be more difficult to settle such cases by giving/receiving undertakings unless the Court is prepared to find that the applicant or relevant child would be "adequately protected" without a power of arrest.

Enforcement of undertakings

1. Extent of powers

3–56   An undertaking given to the Court is enforceable as if it were an order of the Court: section 46(4). See *Hussain v. Hussain* [1986] 1 All E.R. 961, CA; *Roberts v. Roberts* [1990] 2 FLR 111, CA.

2. No power of arrest

The Court cannot attach a power of arrest to an undertaking: section 46(2), *Carpenter v. Carpenter* [1988] 1 FLR 12, CA. However, as an undertaking is otherwise enforceable as if it were an order of the Court, an applicant would, it seems, be able to apply for a warrant of arrest under section 47(8) if she considered that the respondent was in breach.

3. No appeal

There cannot be an appeal against an undertaking—the Court of Appeal "can 3–57 only operate on orders": *McConnell v. McConnell* (1980) 10 Fam. Law 214.

E. Injunctions and Children

Family Law Act 1996: Public Law

1. CA 1989 amendments

Section 52 and Schedule 6 to FLA 1996 amend Parts 4 and 5 of CA 1989 3–58 relating to interim care orders and emergency protection orders by inserting section 38A and B and section 44A and B.

2. Emergency ousters

The Court has the power, on making an interim care order or emergency 3–59 protection order, also to make an order excluding a named individual from the child's home or a defined area around the home—an "exclusion requirement".

3. When?

This power will enable the Court to protect children *e.g.* by excluding an abuser 3–60 or suspected abuser from the home in circumstances where the child will be at risk as long as that person lives in the home, but where it would be damaging or traumatic for the child to be removed pending further enquiry or assessment. Hitherto, Local Authorities had encountered difficulties in seeking to achieve such a result: See *Nottinghamshire County Council v. P* [1994] 2 FLR 134, CA (not appropriate for Local Authority to apply for prohibited steps order to oust a father from family home); *Re. S* (Minors) (inherent jurisdiction: ouster) (1994) (not appropriate to oust a parent by making a "no contact" order under C.A. 1989 section 34: below case 9); see also *Devon County Council v. S* [1995] 1 All E.R. 243, Fam. Div.

4. Range of powers

By including an exclusion requirement, the Court may do one or more of the 3–61 following:

(a)   require the named person to leave the dwellinghouse in which he is living with the child;

(b)   prohibit the named person from entering a dwellinghouse in which the child lives;

(c)   exclude the named person from a defined area around the dwellinghouse in which the child lives: CA 1989, ss.38A(3), 44A(3).

5. A two stage process

3–62   If the Court decides to make an interim care order or emergency protection order, it may go on to include an exclusion requirement where the statutory criteria are met: section 38A(1); section 44A(1). This is a supplementary power; the Court cannot make a free-standing exclusion requirement under section 38A or 44A CA 1989, as an alternative to making an interim care order or emergency protection order. It is to be noted that an exclusion requirement may be added to an interim care order made on the basis of the threshold criteria in CA 1989, s.31(2)(a) or (b)(i)—but not (b)(ii) (the child being beyond parental control). An exclusion requirement may be added to an emergency protection order whether it is granted under CA 1989, s.44(1)(a)(b) or (c).

6. Exclusion order criteria

3–63   Before adding an exclusion order to an interim care order or emergency protection order, the Court must be satisfied that there is reasonable cause to believe that if the relevant person is excluded from the dwellinghouse in which the child lives, then:

(a)   (for ICO's) the child will cease to suffer or cease to be likely to suffer significant harm; *or*
        (for EPO's) the child will not be likely to suffer significant harm, or the applicant's enquiries will cease to be frustrated; *and*

(b)   (for both) that another member of the household (whether a parent of the child or some other person) is able and willing to give the child the care which it would be reasonable to expect a parent to give him and consents to the exclusion order being made.

7. Duration of ouster

3–64   The maximum duration of the exclusion requirement is the duration of the order to which it is supplementary; the Court may specify a shorter period which may be extended: See CA 1989, s.38A(4),(7) and s.44A(4), (7).

8. Power of arrest may be attached

(a) Jurisdiction

3–65   The Court may attach a power of arrest to an exclusion requirement under CA 1989, s.38A(5), s.44A(5). These sections are silent as to the criteria, but the Law Commission considered that the Court should have such a power where this was necessary to protect the child from an immediate risk of significant harm (Law Com. No.207 para. 6.22).

(b) Duration

The maximum duration of the power of arrest is the duration of the exclusion order to which it is added; the Court may specify a shorter period which may be extended: section 38A(6), (7); section 44A(6), (7).

(c) Police powers

A constable may arrest without warrant a person whom he has reasonable cause to believe to be in breach of the exclusion requirement: section 38A(8); section 44A(8).

(d) Procedure after arrest

The same procedure applies as if the person had been arrested under a power of 3–66 arrest pursuant to FLA 1996, s.47(6). In particular, the person arrested:

(1) must be produced before the appropriate Court within 24 hours from arrest (taking no account of Christmas Day, Good Friday or Sundays);
(2) may be remanded on bail or in custody; Court may impose requirements if bail granted;
(3) may be remanded for medical examination and report;
(4) may, in appropriate circumstances, be remanded for report as to his mental condition.

See CA 1989, s.38A(9); s.44A(9).

9. Lapse of exclusion order

If the Local Authority (or other applicant) places the child outside the home for a 3–67 continuous period of more than 24 hours, the exclusion order will cease to have effect: section 38A(10); section 44A(10).

10. Duration and variation of order

The person ousted from the child's home may apply for variation or discharge of 3–68 the exclusion requirement, and/or of the power of arrest attached to the exclusion requirement: CA 1989, s.39(3A) (3B); s.45 (8A), (8B).

11. Undertakings

If the Court has the power to oust a person by the inclusion of an exclusion 3–69 requirement, it may accept an undertaking from that person; a power of arrest cannot be attached (CA 1989, s.38B(1) and (2); s.44B(1) and (2)). The undertaking is enforceable as if it were a Court order, and will lapse if the local authority (or other applicant) places the child outside the home for a continuous period of more than 24 hours.

12. Consent of carer required

3-70   Before making an exclusion requirement the Court must be satisfied, *inter alia*, that the person caring for the child consents. As the ouster is supplementary to the interim care order or emergency protection order, the local authority retains the power to remove the child from the home where, for example, the carer withdraws consent or cooperation, or colludes with the excluded person, or where the excluded person breaches the exclusion order.

Children bringing or defending injunction proceedings under FLA 1996

1. The General Rule

3-71   A child may neither bring nor defend civil or family proceedings otherwise than through a next friend or guardian *ad litem*: RSC Ord. 80, r.2; FPR 1991, r.9.2; CCR Ord. 10, r.1.

2. Exception to the rule

3-72   "An exception to that long-established principle has been introduced, uniquely, into family law by FPR, r.9.2A in certain specified instances. Those are:

(1)   Where the Court has given leave at the outset for a minor to begin or defend proceedings without a next friend or guardian *ad litem*. Such leave is only to be granted if the Court considers that 'the minor concerned has sufficient understanding to participate as a party in the proceedings . . . without a next friend or guardian *ad litem*' (r.9.2A(1)(a), (6)).

(2)   Where a minor has a next friend or guardian *ad litem* in proceedings that are already on foot and applies successfully for leave to prosecute or defend the remaining stages of the proceedings without a next friend or guardian *ad litem*. Leave for that purpose is only to be granted if the Court reaches the same conclusion as in case (1) (r.9.2A) (4), (6)).

(3)   Where a Solicitor has accepted instructions from the minor to act in the proceedings, and where that Solicitor considers that the minor is able, having regard to his understanding, to give instructions in relation to the proceedings (r.9.2A(1) (b) (i), (ii))."

(*Re CT (A minor)* (Wardship: representation) [1993] 2 FLR 278, CA *per* Waite L.J. at p.281).

3. Applying for injunctions

3-73   Under FLA 1996, s.43, a child under 16 cannot apply for an occupation order or non-molestation order without the leave of the Court. The Court may only grant leave if it is satisfied that the child has sufficient understanding to make the proposed application.

4. Court assessment of understanding

In *Re S (a minor)* (independent representation) [1993] 2 FLR 437, CA, Sir 3–74 Thomas Bingham M.R. made the following observations in relation to the assessment of a child's understanding:

(a) the issue is the child's understanding, not his age (see also *Re H (A Minor)* (Care proceedings: child's wishes) [1993] 1 FLR 440 at 449 *per* Thorpe J.);

(b) an understanding is not absolute—it must be assessed relatively to the issues in the proceedings; where any sound judgment on these issues calls for insight and imagination which only maturity and experience can bring, the Court will be slow to conclude that the child's understanding is sufficient;

(c) when considering the child's application for leave, the Court has a discretion to hear any party whom he thinks it necessary or desirable to hear in the interests of justice;

(d) the Court should balance two considerations: first, that children are human beings in their own right with individual minds and wills, views and emotions, which should command serious attention; secondly, a child is, after all, a child. The judge has to do his best, on the evidence before him, to assess the understanding of the individual child in the context of the proceedings in which he seeks to participate.

5. What is sufficient understanding?

Lord Scarman in *Gillick v. West Norfolk and Wisbech AHA and anor* [1986] A.C. 3–75 112 at 188A expressed it as "the attainment by a child of an age of sufficient discretion to enable him or her to exercise a wise choice in his or her own interests". This was re-stated by Sir Thomas Bingham MR in *Re S* (above) who also referred to those qualities that children often lack:

(a) maturity to weigh the longer term against the shorter;

(b) insight to know how they will react in certain situations;

(c) imagination to know how others will react in certain situations;

(d) experience to measure the probable against the possible.

6. Role of Solicitor in assessing understanding

By virtue of FPR 1991, r.9.2(10) it is for the Court to decide whether a child who 3–76 comes before it as a party without a next friend or guardian has the necessary ability, having regard to his understanding, to instruct his solicitor—the solicitor's judgment and his acceptance of instructions is not conclusive: *Re CT (A minor) (Wardship: representation)* (1993) (above). However, Sir Thomas Bingham M.R. observed that the solicitor's judgment should be respected and given great weight: "Judges should be very slow to go behind or question the professional judgment of a responsible solicitor" (at p.291). Also see *Re T* (Application by child) [1993] 1 FCR 646.

7. Nature of enquiry

In *Re CT* (above), Waite L.J. observed (at p.289): 3–77

"I would hope and expect that instances where a challenge is directed to a solicitor's view of his minor client's ability to instruct him will be rare, and that cases where the Court felt bound to question such ability of its own motion would be rarer still. If and when such instances do arise, I would expect them to be resolved by a swift, pragmatic inquiry conducted in a manner which involved the minimum delay and the least possible distress to the child concerned. It would be very unsatisfactory if such issues themselves became the subject of detailed medical or professional investigation".

In *Re H (A minor) (care proceedings: child's wishes)* (1993) (above) Thorpe J. considered that a child's ability to give instructions may need to be assessed by expert evidence in light of emotional disturbance which may remove a degree of rationality required for coherent and consistent instructions.

8. "Participate as a party"—meaning

3–78   In *Re. H (A minor) (role of official solicitor)* [1993] 2 FLR 552, Booth J. made the following observations:

(a)   consider all the circumstances of the case: the question whether a child has sufficient understanding to participate as a party without a guardian is to be considered in light of what *has* happened, and what may happen in the proceedings in future;

(b)   "Participating as a party": it means much more than instructing a solicitor as to his own views . . . "He may give evidence and he may be cross-examined. He will hear other parties, including in this case his parents, give evidence and be cross-examined. He must be able to give instructions on many different matters as the case goes through its stages and to make decisions as need arises" (at p.555).

9. Child's interests—not paramount

3–79   When assessing the sufficiency of a child's understanding, it is not for the Court to take into account what it may or may not consider to be in the child's best interests: *Re H (A minor)* (1993) above, *per* Booth J. The child's welfare is not paramount when determining a child's application for leave to apply for an order in family proceedings: *Re SC (A minor) (leave to seek residence order)* [1994] 1 FLR 96 Booth J.

10. Court retains discretion to grant leave

3–80   Where a child is found to have sufficient understanding to make an application, the Court has a discretion whether to grant leave: *Re SC* (1994) (above). An application for leave to apply should not be made *ex parte*, but on notice to all those with parental responsibility (*ibid.*).

11. Role of Official Solicitor

3–81   Where a child is allowed to instruct his own Solicitor and present his own case, the Court may ask the Official Solicitor for his continuing assistance as amicus in difficult cases: See *Re S (A minor)* (1993) (above) at p.448 and *Re H (A minor)* (1993) (above) at p.557 *per* Booth J. It would not be appropriate to join the Official Solicitor as a party in such circumstances.

12. Joining children as parties

Where children intervene in High Court family proceedings and separate 3–82 representation is required, they should be made parties to the proceedings for practical reasons, and to make their position clear: *L v. L (Minors) (separate representation)* [1994] 1 FLR 156, CA.

The Children Act 1989

1. Restriction on removal

Under CA 1989, s.13(1) (and s.33(7)) where a residence order (or care order) is in 3–83 force with respect to a child, no person may remove the child from the United Kingdom without the written consent of every person who has parental responsibility for the child *or* the leave of the Court, save for the person in whose favour the residence order is made (or the authority in whose care she/he is), who may take the child for a period of "less than one month": section 13(2), section 33(8).

2. The threatened snatch

If a person has reasonable grounds for believing that another person is intending 3–84 to remove a child from their care, the following orders may be sought under CA 1989 to restrain that other person from removing the child(ren):

(1)   a residence order under section 8 with its automatic restriction on removal from the United Kingdom;

(2)   conditions under section 11(7) which may be imposed (*e.g.* to a new or existing residence order) restricting removal (*e.g.* from the applicant, United Kingdom, etc.)

(3)   a prohibited steps order under section 8, specifically prohibiting any person from removing the child (*e.g.* from the applicant, United Kingdom, etc.).

3. Reasonable grounds for belief

In *Re S (Minors)* (1996) 10 CL 38, CA, a father sought to take his children on a 3–85 foreign holiday; the mother obtained an *ex parte* prohibited steps order which was discharged at an *inter partes* hearing. The Court of Appeal, upholding the discharge of the order, observed that although the mother feared that the children would not be returned to the jurisdiction, there was no evidence to support her concerns. Contrast *Re A—K (Minors)* (foreign passport: Jurisdiction) *The Times*, March 7, 1997, in which the High Court exercised its inherent jurisdiction to order a father to surrender his Iranian passport, to be kept by his solicitors and only released by order of the court or with the mother's consent. Such power is not limited to United

Kingdom nationals. The order was made in response to the mother's anxiety that the father, who had previously abducted one of their children, might do so again.

4. *Extent of powers*

3–86   The County Court cannot restrain a local authority or the Police from exercising their statutory powers under CA 1989 or their common law powers in respect of children. The Court may restrain a party to proceedings, by means of a prohibited steps order, from exercising his parental responsibility and involving those agencies if the Court is satisfied that to do so would be detrimental to the child's welfare: *D v. D* (County Court jurisdiction: injunctions) [1993] 2 FLR 802, CA. (Followed in *Devon County Council v. B*, *The Times*, January 7, 1997, CA).

5. *"Snatched" child—within the jurisdiction*

3–87   The person from whose care the child has been removed may apply for the following:

(1)   an *ex parte* residence order, and
(2)   a direction (or specific issue order) that the child be returned to the applicant's care, and
(3)   a direction that the child remain with the applicant pending an *inter partes* residence hearing (or prohibited steps order prohibiting further removal of the child).

See *Re B (Minors)* (residence Order) [1992] 3 All E.R. 867, CA; *Re G (Minors) The Times*, October 9, 1992, CA.

6. *"Snatched" child—outside the jurisdiction*

3–88   The Court may make an *ex parte* residence, specific issue and/or prohibited steps order even though the child has been taken abroad, where it may assist the applicant in any proceedings in a foreign country for the return of the child: *Re D (a minor)* [1992] 1 All E.R. 892, CA.

7. *Is it a "snatch" case?*

3–89   Where one parent takes the child from the other due to genuine concern for the child's welfare, it may not amount to a "snatch" case, and it may not necessarily be appropriate to order the immediate return of the child under an interim residence order: *Harvey v. Beavis* (1993) 11 C.L. 97, CA.

8. *Principles to be applied*

3–90   When determining an application to obtain, vary or discharge a section 8 Order, the Court should apply the following:

(a)   the principle that the child's welfare shall be the Court's paramount consideration (CA 1989, s.1(1));

(b)   the "delay principle" (section 1(2));

(c)   the welfare checklist set out at section 1(3) (opposed applications); and

(d)   the "no order" principle (section 1(5)).

9. Ex parte orders

An application for a section 8 order may be made *ex parte*, but *ex parte* orders 3–91 should be rare. The case must be compelling and an early return date should be fixed for an *inter partes* hearing: *Re M v. C* (children orders: reasons) [1993] 2 FLR 584: *Re Y (A minor) (ex parte residence order)* [1993] 2 FCR 422. *Ex parte* residence orders should only be made in exceptional circumstances, and should not be made unless there is compelling evidence that the child requires short term protection *e.g.* from physical or moral danger: *Re G (Minors) (ex parte interim residence order)* [1993] 1 FLR 910, CA; *Re P (A minor) (ex parte interim residence order)* [1993] 1 FLR 915, CA. Those seeking *ex parte* orders should behave with scrupulous care both as regards the application and the implementation of any order made: see *Re J (Minors) (ex parte orders)* (1997) (below case 10).

10. Applications

Section 8 Orders may be sought by making a free-standing application (CA 1989, 3–92 s.10(2)), or within any existing "family proceedings" which includes proceedings under FLA 1996, Pt 4 (CA 1989, s.8(3), (4) (h)). This is subject to:

(a)   any relevant restrictions set out in section 9;

(b)   obtaining leave where necessary to apply for the order sought (see section 10).

11. Applying for leave

Although the Courts are traditionally reluctant to grant leave *ex parte* (*Re M (prohibited steps order: application for leave)* [1993] 1 FLR 275), an *ex parte* application may be allowed in cases of emergency: *Re O (Minors) (leave to seek residence order)* [1994] 1 FLR 172.

12. Applying for leave—criteria

The Court will have "particular regard" to those factors set out at section 10(9). 3–93 It can take other matters into account, although it should be noted that the welfare of the child is *not* the Court's paramount consideration in an application for leave: *Re A (Minors)* (residence orders: leave to apply) [1992] 3 All E.R. 872, CA; *G v. Kirklees Metropolitan Borough Council* [1993] 1 FCR 357; *Re SC (A minor) (leave to seek residence order)* [1993] Fam. Law 618.

13. Age of the child—relevance

Section 8 orders can neither have effect beyond, nor be made after, the child's sixteenth birthday unless the Court is "satisfied that the circumstances of the case are exceptional" CA 1989, s.9(6), (7).

14. Enforcement of section 8 Orders

(a) Family Law Act 1986, s.34

3-94   Where the Court has made a section 8 order requiring a person to give a child to another person, and that Court is satisfied that the child has not been "given up in accordance with the order", it may authorise an officer of the Court or a constable to recover the child and deliver him to the person concerned.

(b) High Court and County Court

The Judge has a discretion to attach a penal notice to a section 8 order which is "enforceable by committal" on application; FPR 1991, r.4.21A; *Re N (A Minor) (access: penal notice)* [1992] 1 FLR 134, CA. To be enforceable by committal the order must be in injunctive (and not merely declaratory) terms; orders should therefore be specific as to what a party is required to do or prohibited from doing: *D v. D* (access: contempt: committal;) [1991] 2 FLR 34, CA. To remove a child from the jurisdiction in breach of a Court order and an undertaking was held to be as serious a contempt as it is possible to imagine in *M v. M (contempt: Committal)* [1992] 1 FCR 317, CA (upholding 12 months' imprisonment).

(c) Magistrates' Courts

3-95   Breaches of prohibited steps orders or specific issue orders fall within the Courts general enforcement powers under MCA 1980, s.63(3), where they order a person to do, or abstain from doing, something. Residence orders are expressly brought within the provisions of s.63(3) by virtue of CA 1989, s.14. As to whether an order is capable of founding a complaint under s.63, see *Re H* [1996] 1 FLR 614.

15. Seeking leave to remove child

3-96   Under CA 1989, s.13(3), when the Court makes a residence order, it may grant leave to any person to remove the child from the United Kingdom: such leave may be granted for specified purposes or may be in general terms (*e.g.* for temporary visits abroad) so that special leave need not be sought for each visit.

16. Application to remove—forum

3-97   An application for leave to remove a child from the United Kingdom may be made to a Family Proceedings Court, a County Court or the High Court.

An application for leave to remove a child permanently from the jurisdiction of the Court may be determined by either the High Court or the County Court depending on the difficulty and complexity of the decision: *MH v. GP (child: emigration)* [1995] 2 FLR 106, Fam. Div. Such applications should not be determined by Magistrates: *Re. L (A minor) (removal from jurisdiction)* [1993] 1 FCR 325 at 330. (For applications relating to Wards of Court, see Practice Direction (Family Division: Distribution of Business) [1992] 1 W.L.R. 586 (Appendix C). Such applications should not be made/granted *ex parte*: *Re. C (A Minor)* (1976) 6 Fam. Law 211, CA).

17. Application to remove—principles

In determining an application for leave to remove a child, the Court's paramount 3–98 consideration must be the child's welfare (CA 1989, s.1(1)).

In *MH v. GP* (1995) (above), in determining (and refusing) a mother's application for leave to permanently remove her child (D) from the jurisdiction, Thorpe J. stated (at p. 110):

> "I come to my first finding. I am quite satisfied, having seen and heard the mother, that the application for leave is not reactionary and strategic . . . So in approaching the first question, whether or not there should be leave for permanent removal, I apply the principles which have stood largely unchanged since the decision of the Court of Appeal in *Poel v. Poel* [1970] 1 W.L.R. 1469. In the later case of *Chamberlain v. de la Mare* (1983) 4 FLR 434, a strong Court of Appeal stated that, in considering whether to give leave, the welfare of the child was the first and paramount consideration, but that leave should not be withheld unless the interests of the children and those of the custodial parent were clearly shown to be incompatible.
>
> That statement of principle creates a presumption in favour of the reasonable application of the custodial parent, but in weighing whether the reasonable application is or is not incompatible with the welfare of D, I have to assess the importance of the relationship between D and his father, not only as it is but as it should develop . . ."

For other cases where *Poel v. Poel* was applied, see *Re K* [1992] 2 FLR 98; *M v. A* [1993] 2 FLR 715; *Re W* [1994] 1 FCR 842; *H v. H* [1995] 1 FLR 529, CA. Also see *M v. M* [1993] 1 FCR 5, CA (consider child's wishes and feelings) and *Re M, The Times*, December 11, 1991, CA (consider damage to respondent parent's relationship with child); *Re B* (1994) 2 FCR 309, CA.

However in *Re S* (Minors) C.A.T. April 2, 1996, Waite L.J. considered that although pre–CA 1989 cases are useful for guidance, they do not provide definite principles or binding tests to apply.

F. Miscellaneous practice points

Hearings

1. Advocates duty

In family proceedings advocates are under a duty to advise the justices if they 3–99 consider that a procedurally inappropriate course was being embarked upon: *Re F (A minor) The Times*, October 27, 1993, Wall J.

2. Judicial Continuity

This is important, particularly in cases involving children: *Re M (Minors) (Judicial continuity)* [1993] 1 FLR 903 at 909 *per* Butler-Sloss L.J.:

"In family cases, especially but by no means only in children cases, it is a positive advantage to have continuity of the judge or district judge. A party who has been criticised by a judge in earlier proceedings will frequently find himself or herself before the same judge on subsequent applications. For that to happen is not a reason for requesting that the matter be heard by a different Judge".

See also *W v. Wakefield City Council* [1994] 2 FCR 564 Wall J.

3. Cross-examination

3–100 One aim of cross-examination is to discredit witnesses. Where this has been achieved (*e.g.* by showing a witness has perjured himself) the justices should not withdraw in favour of a second bench, but should draw such conclusions from the perjury as are appropriate: *R. v. Plymouth J.J. exp. W* [1993] 2 FLR 777 (Ewbank J.).

4. Children—swearing affidavits

3–101 A child should not be asked to swear an affidavit to enhance either of his parents' prospects of success in private law proceedings regarding his upbringing: *Re M* (Family proceedings: Affidavits) [1995] 2 FLR 100 at pp.102–3, *per* Butler-Sloss L.J.:

". . . speaking entirely for myself I would very seriously deprecate any attempt by solicitor and counsel to boost the father's or mother's case in the Court of Appeal by involving the daughter or, in another case, a son of any age, but particularly not as young as 12, in swearing an affidavit at this stage or indeed at any stage. It is not the practice in family proceedings, and I say nothing about care proceedings, as I understand it, for children to be giving evidence. That may come. It has not come yet. Counsel suggested that because children had the right to make an application for leave to be involved, it would be perfectly acceptable for them to swear affidavits when they do not apply to become parties. But as I understand it, and no doubt my Lord will confirm, it is not the practice in the Family Division to allow children to intervene in family proceedings between their parents, and for very good reason. It is not fair on children that they should be dragged into the arena, that they should be asked specifically to choose between two parents, both of whom they love, and they ought not to be involved in the disputes of their parents."

5. Hearsay evidence

3–102 In:

(a) civil proceedings in the High Court or County Court, and
(b) (*inter alia*) family proceedings in Magistrates Courts

hearsay evidence shall be admissible where it is given in connection with the upbringing, maintenance or welfare of a child: Children (Admissibility of Hearsay) Ord. 1993 (S.I. 1993 No. 621).

6. Representation of litigants in person

Applications under CLSA 1990 by lay representatives for rights of audience will 3–103
only be granted, in the exercise of the Courts discretion, in exceptional circumstances, not merely on the consent of the parties, and notwithstanding the
applicant's claim that he had requisite knowledge and experience: *D v. S* (rights of
audience) *The Times*, January 1, 1997, CA, Lord Woolf M.R.

Appeals

1. Legal advisers—duty

A detached view should be taken of the merits of family cases. Appeals should 3–104
not be brought where there were no prospects of success, irrespective of the wishes
of the dissatisfied losing party: *Re D (Minors) (family appeals)*, *The Times*, October 28,
1994, CA; *Re N (Minors) (residence)*, *The Times*, April 6, 1995, CA.

2. Fresh evidence—general rule

Where a party seeks to adduce new evidence on appeal to the Court of Appeal he 3–105
must generally satisfy the following conditions, *i.e.* he must show that:

(a)   the evidence could not have been obtained with reasonable diligence for use at
        the trial;
(b)   the evidence would, if given, probably have an important influence on the
        result of the case (it need not be decisive);
(c)   the evidence must be apparently credible, although it need not be
        incontrovertible.

(*Ladd v. Marshall* [1954] 3 All E.R. 745 at 748 *per* Denning L.J.).

3. Fresh evidence—welfare of children

The conditions for the admission of fresh evidence set out in *Ladd v. Marshall* 3–106
(above) do not necessarily have to be fulfilled in cases where the welfare of children
is concerned: in such cases, the Court of Appeal should consider:

(a)   whether the appeal should be allowed without consideration of the fresh
        evidence, applying the paramountcy principle;
(b)   if the judge's decision is not found to be plainly wrong within *G v. G (Minors)
        (custody appeal)* [1985] FLR 894, the Court should then consider the fresh
        evidence, bearing in mind that the evidence is in affidavit form and untested
        in cross-examination at that stage: *Re B (Minors)* (custody) [1991] 1 FLR 317,
        CA; *Re W (A Minor) (residence order)* [1993] 2 FLR 625, CA.

4. Consent orders—no appeal

A party cannot appeal against a perfected and subsisting order where he is 3–107
expressed to have consented to it—the proper course is to apply to vary or set aside
the order: *Re F (A minor) (custody: consent order: procedure)* [1992] 1 FLR 561, CA.

However, the Court decided in *Re R (A Minor) (contact: consent order)* [1994] 2 FCR 1251, CA, that a party could appeal where she had consented to the order only after the judge had warned her that she would be at risk of costs should she continue to oppose the application.

5. *"Academic" appeals*

3–108 It is an abuse of process to bring a legally aided appeal where it was of academic interest to lawyers only, and where the outcome will not affect either party in the case: *S v. S (abuse of process of appeal)* [1994] 2 FCR 941, CA.

6. *Appeal—not a stay*

The commencement of an appeal does not operate as a stay of execution on the order being appealed—any application for a stay should be made to the Court appealed from, not the House of Lords: Practice Direction (Civil Procedure: stay of execution) (1996) 10 C.L. 58, HL.

7. *Appeals—Magistrates*

3–109 Under FLA 1996, s.61(1), an appeal lies to the High Court against a Magistrates' Court decision to make, or refuse to make, an order under Pt 4 of the FLA 1996. There is no appeal against a Magistrates' Court decision to decline jurisdiction under section 59(2)—*i.e.* where it considers that the case can "more conveniently be dealt with by another Court". On an appeal brought under section 62, the High Court may make such orders as may be necessary to give effect to its determination of the appeal, and also make such incidental or consequential orders as appear to be just (section 62(2), (3)). Any order made by the High Court shall be treated, for specified purposes, as if it were an order of the Magistrates' Court from which the appeal was brought; See section 62(4).

8. *Appeals—notes of evidence*

3–110 On an appeal from the Family Proceedings Court it is the duty of the Clerk to the Justices to provide the appeal court with clear, legible typescript notes of evidence, so that the appeal may be dealt with expeditiously: *S v. S (notes of evidence)*, *The Times*, September 8, 1992, Bracewell J.

Applications and Orders under the "Old Law"

1. *Pending applications unaffected*

3–111 The provisions of FLA 1996, Pt 4 (and the amendments and repeals set out in Sched. 8, Pt 3 and Sched. 10) will not effect any application for a non molestation or ouster injunction under DVMPA 1976, DPMCA 1978, ss. 16–18, or MHA 1983, ss.1 and 9, where such application is "pending immediately before the commencement of the repeal of that enactment" (FLA 1996, Sched. 9, para. 8.)

2. Existing Orders—Status?

Where an existing order or injunction made under DVMPA 1976, DPMCA 3–112
1978, ss. 16–18, or MHA 1983, ss. 1 and 9 is either:

(a)   in force immediately before the repeal of the relevant Act, or
(b)   was made after such repeal, in proceedings brought before that repeal,
the provisions of FLA 1996, Pt 4, Sched. 8, Pt 3 and Sched. 10 will not prevent the
order from remaining in force, or affect its enforcement: FLA 1996, Sched. 9, para.
10.

3. Existing orders—effect of FLA 1996

Where application is made to extend, vary or discharge an existing order, the court
may treat it as an application for an order under FLA 1996, Pt 4 if it thinks it just
and reasonable to do so (Sched. 9, para. 10(3)). The making of any order under FLA
1996, Pt 4 will discharge any existing order in force between the parties (*ibid.*, para.
10(4)).

CHAPTER FOUR

Tortious injunctions

A. Practice And Procedure

Commencing proceedings

1. Forum

An application for a tortious injunction may be made either in the High Court, or 4–01 in a County Court for the district in which the defendant lives or where the cause of action arose in whole or in part: CCR Ord. 4, r.2(1).

2. Documents

The action is commenced in a County Court by issuing a summons together with 4–02 Particulars of Claim: CCR Ord. 3, rr.1, 2(1), 3(1) and Ord. 6, r.1. Further the application should be set out in Form N16A, and be supported by an affidavit: CCR Ord. 13, r. 6(3). The plaintiff may seek a "freestanding" injunction and need not include a claim for damages or other relief: CCA 1984, s.38 as amended by CLSA 1990, s.3. In the High Court a summons is issued with a Statement of Claim and affidavit in support: RSC Ord. 29, r.1(2).

3. Notice—General Rule

CCR Ord. 13, r.6 and RSC Ord. 29, r. 1(2) provide that where the case is one of 4–03 urgency, the application may be made *ex parte* on affidavit. There must be strong grounds for making an *ex parte* application, which should be made promptly.

4. Affidavit practice

Where the applicant proceeds by way of *ex parte* application, the affidavit in 4–04 support should:

(a)   show the degree of urgency;

(b)   sufficiently explain any delay in making the application;

(c)   disclose all material facts;

(d)   explain the lack of proper notice/why it is impracticable to wait for an *inter partes* hearing.

See CCR Ord. 13, r.6(3A); RSC Ord. 29, r.1(2) (3).

5. Informal notice possible?

4–05   Giving short notice or informal notice to the other side is preferable to giving no notice at all: *G v. G* [1990] 1 FLR 395.

6. Exception to general rule—real emergency

4–06   In real emergencies, an *ex parte* injunction may be granted on the plaintiff's undertaking to issue an application or affidavit within a specified limited period *e.g.* 24 hours. In such cases the evidence may be given orally. It is the responsibility of the plaintiff's solicitor to ensure that the undertaking is complied with—long delay in carrying it out is serious contempt by the solicitor and may be punished as such.

7. Pleadings

The appropriate cause(s) of action must be properly asserted in the pleading. In an appropriate case, the Court may allow the pleading to be amended "or if technically necessary a further action can be started and the two can be consolidated" (*Khorasandjian v. Bush* [1993] 2 FLR 66 at 69 *per* Dillon L.J.).

8. Draft Order

4–07   Except where the case is one of urgency, a draft of the injunction should be prepared beforehand by the plaintiff and, if the application is granted, the draft should be submitted to the judge by whom the application was heard and shall be settled by him/her (CCR Ord. 13, r. 6(6)).

9. Parties to a marriage

4–08   Spouses may each bring an action in tort against the other by reason of Law Reform (Husband and Wife) Act 1962, s.1(1), although the Court has the power to stay the action where it considers that no substantial benefit will accrue to either party from continuation of the proceedings (s.1(2) (a)). See also RSC Ord.89, r.2.

Service of Application

1. Time for service

4–09   The defendant is entitled to at least two clear days between service of the application and affidavit and the hearing: CCR Ord. 13, r. 6(3), Ord. 1, r. 9(4). The Court has power to abridge that period: CCR Ord. 13, r.4(1). It is to be noted by virtue of CCR Ord. 7, r.3 that:

"no process shall be served or executed within England and Wales on a Sunday, Good Friday or Christmas Day except, in the case of urgency, with leave of the court". (See RSC Ord. 65, r.10).

2. Service—by whom

By virtue of CCR Ord. 7, r.2(b) where the document is served personally, it may 4–10 be served by:

(a) a bailiff of the Court or, if the person to be served attends the office of the Court, any other officer of the Court; or
(b) a party to the proceedings or some person acting as his agent; or
(c) the solicitor of a party or a solicitor acting as an agent for such solicitor or some person employed by either solicitor to serve the document.

Service should not be effected by any person under the age of 16 years.

3. The violent response to service

Where the bailiff is prevented either by violence or threats of the person to be 4–11 served or any other person acting in concert with him from serving a document it should be sufficient service to leave the document as near as practicable to the person served (CCR Ord. 7, r.5.) Documents may be properly served even where the defendant does not accept them: *Walters v. Whitelock* (1994) (below case 13).

4. Affidavit of service

Once documents have been served, an affidavit of the service of those documents 4–12 should be sworn by the person serving them: CCR Ord. 7, r.6. If such affidavit of service is not available at the hearing, oral evidence of service may be given. In the High Court the affidavit must state by whom the document was served, the day of the week and the date on which it was served, where it was served and how. (RSC Ord.65, r.8).

The Hearing

1. Forum

The application for injunctive relief will be heard in open court, unless the order is 4–13 being made *ex parte*: CCR Ord. 13, r.6(5). In the County Court, a District Judge has jurisdiction to deal with the application where the value of the claim is £5,000 or less: CCR Ord. 21, r.5(1).

2. Evidence

Once served with the application and affidavit the defendant may prepare and file 4–14 an affidavit in reply; however, the rules do not require him to do so.

3. No power of arrest

4–15   The Court cannot attach a power of arrest to an injunction made in a tortious action. The FLA 1996, s.47 confers jurisdiction to attach a power of arrest to orders made under the FLA 1996; actions in tort are not "family proceedings" within the meaning of s.63(1), (2).

4. Proceedings in absence

4–16   Since an injunction will restrict a person in his actions and the Court may deprive him of certain rights, the Courts much prefer to give that person a chance to be heard.

However, pursuant to CCR Ord. 13, r.1(5), the Court has the power to proceed in the defendant's absence:

> "Where any party to the application fails to attend on the hearing the Court may proceed in his absence if, having regard to the nature of the application, the Court thinks it expedient to do so."

5. Duration of injunction

If the matter is adjourned *sine die*, the injunction should only be granted for a limited period *i.e.* a matter of months.

6. Service of injunction

4–17   The general rule is that the injunction order must be served personally upon the party against whom the order was made: RSC Ord. 45, r.7; CCR Ord. 29, r.1(2). An order requiring an act to be done must be served within the time limit fixed for compliance; CCR Ord. 29, r.1(2)(b). Those provisions re dispensing with service/ substituted service are set out in Chapter 5.

B. General Principles

Jurisdiction

1. Tortious injunctions - when?

4–18   Generally, where an application cannot be launched under the FLA 1996, it will be necessary to rely on the tort of trespass, assault, nuisance or harassment; for example, in those cases at para. 2–21 where the parties are not "associated persons" within section 62(3)–(5).

2. *Jurisdiction—statutory formula*

County Courts: CCA 1984, s.38(1) provides that a County Court "may make   4–19
                 any order which could be made by the High Court if the
                 proceedings were in the High Court". Under section 38(2) any
                 order made by a county court may be:
                 (a) absolute or conditional;
                 (b) final or interlocutory.

High Court: SCA 1981, s.37(1) provides "the High Court may by order
                 (whether interlocutory or final) grant an injunction . . . in all
                 cases in which it appears to the Court to be just and convenient
                 to do so"

Pre-requisites to applications

1. *A legitimate interest*

Despite the width of the Courts' powers, an injunction cannot properly be   4–20
granted at common law unless the plaintiff can show "at least an arguable cause of
action to support the grant" (*Burris v. Azadani* [1995] 4 All E.R. 802 *per* Sir
Thomas Bingham M.R.). Further, the order sought must reasonably be regarded as
necessary for the protection of the plaintiff's legitimate interest.

2. *Intervention of Court warranted*

The Courts are not concerned with trivia: "the law expects the ordinary person to   4–21
bear the mishaps of life with fortitude and . . . customary phlegm . . ." (*Khorasandjian v. Bush* (1993) *per* Lord Dillon)

3. *The defendant*

The person against whom the injunction is sought must be someone who can
properly be made a party to the action.

Interlocutory relief

1. *When, in principle*

A permanent injunction may be granted only after trial of the action but in order   4–22
to give more immediate protection to the plaintiff he/she may apply for an
interlocutory injunction. In *The "Siskina"* [1979] A.C. 210 the Court considered that
the interlocutory order must be made in an action claiming substantive relief which
the Court has jurisdiction to grant and to which the interlocutory order is but

ancillary. It is, however, frequent in these situations to apply for an interlocutory injunction with a view to the full application being adjourned *sine die*.

2. Scope of interlocutory relief

4–23   In *Khorasandjian v. Bush* (1993) Dillon L.J. observed that "the form of an interlocutory injunction does not have to follow slavishly the form of the substantive relief which would be likely to be granted at the trial if the plaintiff succeeds." See also *Fresh Fruit Wales Ltd v. Halbert, The Times*, January 29, 1991, CA.

The majority of the Court in *Khorasandjian* found that the injunction which restrained the defendant from "harassing pestering or communicating with" the plaintiff was justified in law, and the order was confirmed without variation. The order would have been similarly approved had it restrained the defendant from "molesting" the plaintiff.

Powers of the court

1. Restrain tortious conduct

4–24   The Court may, in an appropriate case, grant an injunction to restrain a tort which has been, or is likely to be, committed. An injunction may be made *quia timet* in appropriate cases, before an actual tort has been committed, *i.e.* where there is a real possibility that the conduct complained of, if not restrained, would cause damage to the plaintiff (see *Khorasandjian v. Bush* (1993)). Such power applies to mandatory and prohibitory injunctions, but will not be exercised prematurely—the Court aims to do justice between the parties.

2. Restrain non-tortious conduct?

4–25   In *Burris v. Azadani* (1995) the Court of Appeal held that the Court's powers were not limited to restraining conduct which was in itself tortious or otherwise unlawful—the question is whether the order is reasonably regarded as necessary to protect the plaintiff's legitimate interests.

3. Exclusion Zones in tort?

4–26   In *Patel v. Patel* [1988] 2 FLR 179, the Court of Appeal approved the deletion of an exclusion zone order from an injunction. However, in *Burris v. Azadani* (1995) the Court of Appeal did not interpret *Patel* as laying down any general principle forbidding the making of exclusion zone orders in a proper case *e.g.* "where the commission of a tort was reasonably to be apprehended and where an exclusion zone was reasonably judged to be necessary for the protection of the plaintiff as the potential victim of tortious conduct" (*per* Sir Thomas Bingham M.R.).

4. Exclusion zones—not readily imposed

4–27   Such an order should not be readily imposed, or made without very good reason as it operates to restrain otherwise lawful conduct. When considering whether to create an exclusion zone around the plaintiff's property, the Court must reconcile the respective rights of the parties and must not interfere with the defendant's right (to move freely along the highway) more than is necessary to protect the plaintiff's right (not to be harassed): See *Burris v. Azadani, per* Schiemann L.J.

5. Exclusion zones—liberty to apply

A permanent injunction containing an exclusion zone order should include a 4–28 liberty to the defendant to apply to discharge it (*ibid., per* Schiemann L.J.). It is suggested that this should also be included where such an order is included in an *ex parte* interlocutory injunction.

C. Heads of Tort

Assault and battery

1. Jurisdiction

The plaintiff must show that he or she has been, or is about to be, the victim of a 4–29 battery and/or an assault:

(a) Battery: deliberate or negligent direct, unwanted physical contact with the plaintiff (save for the generally acceptable, ordinary physical contact of everyday life: *F v. West Berkshire Health Authority* [1990] 2 A.C. 1).

(b) Assault: "an overt act indicating an immediate intention to commit a battery, coupled with the capacity of carrying that intention into effect . . . an act causing reasonable apprehension of a battery . . ." (*Clerk and Lindsell on Torts* (17th ed.), paras 12–12, 12–13).

2. Actionable per se

Assault and battery are actionable without proof of damage; the plaintiff need not 4–30 prove an intention to injure: *Wilson v. Pringle* [1987] Q.B. 237. Threats to assault or threats of violence may be restrained *per se* by injunction "because they are threats to commit a tort" even where they do not cause injury or illness, and whether or not they were calculated to cause the plaintiff harm (*per* Dillon L.J., *Khorasandjian v. Bush* (1993) at p.72E).

3. Evidence

If the plaintiff has sustained injury, medical and/or photographic evidence should be obtained where possible.

4. Criminal cases

It is to be noted that psychological injury can amount to actual bodily harm: *R.v.* 4–31 *Chanfook* [1994] 1 W.L.R. 689; *R. v. Burstow, The Times,* July 30, 1996, CA. In *R. v. Ireland, The Times*, May 22, 1996, CA, a defendant telephoned women on a number of occasions and remained silent when the telephone was answered. The Court considered that it was a question of fact whether such act amounted to an assault: the victims were in fear as they did not know what D would do next. Also see the case of *Constanza* (1997), (below case 37).

Trespass to property

1. Jurisdiction

4–32   The plaintiff must show that there has been—or is threatened—a wrongful voluntary entry by the defendant upon property in the exclusive possession of the plaintiff, *i.e.* the plaintiff is the freehold or leasehold owner, or the tenant or licensee with rights of occupation in the property in question.

2. Co-ownership

4–33   The defendant should have no right to possession of the property in question— indeed it is a trespass for one co-owner (or tenant in common) to exclude the other from the property, or part of it.

3. Actionable per se

4–34   Trespass is actionable without proof of damage: *Stoke-on-Trent Council v. W & J Wass Ltd* [1988] 1 W.L.R. 1406 at 1411 *per* Nourse L.J. The plaintiff is entitled to undisturbed occupation of the property.

Private Nuisance

1. Jurisdiction

4–35   ". . . the essence of nuisance is a condition or activity which unduly interferes with the use or enjoyment of land" (*Clerk and Lindsell on Torts* (17th ed.) para. 18–01). A person may sue in private nuisance where he or she has an interest (freehold or leasehold) in land or a right to occupy land (*Malone v. Laskey* [1907] 2 K.B. 141, CA; *Nunn v. Parkes* (1924) 158 L.T. Jo 431, D.C.; and see *Metropolitan Property v. Jones* [1939] 2 All E.R. 202). Further, a person in *de facto* possession of land may maintain an action in nuisance (*Foster v. Warblington UDC*) [1906] 1 K.B. 648). So too may a licensee with an exclusive right to possess land (*Newcastle-under-Lyme Corporation v. Wolstanton* [1942] Ch. 92).

2. What about a mere licensee?

4–36   In *Khorasandjian v. Bush* [1993] 3 All E.R. 669; [1993] 2 FLR 66, the Court of Appeal held by a majority that harassment by persistent unwarranted telephone calls was an actionable interference, under the head of private nuisance, with the plaintiff's ordinary and reasonable use and enjoyment of property where she was lawfully present, even though she had no proprietary right or interest in property.

Dillon L.J. stated (at p.675; 70):

> "To my mind, it is ridiculous if in this present age the law is that the making of deliberately harassing and pestering telephone calls to a person is only actionable in the civil courts if the recipient of the calls happens to have the freehold or a leasehold proprietary interests in the premises in which he or she has received the calls . . . The Court has at times to reconsider earlier decisions in the light of changed social conditions".

These views were applied in *Hunter v. Canary Wharf Ltd* [1996] 1 All E.R. 482, **4–37** CA, which held that occupation of property as a home confers upon the occupant a capacity to sue in private nuisance. *Per* Pill L.J. at p.498:

> "There has been a trend in the law to give additional protection to occupiers in some circumstances. Given that trend and the basis of the law of nuisance in this context, it is no longer tenable to limit the sufficiency of that link by reference to proprietary or possessory interests in land. I regard satisfying the test of occupation of property as a home provides a sufficient link with the property to enable the occupier to sue in private nuisance. It is an application in present-day conditions of the essential character of the test as contemplated by Lord Wright. It appears to me, as it did to Dillon L.J., to be right in principle and to avoid inconsistencies, for example between members of a family, which in this context cannot now be justified."

3. Must prove damage

In *Khorasandjian v. Bush*, the Court accepted that damage was a necessary **4–38** ingredient of the tort of private nuisance. Dillon L.J. considered that:

> "the inconvenience and annoyance to the occupier caused by such calls, and the interference thereby with the ordinary and reasonable use of the property are sufficient damage. The harassment is the persistent making of the unwanted telephone calls, even apart from their content; if the content is itself, as here, threatening and objectionable, the harassment is the greater".

Wrongful interference with goods.

1. Jurisdiction

The Court may grant an injunction to restrain the defendant from interfering with the plaintiff's property.

2. Examples

"Wrongful interference with goods such as the taking of the plaintiff's handbag, **4–39** or . . . malicious damage to property, such as, if sufficiently proved, the making of the scratches on the paint work of the plaintiff's car". (*Khorasandjian v. Bush* (above) at p.70).

Harassment

1. Statutory Creation of Civil Tort

4–40 The Protection from Harassment Act 1997, s.1 prohibits a person from pursuing a "course of conduct" which

(a)   amounts to harassment of another, and
(b)   he knows/ought to know amounts to harassment of another.

He ought to know it amounts to harassment of another if a reasonable person in possession of the same information would think the course of conduct amounted to harassment of the other (s.1(2)).

2. Definitions: PHA 1997, s.7

4–41 "Harassment"   not defined, but includes alarming a person or causing the person distress

"Course of Conduct"   must involve conduct on at least two occasions

"Conduct"   includes speech.

3. Civil remedy

Under section 3, an actual or apprehended breach of the section 1 prohibition of harassment may be the subject of a civil claim by the person who is/may be the victim of the course of conduct in question. The Court may (inter alia) award damages for any anxiety caused by, or any financial loss resulting from, the harassment (section 3(2)).

4. Criminal offences created

4–42   The PHA 1997, ss.2 and 4 make it an offence in England and Wales to pursue a course of conduct which:

(a)   amounts to harassment of a person, or
(b)   causes a person to fear, on at least two occasions, that violence will be used against him.

The Act provides for three statutory defences, the Courts powers of sentence, and the power to make "restraining Orders" to prevent further harassment with criminal consequences for breach of such Orders (see Appendix D below).

CHAPTER FIVE

Committal

A. General principles

Jurisdiction

1. Contempt

Breach of an injunction, whether a mandatory or prohibitory order, is a contempt **5–01** of Court (RSC Ord. 45, r.5–7, Ord. 52 and CCR Ord. 29).

2. FLA 1996

Section 58 provides that the power to deal with contempt of Court arising out of breach of orders made under FLA 1996, Pt 4 may be exercised by the "relevant judicial authority" *i.e.*, a High Court Judge, a District Judge or County Court Judge, or a Magistrates' Court, according to the level of Court where the order was made (see section 63 (1)).

3. Purpose of contempt proceedings

Committal proceedings are intended to: **5–02**

(a)   uphold the authority of the Court;
(b)   punish the contempt;
(c)   ensure that orders are obeyed;
(d)   demonstrate that respondents disobey orders at their peril:

See *James v. Cliffe, The Times,* June 16, 1987, CA; *Johnson v. Walton* [1990] 1 FLR 350, CA (below case 2). They are not intended to provide solace or compensation to the applicant.

4. Undertakings

An undertaking has all the force of an injunction. Breach of an undertaking is a **5–03** contempt, is enforceable as if it were a Court order, and can attract equally severe punishment: *Hussain v. Hussain* [1986] 1 All E.R. 961, CA, *Roberts v. Roberts* [1990]

2 FLR 111, CA, FLA 1996, s.46(4). To be effective, an undertaking has to be given and recorded in Court (*Gandolfo* [1981] Q.B. 359, CA). *Hussain*, however, is authority for the proposition that the procedural requirements for the enforcement of undertakings given to the Court are not as strict as those applying to formal orders of the Court. In that case, an order committing the husband for breach of an undertaking was held to be valid notwithstanding that the original order in which the undertaking was recited was neither served on him nor endorsed with a penal notice.

5. Drafting the injunction order

5–04   If an injunction order is not indorsed with a penal notice it cannot be enforced by way of committal (but see *Cleveland County Council v. L, The Times*, April 8, 1996, CA – below case 14). In the High Court, where an undertaking is voluntarily given to the Court, there is no requirement for a penal notice: *D v. A & Co.* [1900] 1 Ch. 484; *Hussain v. Hussain* [1986] 1 ALL E.R. 961. But as Sir John Donaldson M.R. said in *Hussain* at p.964:

> ". . . it is in all cases highly desirable that any undertaking to the Court shall be recorded and served on the giver personally, in order to remove all scope for argument as to the precise terms of the undertaking and as to the extent of his knowledge".

In the same case, Neill LJ observed that the undertaking should be recited as a preamble to an order of the Court, which should explain the possible consequences of breach.

In the County Court, the effect of CCR Ord. 29, r.1(3) and r.1A is to require orders of the Court *and* undertakings given by a party to be indorsed with a penal notice and served in accordance with Ord. 29, r.1(2) (orders) or r.1A(2) (undertakings).

6. Mandatory injunctions—drafting

5–05   To be enforceable, an order requiring the respondent to do an act, or an undertaking to do an act (*e.g.* leave the property) must state the time within which the act is to be done (RSC Ord. 42, r.2(1); RSC Ord. 45, r.5(1) (a); CCR Ord. 22, r.3 and CCR Ord. 29, r.1 (1)). Where a mandatory injunction does not specify a time within which the act is to be done, an application may be made to the Court to fix a time: RSC Ord. 45, r.6(3).

An application for such a "time limit" must

(a)   be made by Summons;
(b)   be personally served on the person required to do the act in question;
(c)   state the "time limit" sought for performance of the required act; and
(d)   should be supported by affidavit.

5–06   The Court may fix such time as it thinks fit, although the order or undertaking should be precise as to:

(1)   the person to whom the order is directed,

(2)   the act(s) to be done,

(3)   the time within which the act(s) must be done; (*e.g.* "not later than 2 p.m. on
..... day, the ..... day of ..... 19 .....");

(4)   consequences of breach.

The Court cannot commit the defendant for breaching an injunction which failed to clearly specify the act(s) to be done and does not specify a time for compliance: *Parsons v. Nasar* [1990] 2 FLR 103, CA; *Temporal v. Temporal* [1990] 2 FLR 98, CA; *Re P (minors) (Custody Order: penal notice)* [1990] 1 W.L.R. 613, CA.

7. Mandatory injunctions—enforcement

A mandatory injunction order must be served personally upon the party against 5–07
whom it is sought to enforce the order "before the expiration of the time within which he was required to do the act": RSC Ord. 45, r.7(2) (b), together with any order specifying, extending or abridging the time limit for doing the act: RSC Ord. 45, r.7 (5); *Re Seal* [1903] 1 Ch.87. Where the time limit has expired before personal service can be effected, an order should be obtained extending the time for doing the required act.

8. Sentencing powers

The power to imprison is explored below. There is also a power to fine: 5–08
Phonographic Performance Ltd v. Amusement Caterers (Peckham) Ltd [1963] 2 All E.R. 493. Non-compliance with a mandatory order, by failing to perform an act within a specified period, is a single breach—the respondent should not be committed/ sentenced for the same offence twice—see *Kumari v. Jalal* [1996] 4 All E.R. 65, CA (below case 15).

Invalid defence to committal applications

1. Merits of the order—irrelevant to question of contempt

It is no defence to allege that the order should not have been made or has since 5–09
been discharged. An order of the Court must be obeyed whilst it stands, and a breach is still contempt even if, at a later stage, the order is discharged: *The Eastern Trust Co. v. McKenzie, Mann & Co. Ltd* [1915] A.C. 750, PC; *Roberts v. Roberts* [1990] 2 FLR 111, CA (below case 16).

2. Applicant cannot waive contempt

Similarly, a voluntary undertaking can only be discharged or obeyed—not consen- 5–10
sually varied: *Cutler v. Wandsworth Stadium Ltd* [1945] 1 All E.R. 103, CA. Breach of the undertaking is contempt even if the other party is prepared to agree to the particular action. The respondent cannot negotiate with the applicant to negate the

effect of an injunction ordered by the Court. One party cannot give "permission" to the other to act in breach: *R v. Inland Revenue Commissioners ex p. Kingston-Smith, The Times*, August 15, 1996.

3. Propriety of order—irrelevant to question of contempt

5–11   It is no defence to allege that the original order is irregular. The proper course is to appeal against it or apply to set it aside: *Isaacs v. Robertson* [1985] A.C. 97 (for powers of the Court to set aside, see RSC Ord. 2 and CCR Ord. 37, r.5); *M v. Home Office* [1992] 4 All E.R. 97. See also *Johnson v. Walton* [1990] 1 FLR 350 at 352 *per* Lord Donaldson of Lymington M.R:

> "It cannot be too clearly stated that, when an injunctive order is made or when an undertaking is given, it operates until it is revoked on appeal or by the Court itself, and it has to be obeyed whether or not it should have been granted or accepted in the first place".

As Romer L.J. said in *Hadkinson* [1952] P. 285 at 288:

> "It is the plain and unqualified obligation of every person against, or in respect of whom, an order is made by the Court of competent jurisdiction, to obey it unless and until the order is discharged. The uncompromising nature of this obligation is shown by the fact that it extends even to cases where the person affected by an order believes it to be irregular or even void".

4. Impropriety of order—can be relevant

5–12   In *Holtom v. Holtom* (1981) (below case 17) the husband undertook not to return to the former matrimonial home and the wife gave an undertaking not to cohabit with another man at the home. The Court of Appeal held that the wife's undertaking was bad and should never have been accepted by the Court in the first place. It was further held that it was otiose to hear committal proceedings which were bound to be stayed.

5. Acting on legal advice

5–13   It is no defence to allege that an undertaking was breached by acting on legal advice, although this may be a mitigating factor when considering punishment: *Re Mileage Conference Group of the Tyre Manufacturers' Conference Ltd's Agreement* [1966] 2 All E.R. 849, RPC.

6. Misunderstanding

It will usually be no defence for a party to assert that he was misunderstood or did not think he was giving an undertaking where he has conveyed to the Court (*e.g.* by his own acts, or those of his Solicitor/Counsel) the clear belief that an undertaking has been given: *M v. Home Office* [1992] Q.B. 270, CA.

7. Forum non convenients

5–14   Where an order is made in proceedings with a foreign element, which have continued for some time, and an application to commit is made for an alleged breach of that order, it may be too late for the alleged contemnor to stay the action and/or set aside the committal application on the ground of forum non conveniens. In *Mansour v. Mansour* [1989] 1 FLR 418, CA at 419, Lord Donaldson M.R. observed:

> "If people want to raise the issue that the action would be more conveniently tried in a foreign Court, they should do so at the very outset before costs are incurred in the proceedings . . . I think it is of paramount importance that any application of this nature, which in effect is in much the same position as an application based upon the proposition that the Court has no jurisdiction, should be made at the outset and that no steps, or very minimal steps, should be taken in the action before it is made."

Pre-requisites to committal applications

1. The need for strict compliance with the rules

As the power to commit to prison is a draconian remedy which affects the liberty 5–15 of the subject, the Court will not exercise its power unless the application is brought strictly in compliance with the rules of Court (*per* Lord Denning M.R. in *McIlraith v. Grady* [1968] 1 Q.B. 468 at 477). These rules have the binding effect of statute and there is no power to waive them, save where expressly provided in the rules themselves. The importance of compliance was emphasised by Cumming-Bruce L.J. in *Nguyen v. Phung* [1984] FLR 773:

> "In spite of repeated pronouncements of this Court and an instruction from the Lord Chancellor it is still necessary quite frequently to quash orders for committal on the ground that the procedure in relation to bringing into existence valid orders for committal has been slapdash and contrary to law".

In *Kumari v. Jalal* (1996) (below Case 15) Neill L.J. observed (at p.66): 5–16

> "This is another case which demonstrates the care which has to be taken before orders for committal for contempt of Court are made. There are technical rules laid down. An order for committal involves the liberty of the subject. It is therefore important that, before an order is made, the Court should scrutinise with great care not only the facts but the procedure".

2. The effect of non-compliance with the rules

The case of *B v. B* (contempt: Committal) [1991] 2 FLR 588, demonstrates how 5–17 compliance with the rules is not only necessary in order to safeguard the liberty of the defendant. As Purchas L.J. said at p.591:

> "The circumstances in which this appeal comes before the Court demonstrates two regrettable features. The first is the persistent and blatant disregard by the appellant [the Contemnor] of orders of the Court. The second is the persistent and lamentable failure by the staff of the [relevant] County Court to perform the simplest of functions. The concatenation of these features has resulted in

the discharge from prison of a man who ought to be serving the remaining portion of an appropriate committal sentence for contempt of Court of 18 months."

3. The penal clause

5-18   All orders served should contain a penal clause: RSC Ord. 45, r.7 (4); CCR Ord. 29, r.1(3); *Iberian Trust Limited v. Founders Trust & Investment Co. Ltd* [1932] 2 K.B. 87. But see *Cleveland County Council v. L* (1996) (below case 14). In a County Court, when an undertaking is given, a penal notice should be incorporated: CCR Ord. 29, r.1A. Whilst this is not strictly necessary when an undertaking is given in the High Court, it is highly desirable: *Hussain v. Hussain* [1986] 1 All E.R. 961. This avoids argument as to the precise terms of the undertaking and extent of the contemnor's knowledge. When making a judgment or order enforceable by committal the Court must issue the penal notice at the time when the order or judgment is drawn up. The court has no discretion: *Williams v. Fawcett* [1985] 1 W.L.R. 501 at 503, *per* Sir John Donaldson M.R.; *Moerman-Lenglet v. Henshaw, The Times*, November 23 1992. The penal clause should be in the terms specified pursuant to The Supreme Court Practice, para 45/7/6, *i.e.*:

5-19 Positive order: "If you, the within named A.B., neglect to obey this order by the time stated you may be held to be in contempt of Court and liable to imprisonment".

Negative order: "If you, the within named A.B., disobey this order, you may be held to be in contempt of Court and liable to imprisonment.

Service of injunction

1. General rule—personal service of injunction

5-20   The general rule is that the injunction order must be served personally upon the party against whom it is sought to enforce the order: RSC Ord. 45, r.7; CCR Ord. 29, r.1(2). Accordingly, any application to commit for breach of the order must be supported by an affidavit as to its personal service. In the absence of an affidavit a court may be prepared to accept oral evidence as to service. It should be noted that the attendance of the respondent at the committal application does not of itself abrogate the necessity for proper service: *Mander v. Falke* [1891] 3 Ch. 488.

2. General rule—personal service of undertaking

(a) High Court:

5-21   It is not strictly necessary as a person is presumed to have knowledge of his undertaking. But in order to avoid any argument the order incorporating the undertaking with a penal notice should be served: *Hussain, per* Neill L.J. (see above).

The undertaking should be included as a recital or preamble in an order of the Court even where the substantial part of the order is simply adjourned *sine die*.

(b) County Court:

CCR Ord. 29, r.1A requires the document recording the undertaking to be served 5–22 on the respondent by the proper officer either by:

— handing a copy of the document to him before he leaves court; or
— posting a copy to him at his place of residence; or
— through his Solicitor.

If service cannot be effected in any of these ways, the proper officer shall send the document to the applicant, who "shall cause it to be served personally as soon as is practicable".

3. Dispensing with service—in principle

In the County Court, by CCR Ord. 29, r.1(7) the Court may dispense with service 5–23 of the injunction "if the Court thinks it just to do so". This power may only be exercised:

(a)   at the time of making the order, or
(b)   on separate application, after service has been evaded.

There is no jurisdiction to dispense with service retrospectively, after the alleged breach: *Lewis v. Lewis* [1991] 3 All E.R. 251, CA. In the High Court the relevant orders are RSC Ord. 45, r.7(7) and Ord. 52, r.4(3).

4. Dispensing with service—in practice

In the County Court and the High Court in the case of a prohibitory order, as 5–24 opposed to a mandatory order, the Court may dispense with the requirement of service where the judge is satisfied that the person against whom it is sought to enforce the judgment or order has had notice thereof either:

(a)   by being present when the judgment or order was made, or
(b)   by being notified of the terms of the judgment or order whether by telephone, telegram or otherwise: CCR Ord. 29, r.1(6); RSC Ord. 45, r.7(6).

The Court may dispense with service under this narrower provision either at the 5–25 time of making the injunction order, or at the hearing of the application to commit. The exercise of the power should be stated in the appropriate order: *Lewis v. Lewis* (*ibid.*).

The above does not apply to a mandatory injunction order: *Blome* (1976) 6 Fam. Law 215, *per* Faulks J. (below case 29); *Dempster v. Dempster, The Independent*, November 9, 1990. Nor does it apply to undertakings in the County Court (CCR Ord. 29, r.1A).

5. Substituted service

Additionally, in appropriate cases by virtue of CCR Ord. 7, r.8 there may be 5–26 substituted service of an order enforceable by committal: *Worboys v. Worboys* [1953] 1 All E.R. 857. In the High Court, the Court may also order substituted service pursuant to RSC Ord. 65, r.4. The Court should be satisfied that personal service is "impracticable", *e.g.* where the respondent is evading service.

5–27   The affidavit in support of an application for substituted service should set out the following matters:

(a)   the steps that have been taken to effect personal service (see RSC N.65/4/6 for guidance);

(b)   the grounds for asserting that personal service is impracticable and/or that the respondent is evading service (*e.g.* as opposed to a temporary absence);

(c)   the form of substituted service sought (*e.g.* service by post, service on solicitor known to be in communication with the respondent, service on a named person in substitution for the respondent);

(d)   the basis for believing that the proposed service will reach the respondent or come to his knowledge.

Also see *Re De Cespedes* [1937] 2 All E.R. 572 (below case 18)

Service of committal application

(1) General rule—personal service of application

5–28   The general rule requires that the Notice warning the alleged contemnor that an application will be made for him to be committed "shall be served on him personally": CCR Ord. 29, r.1(4); RSC Ord. 52, r.4(2). Documents can be properly served on an alleged contemnor, even though he does not accept them: *Walters v. Whitelock* (1994) (below case 13).

2. Dispensing with service—in principle

In the County Court, by CCR Ord. 29, r.1(7) the Court may dispense with personal service of the Notice to show cause "if the Court thinks it just to do so". The High Court has a discretion under RSC Ord. 52, r.4(3) to dispense with service of the notice.

3. Dispensing with service—in practice

5–29   Personal service should only be waived in exceptional cases where:

(a)   the circumstances are serious,

(b)   the need for relief is urgent,

(c)   the respondent knows of the injunction and possible consequences of breach,

(d)   the respondent has knowledge of the application and/or is deliberately evading service: *Spooner* (1962) 106 S.J. 1034: *Taylor v. Taylor* (1996) (below case 19).

Where the County Court waives personal service of a Notice to show cause, and a committal order is made, the judge "may of his own motion fix a date and time when the person to be committed is to be brought before him or before the Court" (CCR Ord. 29, r.1(8)).

4. Foreign defendant

In *Mansour v. Mansour* [1989] 1 FLR 418, the Court of Appeal held that where an 5–30
application is made to commit a foreign defendant who was out of the jurisdiction
for contempt of Court, the Court's discretion to dispense with service of the Notice
is not barred or fettered by other rules of Court relating to leave to serve out of the
jurisdiction. Service could be dispensed with if the Court considered it just to do
so—the fact that the defendant is resident abroad is an important factor to be taken
into consideration.

5. Ex parte committal applications—only in exceptional circumstances

It is possible that service should be dispensed with and a committal order be 5–31
made *ex parte:* RSC Ord. 45 r.7(7); CCR Ord. 29, r. 1(7). The circumstances should
be exceptional: *Warwick Corporation v. Russell* [1964] 2 All E.R. 337.   Thus in *Lamb*
(1984) (below case 20), where there were flagrant and deliberate breaches of court
orders, the Court of Appeal declined to say that it was wrong in making an *ex parte*
order. Another example is *O'Donovan* [1955] 1 W.L.R. 1086 where the father was in
breach of an undertaking to return a child to England by a specific date. His
whereabouts were unknown, although out of the jurisdiction and he had not been
served with notice of the committal proceedings. The court dispensed with service.
And in *Newman v. Benesch*, [1987] 1 FLR 262, the Court of Appeal held that where
it was alleged that there had been a serious and flagrant breach of an injunction,
restraining a person from assaulting or interfering with his spouse or from entering
the matrimonial home, to which a power of arrest had been attached, it was not
wrong in principle for the judge to make an *ex parte* order committing the
contemnor to prison. Sir John Donaldson M.R. added, however, that a better course
would be for the court to inform the police that the injunction appeared to have
been breached and that the alleged contemnor should be arrested. Also see *Wright v.
Jess* [1987] 2 All E.R. 1067, in which the Court of Appeal confirmed an *ex parte*
order committing the contemnor to prison for two years. There had been serious
breaches of an injunction. It was held to be an exceptional case with a history of
many breaches, where no other course was open to protect the applicant and her
three children and uphold the Court's authority. The Court was entitled to have
regard to a breach of the injunction which occurred on the morning of the hearing
even though it was not included in the Notice to show cause. It was further held
that where the Court waives service, this should be recorded in the order for
committal.

6. Bringing the contemnor before the court

Where an *ex parte* committal order is made and the judge directs that the contemnor 5–32
is to be brought before the court (see above), this gives the judge the opportunity to
review the committal order. He may:

(a)   hear an application by the contemnor to purge his contempt, or
(b)   order an *inter partes* hearing with the defendant to attend so that the
      committal order may be reviewed again (see *B v. B* [1991] 2 FLR 588 at
      602).

However, the defendant should not be sentenced more severely at the second hearing for the same breach: *Lamb* (1984) FLR 278.

Persons under disability

1. Introduction

5–33   A person suffering from a mental disability may be, and a person under 18 is, a "person under disability". The fact that a person is under disability is not of itself a bar to an injunction being made, or a defence to committal proceedings (*Wookey v. Wookey; Re S* [1991] FCR 811, CA). The matters to consider are:

(a)   the level of the respondent's understanding of the nature of an injunction, and
(b)   the feasibility of enforcement.

2. Mental disability

(a) Understanding

5–34   An injunction should not be granted if the respondent is incapable within the M'Naughten Rules of understanding what he is doing or that it is wrong, as he will not be capable of complying with any order made. Such a person would have a clear defence to an application to commit for contempt: *Wookey; Re S* (1991) (above).

(b) Enforcement

5–35   If the respondent is capable of understanding the nature and requirements of an injunction, the court should go on to consider the feasibility of enforcing the order. If it cannot be enforced, it should not be granted as "the court would not grant an injunction which was idle and ineffectual" (*Wookey; Re S (ibid.)*). In *L v. L* (injunction: mental illness) [1993] Fam. Law 522 the respondent suffered from a delusional paranoic disorder. She understood the injunction but continued to breach it. The injunction was discharged as there was no effective way to enforce it—the available methods of dealing with contempt would not affect her behaviour.

3. Children

(a) Understanding

5–36   The Court should satisfy itself that the respondent child understands the order and its consequences.

(b) Enforcement

Where the respondent is under the age of 18, breach of an injunction cannot be enforced by committal: *R. v. Selby J.J. ex p. Frame* [1992] Q.B. 72; CJA 1991, s.63(5).

Where the respondent is aged between 18 to 21 years, he cannot be committed to prison, but an order for detention in a young offender institution may be made under CJA 1982, s.9 (as amended by CJA 1991, s.63(5)); *Mason v. Lawton* [1991] 2 All E.R. 784, CA.

A Writ of sequestration may be issued against a minor, but "in almost all cases concerning minors there will not be the assets available" to justify this course of action: *Wookey*; *Re S (ibid.)* at p.819.

If the respondent is too young to be committed, but has an income or money 5–37 available, an injunction may be enforced by fine; in such a case the penal notice on the injunction should be amended, replacing the threat of imprisonment with the threat of a fine.

(c) Enforcement impossible?

If the respondent cannot be committed, has no property worth seizing, and has 5–38 no employment or income, an injunction should not be granted as it is unenforceable and "equity does nothing in vain" (*Wookey*; *Re S (ibid.)* p.819; *Re P (a minor)* (injunction) [1994] Fam. Law 131 (injunction order discharged).

(d) Representation

In *Re P (a minor)* (above) an *ex parte* non-molestation injunction was ordered 5–39 against a 16 year old—no guardian had been appointed. The court considered that a minor should be protected by a guardian ad litem, as an injunction is the gravest and most immediate form of relief available from a County Court.

B. Procedure

Application

1. Breach of High Court Order

(a) Matrimonial proceedings: Summons plus affidavit,   5–40
(b) Wardship: Notice of motion plus affidavit,
(c) All other proceedings: Notice of motion plus affidavit
     (RSC Ord. 52, r.4(1); FPR 1991, r.7.2)

2. Breach of County Court Order

Form N78 Notice to show cause plus affidavit (CCR Ord. 29, r. 1(4), (4A)).

Requirements of application

1. Compliance with procedure—all important

The notice must be made in the correct form, and must specify each and every 5–41 breach of the order/undertaking relied upon: *Williams v. Fawcett* [1985] 1 All E.R. 787, CA. In the High Court pursuant to RSC, Ord. 52, r.6(3) "except with the leave of the Court", no grounds shall be relied upon save those set out in the Summons or motion. The position is the same in the County Court (County Courts Act 1984, s.76).

In particular it should be noted that:

5–42 (a) The proper officer to the County Court is under a duty to issue the notice to show cause,

(b) the form of notice to show cause must clearly state;

(i) the provisions of the injunction order or undertaking which it is alleged have been breached.

(ii) details of the ways in which the defendant has breached the injunction. Referring to alleged breaches in general terms (*e.g.* "molesting the applicant") is insufficient—particularise acts done, dates, times and locations.

(iii) the name and address of the applicant's solicitors; the notice must require the respondent's attendance at the hearing, and contain clear details as to the time and place of the hearing.

(c) the notice to show cause must be personally served on the alleged contemnor (see above)—any notices of adjourned hearings must also be served personally, unless the defendant heard the time, place and date of the adjourned hearing by virtue of being in court when the committal application was adjourned: *Phonographic Performance Ltd v. Tsang* (1985) 82 LS Gaz. 2331, CA.

2. Failure to obey—can be fatal

5–43 (a) *Williams v. Fawcett* [1985] 1 All E.R. 787, CA. The notice failed to specify the breaches alleged and was signed only by the applicant's solicitor. The particulars of breach were not provided until the day of the hearing and at the hearing the respondent requested an adjournment which was refused. The judge made the committal order but this was set aside on appeal. As Sir John Donaldson M.R. said at p.791:

"The matter was stood over by consent until January 9, and on that day [the respondent] duly attended court. Then, for the first time, he was provided with particulars of the five breaches of the undertaking which were alleged. Not surprisingly, counsel appearing on his behalf applied for an adjournment. That adjournment was refused, and evidence was called. There is some doubt in the minds of those who recollect the proceedings as to whether or not there was an indication by the judge that the application for an adjournment could be renewed; but, in my judgment, that is plainly immaterial, because to ask somebody to respond to allegations as serious as breaches of an undertaking without any reasonable notice is wholly wrong. It could not be cured by offering him an adjournment after the evidence had been taken or partly taken, both because it was then too late and because the rules require that particulars of the breach or breaches alleged appear in the notice to show cause."

5–44 (b) *Dorrell v. Dorrell* (1985) FLR 1089, CA. In that case the wife applied for the husband to be committed to prison for breach of a non-molestation order and an order restraining him from entering or attempting to enter the house. The husband in his affidavit admitted a relevant breach of the order. The judge dismissed the application and on appeal it was held that he was entitled so to do as the committal application contained no allegation as to the nature of the acts which were alleged to amount to a breach of the order. That was fatal to the success of the application. The defective notice could not be rectified either by the applicant's affidavit or the respondent's admission. When an application for committal is rejected, not on the merits but because it fails to set out in detail the alleged infringements of the original order, the court has jurisdiction to entertain a further application in proper form founded on the same contempt: *Jelson (Estates) Ltd v. Harvey* [1984] 1 All E.R. 12, CA.

(c)   *Harmsworth v. Harmsworth* [1987] 3 All E.R. 816, CA: The notice to show   5–45
cause itself must give the respondent "enough information to enable him to meet the charge" *(per* Nicholls L.J.). The information required by the rules must be available to the respondent "within the four corners of the notice itself", so that he knows "with sufficient particularity what are the breaches alleged". If lengthy particulars of breach are necessary, they may be set out in a Schedule attached to the notice, rather than being set out in the body of the notice itself.

3. Failure to obey—may be adjourned

Where the notice to show cause does not comply with the requirements, the judge   5–46
can decide whether or not to grant an adjournment for an amended notice to be prepared. Where an adjournment is granted for this purpose, the following questions should also be answered:

(1)   does the respondent need additional time to prepare his case?
(2)   who should bear the costs? (see *Bluffield v. Curtis* [1988] 1 FLR 170, CA).

The Court may, in exceptional circumstances, waive a defect in an application to commit under CCR Ord. 37, r. 5(1) (*Harmsworth* [1987] 3 All E.R. 816, CA)—but see *Linkleter* (1988) and *Clarke* (1990) below.

4. Summary

In *Williams v. Fawcett* [1985] 1 All E.R. 787, CA, Sir John Donaldson M.R.   5–47
concluded by summarising the requirements for a notice in Form N. 78. The Master of the Rolls said at p.796:

(a)   "First, a notice in form N. 78 does not have to be signed by the proper officer and, in so far as the decisions of this court suggest the contrary, they should not be followed"
(b)   "Second, the notice has to be addressed to the respondent, but it is undesirable that it should be addressed in addition to the registrar [now district judge] or to the proper officer. On the other hand, if this is done, it should not be regarded as fatal but should be accepted as a reflection of the fact that these documents start life as, in effect, requests to the court to issue

the notice. It is an undesirable practice, but it is not a ground for refraining from making a committal order."

(c) "Third, I think that it is equally undesirable—for the same reason, namely that it may cause the respondent to wonder whether or not the notice is the order of the court—that the notice should be signed by the applicant's solicitor unless he qualifies his signature with some such rubric as: 'This order is made on the application of'. But, again, I do not think his failure so to qualify his signature is a ground for refusing to make a committal order."

5–48 (d) "Fourth, particulars of the alleged breaches must appear in the notice. This has been said over and over again by this court, and I mention it merely to reaffirm it."

(e) "Fifth, the notice must be in Form N. 78 and must call on the respondent to show cause why he should not be committed to prison. Again, this is merely a reaffirmation of the law as it has been stated on many occasions."

(f) "Sixth, I think that the County Court Rule Committee should consider amending Form N. 78 to accommodate the many applicants' solicitors whose practice is to sign these forms. I do not suggest that solely for the convenience of those solicitors, but because I believe that the practice may be a convenience to respondents. If they have any objection to the notice, they can take it up with the applicants' solicitor straight away, and it may in some cases save further proceedings."

(g) "Seventh, and last, I would invite the County Court Rule Committee to consider amending Form N.79 which is the committal form itself, in order to provide an appropriate space for recording dispensation pursuant to Ord. 29 r.1(6) or (7)."

5. Committal orders set aside for defect of form

5–49   (a) Failure to state in the order the allegations of contempt proved against the defendant; failure to specify the individual acts of contempt/breaches on the face of the committal order: *McIlraith v. Grady* [1968] 1 Q.B. 468, CA; *Chiltern District Council v. Keane* [1985] 2 All E.R. 118; *Re C (a minor), The Times*, November 15, 1985; *Parra v. Rones* (1986) 16 Fam. Law 262; *Linkleter v. Linkleter* [1988] 1 FLR 360; *O'Neill v. Murray, The Times*, October 15 1990, CA; *Re M (minors) (access: contempt)* [1991] 1 FLR 355, CA; *Smith v. Smith* [1992] 2 FLR 41, CA; *Lewis v. King* [1992] 2 FCR 149, CA.

(b) Referral to matters which were not comprised in the affidavit sworn in support of the application for committal since there were matters on which the alleged contemnor had not been given notice as required by the County Court Rules: *Tabone v. Seguna* [1986] 1 FLR 591, CA.

(c) Failure to specify which of the chattels ordered to be delivered up the defendant has failed to return: *Sondhis* (1982) 133 New L.J. 420, CA.

5–50   (d) Failure to record the period of imprisonment which has been imposed: *Wellington* (1978) (below case 21). *Cinderby* (1978) (below case 22).

(e) The order should not be left completely blank, the judge merely signing it at the bottom: *Wellington* (see above).

(f) The order should not impose a suspended indefinite sentence of imprisonment: *Re C (a minor)* (see above). The period of suspension must be for a finite period: *Pidduck v. Molloy* [1992] 2 FLR 202, CA.

(g) The order should be announced in open court: *Re C (a minor)* (see above.)

(h) The order should be clear as to whom it is addressed and what is required to comply with it: *Re C (a minor)* (see above).

(i) The order should not be such as in effect to sentence a defendant twice for the same offence: *Lamb* (1984) (below Case 20); *Kumari v. Jalal* (1996) (below case 15).

(j) Failure to treat the parties and their evidence equally: *Aslam v. Singh* [1987] 1 FLR 122, CA.

(k) The committal order should not be based on contempts which are not set out   5–51
in the committal notice: *Javadi-Babreh v. Javadi-Babreh, The Independent*, November 16, 1992.

(l) Failure to include in the committal order a sentence informing the contemnor that he may apply to the court to purge his contempt and seek release: *B v. B (contempt: committal)* [1991] 2 FLR 588, CA—the court cannot limit or restrict his right to make such application: *Vaughan* (1973) (below case 28); *Delaney v. Delaney The Times*, November 2, 1995, CA.

6. Committal orders not set aside—despite defects of form

(a) Defects in the formal wording of a committal order do not affect its validity: 5–52
     Palmer v. Townsend (1979) 123 Sol.Jo 570; *Burrows v. Iqbal (No 2)* (1985)
     Fam. Law 188, CA.

(b) Breach of an order to vacate the matrimonial home, admitted by the husband,
     need not be particularised: *Kavanagh v. Kavanagh* (1978) 128 NLJ 1007, CA
     (below case 23).

(c) Failure to specify the date of breach when the contemnor had been arrested
     on the same day that he was released from prison and committed the breach;
     and accordingly the scope for breaching the order had been restricted to that
     day: *Burrows v. Iqbal* (above).

(d) Inadequate findings of fact recorded in the order for committal, where there
     was no injustice as the contemnor was present when judgment was given in
     which the judge expressly set out those facts he found proved and those not
     proved: *Miller v. Juby* [1991] 1 FLR 133, CA.

(e) Failure to particularise breaches had not caused injustice—contemnor had
     admitted the breaches to the judge—Court of Appeal exercised its discretion
     to vary the order by particularising the offences: *C v. Hackney L.B.C.* [1995] 2
     FLR 681.

Requirements of the affidavit in support

1. Contents

The affidavit filed in support of the application should set out as fully as possible   5–53
all the allegations which are sought to be made against the respondent. This is so he can know fully the nature of the case which he must meet. The court will then also have an opportunity to assess the strength and seriousness of the applicant's case.

2. Form

The rules of court dealing generally with the form and contents of affidavits are RSC Ord. 41, and CCR Ord. 20, r.10.

3. Service

5–54   The affidavit in support should be served on the respondent as early as possible so as to afford him the opportunity, if he wishes, to serve an affidavit in reply.

4. Delay—the risk of an adjournment

If the affidavit is only served at the last moment, a respondent can apply to a court for an adjournment since deprivation of his liberty is involved. The court may well look upon such application with sympathy.

The respondent's riposte

1. Evidence

5–55   The respondent and any witnesses he may choose to call may file affidavits in reply. The respondent must be given a proper opportunity to instruct his solicitor and present his evidence, even where he has been deliberately avoiding receiving notice of the committal hearing, as justice must be seen to be done: *Duo v. Duo* [1992] 3 All E.R. 121, CA.

2. Unrepresented respondent

Where the respondent is unrepresented, the court should:

(a)   warn him of the possible penalty should the alleged breach(es) be proved;
(b)   ask him to consider whether he wishes to be legally represented;
(c)   after he has given evidence, ask him if he wishes to present any other evidence;
(d)   allow him to address the court in respect of the appropriate penalty, and to apologize to the court for the breach(es).

(*Shoreditch County Court Bailiffs v. de Madeiros, The Times*, February 24, 1988, CA)

3. Mitigation

5–56   If the breaches are admitted in part or at all, the admissions will no doubt be coupled with apologies to the court and assurances as to future behaviour. Further mitigating circumstances can be put forward. Where a contemnor is liable to imprisonment, he should be given a proper opportunity to address the court in mitigation, whether he is legally represented or not: *Taylor v. Persico, The Times*, February 12, 1992, CA; *Naring v. Dhami* 1995 CLY, para. 3952.

4. Oral evidence

The alleged contemnor is entitled to give oral evidence (RSC Ord. 52, r. 6(4);   5–57
CCA 1984, s.76) but he cannot be compelled to do so against his will so as to
incriminate himself, as committal proceedings are criminal in nature. However, if
the alleged contemnor has sworn an affidavit which is "filed and used before the
court . . . then he is liable to be cross-examined on it if the court thinks it right so
to order". Moreover, "when he is threatened with cross-examination [he] cannot get
out of it by saying that he will withdraw his affidavit"—*Comet Products U.K. Ltd v.
Hawkex Plastics Ltd* [1971] 1 All E.R. 1141 at 1144 *per* Lord Denning M.R. The
court has a discretion whether or not to allow cross-examination on the affidavit,
although a *bona fide* application to do so "should normally be granted" (*ibid., per*
Megaw L.J. at p.1146 G) In *Titmarsh v. Titmarsh* (1996) 6 C.L. 259, the Court of
Appeal upheld the decision to allow cross-examination of a respondent husband on
his unsigned statement (which contained a false alibi), which his solicitors had sent
to the applicant's solicitors in the course of proceedings—privilege had been waived.

5. Submission of no case to answer

The alleged contemnor may wish to submit that there is no case to answer at the   5–58
conclusion of the applicant's case. However, upon making such an application, he
may at the same time be put to his election as to whether he would give evidence
should the submission fail. Even though committal proceedings are quasi-criminal in
nature, there is no absolute right to withhold evidence until after the submission of
no case to answer: *Barclays De Zoete Wedd Securities Ltd v. Nadir, The Times*, March
25, 1992.

Powers of the Court

1. Standard of proof

"Contempt of court is an offence of a criminal nature" (*Re Bramblevale Ltd* [1969]   5–59
3 All E.R. 1062 at 1071, *per* Lord Denning). Accordingly, breach of injunction or
undertaking must be proved beyond reasonable doubt: *Deborah Building Equipment
Ltd v Scaffco Ltd and Another, The Times*, November 5, 1986; *Dean v. Dean* (1987)
FLR 517, CA; *Smith v. Smith* (1991) FCR 233; *Re P* (1996) 8 CL 6. Where there is
ambiguity and doubt in the evidence of the parties, then the benefit of the doubt
should go to the defendant: *Goff v. Goff* [1989] 1 FLR 436 at 440 H, CA). A
committal order is not to be made on the basis of the defendant's mere
recalcitrance—it must be based on evidence which establishes to the appropriate
standard that he is in deliberate contempt: *Re D.B and C.B (minors)* (1993) 2 FCR
607, CA.

2. Jurisdiction

The court in its discretion can make the following orders: 5–60

(a) Dismiss the application (*e.g.* for want of evidence or breach of the formal requirements).

(b) Make no order (on the basis, *e.g.* that the respondent has now learnt his lesson) but issue a warning.

(c) Adjourn the application to a fixed dated to see how the respondent complies with the order in question: *Re D.B and C.B (minors)* (above). An adjournment *sine die* is not considered to be a correct exercise of discretion because it leaves unresolved the outstanding question as to whether a man's liberty should be imperilled.

(d) Impose a fine or take security for good behaviour.

(e) Impose a period of imprisonment.

(f) Impose a suspended committal order (*note*: magistrates courts now have power to suspend execution of a committal order under FLA 1996, s.50).

(g) Order a further injunction.

Note There is no civil right to damages, and no power for the court to award compensation for the contemnor's actions to the other party: *Chapman v. Hoenig* [1963] 2 Q.B. 502, CA; *Johnson v. Walton* [1990] 1 FLR 350, CA (below case 2).

3. The judicial discretion: how is it exercised?

5–61   In *Danchevsky* [1975] Fam. 17, CA Lord Denning M.R. said at p.22:

"Whenever there is a reasonable alternative available instead of committal to prison, that alternative must be taken."

In *Smith v. Smith* [1988] 1 FLR 179, CA, Sir John Donaldson M.R. said that the court should not assume that any breach of an injunction will inevitably result in committal to prison. See also *McIntosh v. McIntosh* (1990) FCR 351, CA (court should consider making a suspended order before imposing immediate term of imprisonment).

4. Principles to be applied

5–62   (a) The fact that committal orders are remedies of the last resort in family cases was emphasised in *Ansah* (1977) (below case 11), CA. This case gives useful guidelines to be adopted on committal applications. Ormrod L.J. said at [1977] Fam. 138, p.144:

"Breach of such an injunction is, perhaps unfortunately, called contempt of court, the conventional remedy for which is a summons for committal. But the real purpose of bringing the matter back to the court, in most cases, is not so much to punish the disobedience, as to secure compliance with the injunction in the future. It will often be wiser to bring the matter before the court again for further directions before applying for a committal order. Committal orders are remedies of the last resort; in family cases they should be the very last resort. They are likely to damage complainant spouses almost as much as offending spouses, for example, by alienating the children. Such orders should be made very reluctantly and only when every other effort to bring the situation under control has failed or is almost certain to fail. In most cases, stern warnings, combined with investigation and an attempt to alleviate the offending spouse's underlying grievances or an adjournment to allow tempers to cool will resolve the problem. In some cases, the assistance of the court welfare officer may help to remove some of the tension. The . . . power . . . to attach a 'power of arrest' to an injunction may . . . provide another useful alternative way of dealing with some of these cases . . . The practice of making suspended committal orders may be effective in some cases, but it can be very dangerous. Careful consideration must be given to the question of in what circumstances and how the suspension is to be removed and the committal order activated".

(b) This "last resort" principle was restated in *Re M* (minors) (access: contempt: **5–63** committal) [1991] 1 FLR 355, CA: Committal orders should only be made where there was a continuing course of conduct and all other efforts to resolve the situation have failed. However, in *Jones v. Jones* [1993] 2 FLR 377, CA it was observed by Russell L.J. *per curiam*, that there is "little, if any, general principle emerging from the observations of Ormrod L.J."; the order to be made for breach of an injunction is "dependent upon the individual circumstances of the individual case . . ." (at p.381).

(c) In *Goff v. Goff* [1989] 1 FLR 436, CA, in reducing the contemnor's sentence **5–64** from 28 days imprisonment to 14 days suspended for three months, Purchas L.J. considered the following matters to be relevant:

(1)   previous good character
(2)   financial effects of committal to prison
(3)   pressure on respondent due to breakdown of the marriage
(4)   effect of lengthy committal on the attitude of the children towards the respondent husband *and* the applicant wife
(5)   imprisonment should be seen as a drastic measure as emphasised in *Ansah*.

(d) The court should not simply impose a "standard" sentence of 28 days' imprisonment, but should make such order as it considers appropriate in the circumstances of the case (*Wilsher v. Wilsher* [1989] 2 FLR 187, CA).

5. Factors to consider

(a)   Do the matters proved amount to a serious or minor breach of the injunction? **5–65** (*Smith v. Smith* [1988] 1 FLR 179, CA).
(b)   Has the contemnor repeatedly breached undertakings, persistently flouted orders or been committed to prison for earlier contempts? (*Re H* [1986] 1 FLR 558, CA; *Mesham v. Clarke* [1989] 1 FLR 370, CA; *Jones v. Jones* [1993] 2 FLR 377, CA). In *G v. G* (1992) 2 FCR 145, CA, a total sentence of 16 months was justified for persistent breaches of a non-molestation order that did not involve physical violence.
(c)   Has the contemnor had any opportunity to show that he can comply with the order? (*Ansah* (above); *George v. George* [1986] 2 FLR 347, CA).

91

(d) Did the contemnor admit his breach, or were findings made after a contested hearing? (*Re R* [1994] 1 W.L.R. 487, CA; credit due for guilty plea).

(e) Are there any aggravating circumstances? *Jordan v. Jordan* (1992) 2 FCR 701, CA; *N v. N* [1992] FLR 370, CA—defendant breached ouster and non-molestation injunction by breaking into house and raping his wife three days after injunction was made: six months imprisonment justified; *Jones v. Jones* (1993) (above)—blatant and aggravated breaches following warnings re possible custodial sentence in event of breach: immediate imprisonment appropriate.

(f) Has contemnor shown any signs of remorse or contrition? *C v. G, The Times,* October 14, 1996, CA (below case 24).

6. No remorse—relevance

5–66   Where the contemnor shows no signs of remorse or contrition, and/or offers no apology for his breaches, the judge is bound to take this into account when considering sentence. As Butler-Sloss L.J. remarked in *Roberts v. Roberts* [1990] 2 FLR 111 at 113:

> "A total absence of apology is not the way to appear before a court when you are in danger of being committed to prison for a serious breach of an undertaking."

In *Re O (minors)* [1995] 2 FLR 767, CA (below case 25) the respondents' lack of regret for their serious contempt was, *inter alia*, relevant when considering their sentence:

> ". . . there was no question of any regret or contrition, nor any assurance that the conduct would not be repeated if the punishment were not sufficient to deter repetition . . ." (*per* Leggatt L.J. at p.772).

7. No previous breaches—relevance

5–67   In practice, a contemnor will not normally be committed to prison for his first breach of an injunction unless there are exceptional circumstances: *Brewer v. Brewer* (1989) FCR 515, CA; *Ansah* (above). But see *Jones v. Jones* (1993) (above)—no general principle that courts should only impose sanctions as a last resort—immediate imprisonment justified for an aggravated and blatant contempt by someone who had been repeatedly warned of possible consequences of breach.

8. Attitude of the applicant to committal—a relevant factor

5–68   The court should have regard to the future of the family relationships and the approach and attitude of the wife: *Sellars v. Sellars* (1984) (below case 26); *Goff v. Goff* (above). In *Boylan* (1980) 11 Fam. Law 76, CA, Ormrod L.J. stated in a case of committal pursuant to the power of arrest provision:

> "It would seem, as a matter of good practice, very doubtful whether a judge will feel justified in sending a husband to prison for breach of an injunction

(unless it is absolutely gross) without at least finding out what the wife's view is . . . there really are ways in which a more humane approach to the problem can be achieved than by slapping him into prison for 14 days without more ado."

However, in an appropriate case the court must show that it is prepared to exercise its power to commit as orders of the court should not be flouted.

Nature of hearing

1. Forum

Pursuant to RSC Ord.52, r.6, save in certain specified circumstances, the 5–69 application must be heard in open court. If the court does sit in private and makes an order of committal pursuant to Ord. 52, r. 6(2), it shall in open court state:

(a)   the name of the person to be committed;
(b)   in general terms, the nature of the contempt of court in respect of which the order of committal is being made; and
(c)   the length of the period for which he is being committed.

Failure to do so may be rectified by the court under RSC Ord. 2, r.1 by a subsequent statement in open court of the above particulars. However, the Court of Appeal may, in its discretion, set aside the order: *Re C (a minor), The Times,* November 16, 1988, CA. The same applies in the county court: *Re C* (above).

2. Opening the case

On an application to commit it must be shown that: 5–70

(a)   a proper notice of application has been drafted;
(b)   the application and other documents in support have been properly served, giving the respondent the requisite notice of the hearing (any notices of adjournment of which the respondent is not aware must be served personally);
(c)   that the order/undertaking allegedly breached has been properly served on the respondent and/or that he is aware of its provisions and/or that service has been waived or dispensed with;
(d)   that the order/undertaking has been properly drafted, being clear and precise as to what the respondent must (or must not) do and the time fixed for compliance; *O'Neill v. Murray, The Times,* October 15, 1990, CA: *R v. City of London Magistrates' Court ex p. Green, The Times,* March 13, 1997 Scott Baker J., QBD.
(e)   that the order/undertaking has been properly indorsed with a penal notice;
(f)   that the respondent is in breach of the order made or undertakings given.

3. The Court can call evidence

In committal proceedings, the court may, if there is consent or no objection, call 5–71 evidence/serve subpoenas in order to find out whether the defendant is in contempt of court: *Yianni v. Yianni* [1966] 1 All E.R. 231n; there may be no cross-examination without leave.

4. Power to adjourn the hearing

5-72   The court may adjourn the committal hearing where the judge in his discretion considers it necessary to do so in the interests of justice. In *Roberts v. Roberts* (1991) 1 FLR 294, CA, the alleged contemnor was arrested under a power of arrest. He sought, but was refused, an adjournment so that he could call witnesses. Held: the court may adjourn proceedings for a short period if necessary in the interests of justice. The court is not confined to dealing with the contempt (by committal or release) within 24 hours of arrest.

Regard should now be given to FLA 1996, ss.47 to 48 and Sched. 5, regarding the courts' powers to remand if a person is arrested under a power of arrest or warrant of arrest.

The civil/criminal overlap

1. Situation

5-73   Increasingly there is an overlap of jurisdictions where breach of an injunction or undertaking also constitutes a crime. Circumstances occur where the breach of the order involved is exactly the same as a criminal charge which follows.

2. Res judicata—irrelevant

5-74   The penalty imposed in one set of proceedings may be regarded as mitigation in the other set of proceedings—but it cannot be a bar to the other proceedings. Accordingly a person may be sentenced twice for one act of disobedience as it infringes the civil and criminal law: *R v. Kelly* [1996] 1 Cr.App. R.(S.), CA (Crim.Div). In the civil proceedings, the contemnor is punished for his contempt of court, not the criminal offence: *Smith v. Smith* (1991) FCR 233, CA. However, in *Juby v. Miller* [1991] 1 FLR 133, the Court of Appeal held that:

> "there is a difference between a criminal offence against someone who is not subject to the protection of the courts and one who is . . . the court will regard as being in a wholly special category cases in which people commit criminal offences which constitute a breach of the court's orders . . . That sort of conduct is wholly unacceptable and must be met with condign punishment" (at p.135 D–E, *per* Lord Donaldson of Lymington M.R.: 16 months imprisonment imposed for two assaults).

3. Civil/criminal hearing—which proceeds first?

5-75   If a person faces both criminal and civil proceedings for contempt the Court of Appeal has held that the contempt proceedings should not be adjourned to await the outcome of the criminal proceedings. It is important for contempt proceedings to be dealt with swiftly and decisively: *Szczepanski v. Szczepanski* [1985] FLR 468, CA. This of course means that a prospective defendant in criminal proceedings

having to disclose his defence. This approach was followed in *Caprice v. Boswell* (1986) Fam. Law 52, CA. There the facts that the plaintiff was protected by the conditions of the defendant's bail and there had been no trouble since the incident giving rise to the breach were irrelevant to an argument that the civil proceedings should be adjourned until after the criminal proceedings. In *Keeber v. Keeber* [1995] 2 FLR 748, the Court of Appeal held that contempt proceedings should be adjourned pending the conclusion of the criminal proceedings ONLY where there was a "real risk of serious prejudice which might lead to injustice", such test not being met in the circumstances of the case.

It is for the discretion of the judge to decide, on the particular facts of the case, whether or not serious prejudice would be caused by going ahead with the committal hearing before the criminal case: *H v. C* [1993] 1 FLR 787, CA.

C. Sentencing

Imprisonment

1. Enforcement

If the court decides to commit for contempt, the position on seizure of the 5–76 defendant is as follows:

(a)   if the defendant is present, under order of the court, he is taken to prison by a court official (normally the tipstaff or his deputy, or, if a tipstaff is not available, an usher), or by a police officer acting as his assistant;

(b)   if absent, but at a settled known address, the tipstaff travels to that address with the order and arrests him;

(c)   if the contemnor is likely to disappear, the tipstaff may communicate with the local police who hold him and put him in the cells at the police station till the tipstaff arrives and takes him to the prison specified in the warrant.

2. Duration—fixed term

By virtue of section 14(1) of the Contempt of Court Act 1981, a committal to 5–77 prison for contempt of court "shall be for a fixed term". Accordingly, the court cannot commit *sine die*, or pass an indefinite period of imprisonment.

3. Maximum

In both the High Court and County Courts the term imposed "shall not on any 5–78 occasion exceed two years" (section 14 (1) Contempt of Court Act 1981 as amended by the County Courts (Penalties for Contempt) Act 1983 reversing the effect of *Danchevsky* [1974] 3 All E.R. 934, CA, and *Peart v. Stewart* [1983] A.C. 109). Furthermore, both the High Court and County Court have power to impose consecutive sentences of imprisonment in appropriate cases for more than one contempt: *Lee v. Walker* [1985] Q.B. 1191. It will be noted that two years is the maximum total period that the court may impose "on any occasion" (*i.e.* the date of sentence) even where the defendant is being sentenced for more than one contempt committed at different times: *Villiers v. Villiers* [1994] 1 W.L.R. 493, CA. Accordingly, where the contemnor is being sentenced for more than one breach, and is given credit for admitting his breaches, this should be reflected in the total sentence of imprisonment imposed, not merely in each individual consecutive sentence: *Re R* [1994] 2 All E.R. 149, CA.

4. Sentencing guidelines—irrelevant

5–79   In *Re H* [1986] 1 FLR 558, the Court of Appeal stated that it was not possible to lay down sentencing guidelines for such cases and each had to be dealt with on its own facts. There a defendant broke an order in circumstances which caused considerable alarm to the occupants of a house. He was imprisoned for three months. However Balcombe L.J. went so far as to say that if the case was one of repeated disobedience to orders of the court a higher sentence would be called for.

5. Varying the term

5–80   In *Westcott v. Westcott* [1985] FLR 278, CA, it was held that a judge had no power to lengthen his original sentence (the judge had purported to do so after discovering that the effect of prison practice of releasing prisoners early in certain circumstances would be to shorten his sentence). In *Lamb v. Lamb* (1984) (below case 20) the contemnor was committed to prison (14 days) *ex parte* for breach of an injunction. He was brought before the court to show cause where there was no evidence of any further breaches, but the judge passed a higher sentence (three months). The Court of Appeal allowed the contemnor's appeal against the second (three month) order, as he had been sentenced twice for the same breach. Also see *Delaney v. Delaney* (1995) (below case 27); *Kumari v. Jalal* (1996) (below case 15).

Power to suspend execution of committal order

1. Jurisdiction

5–81   Both the High Court (RSC Ord. 52, r 7) and County Courts have existing powers to suspend a committal order conditional on compliance with certain conditions: *Lee v. Walker* [1985] Q.B. 1191, CA. Under FLA 1996, s.50, Magistrates' courts have the power to suspend a committal order (for breach of an occupation/non molestation order, or of an exclusion requirement in an ICO or EPO) for such period or on such terms as may be specified. The length of the suspended sentence and the period of suspension must both be fixed by the court—neither can be for an indefinite term: *Pidduck v. Molloy* [1992] 2 FLR 202, CA; *Re C (a minor)* [1986] 1 FLR 578, CA.

2. Breach of condition—jurisdiction not fettered

5–82   If a committal order is suspended, and it is subsequently discovered that the defendant has not complied with the conditions of the suspended order, the power of the court is not limited to declaring the committal order operative. It retains a discretion to do whatever is just in the circumstances: *Re W (B) (an infant)* [1969] 2 Ch. 50, CA: "it can reduce the length of the sentence or can impose a fine instead. It may indeed not punish at all. It all depends on how serious is the breach, how long has the man behaved himself, and so forth" (at p.56E), see also *Banton v. Banton* [1990] 2 FLR 465, CA.

3. Suspending the committal

Whilst the practice of making suspended committal orders may be effective in **5–83** some cases, it can also be very dangerous: *Ansah* [1977] 2 All E.R. 638, CA, *per* Ormrod L.J. at p.643:

> "The practice of making suspended committal orders may be effective in some cases, but it can be very dangerous. Careful consideration must be given to the question of in what circumstances and how the suspension is to be removed and the committal order activated. In the present case the terms of the suspension were that the warrant for arrest was not to be issued if the wife:
> 'complies with the following terms, namely: that she does not, by herself her servants or agents or otherwise; (1) return to or enter upon the said matrimonial home and/or (2) assault or molest the respondent'.
> The order goes on to provide that upon filing affidavit evidence that the order has been served on the wife and that she has failed to comply with the above terms, the committal order is to be executed without further notice to her. All that is required, therefore, to bring this committal order into effect is the filing of an affidavit at the county court which may or may not be true. In other words, control has passed out of the judge's hands altogether, and the party subject to the order has no means of disputing the alleged failure to comply with the terms of the suspension. It would have been much safer to adjourn the summons to commit, with liberty to restore, in the event of a further breach of this injunction or of a term imposed by the court at the first hearing of the summons".

It should be clear whether the judge has suspended the committal on terms, or has in addition made a further injunction order: *Linkleter v. Linkleter* [1988] 1 FLR 360, CA.

The Order

1. Precision

The order as drawn up must reflect exactly the order of the judge (*Abdi v. Jama* **5–84** [1996] 1 FLR 407, CA). The Court of Appeal has on numerous occasions pointed out the need for meticulous adherence to the required formalities in contempt proceedings (*e.g. Gagnon v. McDonald, The Times*, November 14, 1984), and the need to draw up committal orders with great care (*e.g. Miller v. Juby* [1991] 1 FLR 133).

2. Content

The order itself must state in clear and unambiguous detail the following (*per* Purchas L.J. in *B v. B* [1991] 2 FLR 588 at 591):

(a)   the order of the court or undertaking given to the court in respect of which the contemnor has been found in breach;

(b)   the respects in which it has been alleged that he has been in breach;

(c)   the findings of the judge as to the alleged breaches, specifying the contempt(s) proved;

(d)   the period of committal to which he has been sentenced; and

(e)   that the contemnor may apply to the Court to purge his contempt and seek his release.

(See also *Clarke v. Clarke* [1990] 2 FLR 115, CA; *Howes v. Howes* (1992) 2 FCR 287, CA).

3. Slip rule—not a panacea

5-85   Such orders must be correct when they are made, and cannot subsequently be remedied under the slip rules (*i.e.* RSC Ord. 20, r.11; CCR Ord. 15, r.5): *Cinderby v. Cinderby* (1978) 8 Fam. Law 244, CA (below case 22). The slip rule cannot be invoked to cure a defective order where the case affects the liberty of the subject: *Smith v. Smith* (1984) 134 N.L.J. 603. Nor is it appropriate to use the slip rule to exend injunctions where the respondent is not represented: *Langley v. Langley, The Times*, October 20, 1993, CA.

Service of the committal order

1. General rule—personal service

5-86   Unless the judge orders otherwise, a copy of the committal order must be served on the contemnor either before or at the time of the execution of the warrant of committal: CCR Ord. 29, r.1(5)(a). It is the duty of the court officials to draw up the form giving effect to the order, and to ensure that it is promptly and personally served on the contemnor.

2. Inadequate service

5-87   In *B v. B* [1991] 2 FLR 588 at 594 Purchas L.J. expressed "grave doubts" as to whether it would be sufficient for the court, acting through a solicitor's clerk, to leave the order at a police station with the intention it should be later given or shown to the contemnor. Further, "mere knowledge as a result of previous experience of his rights by a persistent offender would not relieve the court of the duty of complying with CCR Ord. 29, r.1(5) by serving a proper notice on him. . ." (at p.598).

3. Time limit for service

5-88   By virtue of CCR Ord. 29, r.1(5)(b), where "the warrant has been signed by the judge, the order for issue of the warrant may be served on the person to be committed at any time within 36 hours after the execution of the warrant" by the court, unless the judge prescribes a different time limit for service.

4. Failure to serve committal order—may be fatal

". . . Where a requirement affecting the essential rights of a contemnor has not 5–89 been complied with, this court will not use its powers to correct the order" (*Clarke v. Clarke* [1990] 2 FLR 115 at 118 *per* Farquharson L.J.). Further, in *B v. B* (contempt: committal) [1991] 2 FLR 588 at 605, Purchas L.J. stated that:

". . . the total failure to serve the order at any time relevant to the committal to prison disposes of any suggestion that defects in the order might be capable of correction under RSC Ord. 59, r.10 (3) . . . there is no power in the present case to remedy the complete failure to serve the contemnor with the . . . notice".

For the Court of Appeal attitude toward the exercise of its powers, also see *Howes v. Howes* (1992) 2 FCR 287 (committal order quashed in view of non-service on defendant: the requirement of service affected the rights of the contemnor); *Linkleter v. Linkleter* [1988] 1 FLR 360; *Hegarty v. O'Sullivan, The Times*, May 8, 1985. But contrast *M v. P* (contempt: committal), *Butler v. Butler* [1992] 4 All E.R. 833, CA (committal orders not quashed despite non-service on defendant where no injustice suffered—court exercised powers under AJA 1960, s.13(3)).

Discharge from prison of person committed for contempt

1. Jurisdiction

If it is felt by the court that the contemnor has been sufficiently punished for his 5–90 contempt the contemnor may be released upon application: RSC Ord. 52, r.8, CCR, Ord. 29, r.3. See also Contempt of Court Act 1981, s.14(1). On such applications save in exceptional circumstances, the contemnor should be present in court to hear the outcome of the application. (Practice Direction (Family Division: Contempt of Court) [1983] 1 W.L.R 998—see Appendix C below).

2. Practice in the High Court

RSC, Ord. 52, r.8) The application must be made by the contemnor or someone 5–91 acting on his behalf. If possible, the application should be made on motion to the judge who made the committal order, but if that judge is not available, any judge sitting in that division may deal with it. There is no necessity to file an application. Such a motion has priority over all other motions: *Ashton v. Shorrock* (1881) 29 W.R. 117. The court has power to sentence for a fixed term or order release at a future date: *Yager v. Musa* [1961] 2 Q.B. 214, CA. No order should be made which prevents a person applying to the court for this purpose: *Vaughan* (1973) (below case 28)

3. Practice in county court

(CCR, Ord. 29, r.3) The application should be made in writing attested by the 5–92 Governor of the prison (or any other officer of the prison not below the rank of Principal Officer) showing that he has purged or is desirous of purging his contempt. Notice of the application must be served on the party at whose instance the warrant or order was issued not less than one day before the application is made. In certain circumstances the application may be made to a District Judge (Ord. 29, r.3(2)) although generally it is made to a judge and, if possible the judge who made the committal order.

4. Forms

5–93   There is no prescribed form for an application to discharge/purge contempt, but the County Court Practice suggests the following form of words:

> "Take Notice, that I intend on the   day of   19   to apply to the Judge of this court [or to the District Judge of this court as the case may be] at [state place] to discharge me from custody, I having purged [or being desirous of purging] my contempt as follows [give details].
> Dated this   day of   19   . To   etc."

The order of discharge from custody is Form 83 (county court).

5. Early release

5–94   Once the court has sentenced a contemnor to a term of imprisonment, the prison authorities should not (save for remission) release him early without a court order: *Parsons v. Nasar* [1990] 2 FLR 103, CA. However, where a judge discovered that the prison authorities had a practice (quite apart from remission) of releasing prisoners early in certain circumstances, which would effectively reduce the sentence passed, he had no power to lengthen his original sentence: *Westcott v. Westcott* [1985] FLR 278, CA.

Appeals

1. Jurisdiction

5–95   A committal order made by the County Court or High Court may be appealed to the Court of Appeal Civil Division (AJA 1960, s.13; SCA 1981, s.53; RSC, Ord. 59, r.20). An appeal from the Court of Appeal may be made by leave to the House of Lords (AJA 1960, ss. 1, 2 and 13(4)).

2. Fresh evidence on appeal

5–96   Leave will be granted if it is expedient/necessary in the interests of justice. When appealing from an order of committal for civil contempt, the appellant need not fulfill the three conditions set out in *Ladd v. Marshall* [1954] 3 All E.R. 745 at 748, CA: See *Irtelli v. Squatriti* [1992] 3 WLR 218. The normal and proper way to challenge a decision of the county court on the basis of fresh evidence alone is to apply for a rehearing under CCR Ord. 37 rather than appeal to the Court of Appeal: *O'Connor v. Din* [1997] 1 FLR 226, CA.

3. Undertakings—no appeal

Undertakings cannot be appealed to the Court of Appeal (*McConnell v. McConnell* 5–97 (1980) 10 Fam. Law 214, CA: "This court can only operate on orders", *per* Ormrod L.J.—below case 33). If the respondent wishes to be released from his undertaking on the basis that he is no longer prepared to give it, it is submitted that an application should be made on notice to the court which accepted the undertaking: the applicant may for example wish to reinstate the injunction application so that she may apply for an order in the same terms as the undertaking.

4. Academic appeals

It is an abuse of process to bring a legally aided appeal where the appeal was of 5–98 academic interest to lawyers only, was to resolve uncertainty over a point of law, and was of no practical concern or consequence to the parties in the case: *S v. S* (abuse of process of appeal) [1994] 2 FCR 941, CA.

5. Avoidance of delay

As the proceedings involve the liberty of the subject, any appeal against committal should be heard promptly (*Mesham v. Clarke* [1989] 1 FLR 370, CA). Where the contemnor's solicitor thinks that there are grounds for appeal, s/he should lodge the Notice of appeal without delay (*e.g.* caused by waiting for further legal aid: *Jordan v. Jordan* [1992] 2 FCR 701, CA).

6. Power to vary committal orders on appeal

(a) AJA 1960, s.13(3): appeal court has power to "reverse or vary the order or 5–99 decision of the court below" if just to do so in the circumstances;

(b) RSC Ord. 59, r.10(3): Court of Appeal has a general power to "give any judgment and make any order which ought to have been given or made" in the lower court. (For example, see *Hill Samuel & Co Ltd v. Littaur (No.2)* (1985) 129 Sol Jo.433, CA).

7. Judicial discretion to vary order

The court may on appeal consider it just to vary a committal order where there 5–100 has been a purely technical error in drawing up the order *and* no unfairness is caused to the contemnor: *M v. P* [1992] 4 All E.R. 833, CA. Whether a defect is purely "technical" will depend on the facts and circumstances of the particular case (*Clarke v. Clarke* [1990] 2 FLR 115 at 118 *per* Farquharson L.J.). Also see *Nicholls v. Nicholls* (1997) 147 NLJ 61, CA (below case 36).

8. Committal orders varied—despite defects

(a) *Linnett v. Coles* [1986] 3 All E.R. 652, CA (respondent unlawfully committed 5–101 to prison "until further order").

(b) *Wright v. Jess* [1987] 2 All E.R. 1067, CA (failure to record dispensation of service of committal application).

(c) *Mason v. Lawton* [1991] 2 All E.R. 784, CA (where an order committed a young person to prison instead of ordering him to be detained in a young offenders institution for breach of an injunction).

(d) *M v. P; Butler v. Butler* [1992] 4 All E.R. 833, CA (failure to serve copy of committal order on defendant where no injustice caused).

(e) *Abdi v. Jama* (contempt: committal) [1996] 1 FLR 407, CA (amendment made despite procedural irregularity—no injustice suffered by contemnor).

9. Principles to be applied

5–102   The powers of the court to cure defective orders must only be used in exceptional cases: *Linkleter v. Linkleter* [1988] 1 FLR 360; *Clarke v. Clarke* [1990] 2 FLR 115; *Loseby v. Newman* [1995] 2 FLR 754, CA (distinguishing *M v. P* (above)). The Court of Appeal has repeatedly observed that there must be strict compliance with the rules and formalities in committal cases, as the liberty of the subject is at stake: *Re M(minors) (access: contempt: committal)* [1991] 1 FLR 355, CA.

In *Hegarty v. O'Sullivan* (1985) 135 NLJ 557, CA, Kerr L.J. stated that where a defendant had gone to prison, "an appeal against a defective order cannot . . . be allowed to subject him to the risk that this will fail solely on the basis of the exercise of the discretion vested in this court by RSC Ord. 59, r.10(3)".

5–103   In *M v. P; Butler v. Butler* (1993) (above) Lord Donaldson M.R. stated that the critical issue in contempt cases was always one of justice, and the court is required to take account of the interests of (a) the contemnor; (b) the "victim" of the contempt; and (c) other users of the court for whom the maintenance of the authority of the court is of supreme importance. The court should consider whether, notwithstanding any departure from proper procedures, the contemnor has suffered any injustice:

"If he has not suffered any injustice, the committal order should stand, subject, if necessary, to variation of the order . . . In other cases it may be possible to do justice between the parties by . . . 'making such other order as may be just' [s.13(3)]. If . . . justice requires the committal order to be quashed amongst the options available is that of ordering a retrial . . ."

5–104   These observations of Lord Donaldson M.R. were applied in *Abdi v. Jama* (contempt: committal) [1996] 1 FLR 407, in which the Court of Appeal held that a county court has jurisdiction to amend or correct its own orders where there has been an error on the face of the court record (here, a failure to specify whether a committal order sentence was to be concurrent with or consecutive to an earlier committal order); the correction caused no injustice to the respondent—if not corrected, substantial injustice would be done to the victim. As Wall J. said at p.413:

"The courts must, of course, be alert to injustice in these circumstances. My Lord, in argument, posited the situation in which a man committed for contempt had served what he believed to be the term imposed on him and had then been released. In such circumstances the discovery by the court of the error on the record which meant that he had been released prematurely might well constitute an injustice were he to be required to return to prison. But in each case it seems to me a matter for the discretion of the court after a careful scrutiny of the facts. And after a careful scrutiny of the facts in this case, in my judgment, this respondent has suffered no injustice."

D. Magistrates' Courts Powers of committal

Jurisdiction

1. Powers of the court

Where a person disobeys a magistrates' court order to do anything other than the payment of money, or to abstain from doing anything, the court may: 5–105

(a) order him to pay a sum not exceeding £50 for every day during which he is in default or a sum not exceeding £5,000.00; or
(b) commit him to custody until he has remedied his default or for a period not exceeding two months: MCA 1980, s.63(3).

2. Limit on sentence

Where a person is ordered to pay a sum for each day in default, or where he is committed to custody until he has remedied his default, he should not be ordered to pay more than £5,000 or be committed for more than two months—that is without prejudice to the court's powers to punish any subsequent default. 5–106

3. Consecutive orders

The court has no power to impose consecutive committal orders under MCA 1980, s.63(3): *Head v. Head* [1982] 3 All E.R. 14.

4. Suspended committal

The court has no power to make a suspended committal order under MCA 1980, s.63(3); However, under FLA 1996, s.50 a magistrates' court may suspend the execution of a committal order imposed for breach of a "relevant requirement" (*i.e.* an occupation order, non-molestation order or an exclusion requirement included in an EPO or ICO—s.50(2)). Such suspension may be for such period or on such terms and conditions as the court may specify. 5–107

5. Hospital/guardianship orders

By virtue of FLA 1996, s.51(1), a magistrates' court may make a hospital order or guardianship order under Mental Health Act 1983, s.37 or an interim hospital order (*ibid.*, s.38) in the case of a person suffering from mental illness or severe mental 5–108 impairment who could otherwise be committed to custody for breach of a "relevant requirement" as defined in section 50(2) (above).

Exercise of Powers

1. When?

5–109   The courts powers to punish disobedience under MCA 1980, s.63(3) may be exercised either;
(a) of the courts own motion, or
(b) by order on complaint.
See Contempt of Court Act 1981, s.17 and Sched. 3.

2. Applications

5–110   Proceedings alleging breach of a magistrates' court order are commenced by making complaint to a justice of the peace, who may issue a summons directed to the defendant "requiring him to appear before a magistrates' court acting for that area to answer to the complaint": MCA 1980, s.51.

3. No Power to rescind FLA 1996 Orders

Where the court makes an order on complaint to punish disobedience, it does not have the powers under section 63(2) of the MCA 1980 to suspend or rescind any order made under FLA 1996, Pt 4: See FLA 1996, s.59(3).

CHAPTER SIX

Injunctions to Preserve Property

A. Jurisdiction

1. MCA 1973, s.37

"(1) For the purposes of this section 'financial relief' means relief under any of 6–01 the provisions of sections 22, 23, 24, 27, 31 (except subsection (6)) and 35 above, and any reference in this section to defeating a person's claim for financial relief is a reference to preventing financial relief from being granted to that person, or to that person for the benefit of a child of the family, or reducing the amount of any financial relief which might be so granted, or frustrating or impeding the enforcement of any order which might be or has been made at his instance under any of those provisions.

(2) Where proceedings for financial relief are brought by one person against another, the court may, on the application of the first-mentioned person:

(a) if it is satisfied that the other party to the proceedings is, with the intention of defeating the claim for financial relief, about to make any disposition or to transfer out of the jurisdiction or otherwise deal with any property, make such order as it thinks fit for restraining the other party from so doing or otherwise for protecting the claim;

(b) if it is satisfied that the other party has, with that intention, made a reviewable disposition and that if the disposition were set aside financial relief or different financial relief would be granted to the applicant, make an order setting aside the disposition;

(c) if it is satisfied, in a case where an order has been obtained under any of the provisions mentioned in subsection (1) above by the applicant against the other party, that the other party has, with that intention, made a reviewable disposition, make an order setting aside the disposition;

and an application for the purpose of paragraph (b) above shall be made in the proceedings for the financial relief in question.

6–02 (3) Where the court makes an order under subsection (2) (b) or (c) above setting aside a disposition it shall give such consequential directions as it thinks fit for giving effect to the order (including directions requiring the making of any payments or the disposal of any property).

6–03 (4) Any dispositions made by the other party to the proceedings for financial relief in question (whether before or after the commencement of those proceedings) is a reviewable disposition for the purposes of subsection (2) (b) and (c) above unless it was made for valuable consideration (other than marriage) to a person who, at the time of the disposition, acted in relation to it in good faith and without notice of any intention on the part of the other party to defeat the applicant's claim for financial relief.

6–04 (5) Where an application is made under this section with respect to a disposition which took place less than three years before the date of the application or with respect to a disposition or other dealing with property which is about to take place and the court is satisfied:

(a) in a case falling within subsection (2) (a) or (b) above, that the disposition or other dealing would (apart from this section) have the consequence, or

(b) in a case falling within subsection (2) (c) above, that the disposition has had the consequence,

of defeating the applicant's claim for financial relief, it shall be presumed, unless the contrary is shown, that the person who disposed of or is about to dispose of or deal with the property did so or, as the case may be, is about to do so, with the intention of defeating the applicant's claim for financial relief.

(6) In this section 'disposition' does not include any provision contained in a will or codicil but, with that exception, includes any conveyance, assurance or gift of property of any description, whether made by an instrument or otherwise.

(7) This section does not apply to a disposition made before 1st January 1968"

B. Nature of jurisdiction

1. The basis

6–05   There are two limbs to the court's jurisdiction in relation to enjoining the dissipation of assets. The court has both an inherent jurisdiction and jurisdiction pursuant to section 37 of the MCA 1973 to grant an injunction restraining a person from disposing of, or otherwise dealing with, property which has the effect of defeating the other party's claim for financial relief. (The relief provided for under section 37(2) (b) (c)—reviewable dispositions—is not included in this book).

2. Jurisdiction under section 37(2) (a)

6–06   When proceeding under section 37(2) (a) of the MCA 1973 it is necessary to satisfy the following conditions:

(a) Proceedings for financial relief must have been launched. Such proceedings may pray for relief for under sections 22, 23, 24, 25 B/C, 27, 31 and 35 of the Act. If the person seeking the injunction has filed a petition for divorce or judicial separation it is sufficient if such pleading includes a prayer for the formal financial relief which it is sought to protect: *Jackson* [1973] Fam.99.

(b) If no pleading has been filed and/or the pleading that has been filed did not contain such an application, the necessary application must be made prior to seeking injunctive relief.

(c) Under the Act the court must be satisfied that the other party to the proceedings is about to make a disposition or to transfer out of the jurisdiction or otherwise deal with any property.

(d) The court must further be satisfied that the other party is so doing "with the 6–07 intention of defeating the claim for financial relief": *Smith* (1973) 117 S.J.525. Under section 37 of the MCA 1973 though the court must be "satisfied" that the disposition has been made with the intention of defeating the applicants' claim for financial relief, the standard of proof in fraud cases is irrelevant: *K v. K* (1982) 12 Fam. Law 143, CA. Moreover, it is *not* a pre-requisite to the granting of relief that it must have been the *sole* intention: *Dawkins v. Judd* (1986) Fam. Law 295.

(e) Although the court must be satisfied as to the "guilty" intention, subsection 6–08 (5) provides that where the disposition or other dealing would have the consequence of defeating the applicant's claim, it shall be presumed, unless the contrary is shown, that the respondent does have such an intention.

3. What is a disposition?

A disposition does not include any provision contained in a will or codicil. 6–09 However, it does include any conveyance, assurance or gift of property of any description, whether made by instrument or otherwise (section 37(6)). Further, the words "any property" in section 37(2) (a) of the MCA 1973 are not restricted to property in England and Wales. They include real and personal property situated outside the jurisdiction. Accordingly, the court has jurisdiction to make an order in respect of realty abroad: *Hamlin* (1986) Fam. 11, CA. However, it is to be noted that a court will not, in the exercise of its discretion make an order concerning foreign property that cannot be enforced when it decides whether or not to exercise its jurisdiction under section 37.

4. How to bolster a section 37 application

In order to avoid the restrictive provisions of section 37 the application should 6–10 also be made pursuant to the inherent jurisdiction of the court (High Court: SCA 1981, s.37—Mareva injunctions and County Court: CCA 1981, s.38 and regulations made thereunder: County Courts Remedies Regs. 1991). It is not then necessary to prove an intention to dispose of property: *Roche* (1981) 11 Fam.Law 243, CA. This decision appears to make such application easier and avoids the standard of proof required by section 37. In Roche, Ormrod L.J. was clearly influenced by the following features:

6–11   "This is clearly a case where no hardship will be caused whatever to the husband by restraining him from disposing of part of the sum of damages, when he recovers them, provided that proceedings for ancillary relief are dealt with quickly. This court will take steps to see that that is done. I can see no reason why the court should not make such an order and the more the husband protests and refuses to give any assurances that he intends to leave some of his money in a liquid form, the more anxious the court is bound to be. One wonders why all this fuss is being made about such an order."

5. Type of order

6–12   Further, in that case Ormrod L.J. gave a very useful type of order recommending that:—

> "It is ordered that the respondent by himself, his servants, agents or otherwise be restrained from disposing of one quarter of the proceeds of his claim for damages . . . arising out of an accident otherwise than by paying the same into an account in joint names of the parties' solicitors pending determination of the wife's claim for a lump sum under section 23".

The orders which a court can make are very wide, *i.e.* orders may be made preventing a sale, freezing bank and/or other accounts, requiring moneys to be held in the names of solicitors and/or other parties. If an order is granted restraining dealings with a bank account, notice of the injunction should be given to the bank. In this context, the practice and procedure is effectively that now recognised as a Mareva injunction—in relation to which, see Goldrein, Wilkinson and Kershaw, *Commercial Litigation—Pre-emptive Remedies* (1996) and the Practice Direction *(ex parte Mareva Injunctions)* [1994] 1 W.L.R. 1233.

6. Third parties—involvement

6–13   On some occasions it may be necessary to join third parties to the application if a specific direction is required as to payment of monies sought to be restrained. Once the third person has notice of the injunction he will be guilty of contempt if he aids or abets a breach: *Acrow (Automation) Ltd v. Rex Chainbelt Inc.* [1971] 1 W.L.R. 1676.

7. More far reaching:

The inherent jurisdiction may be used to freeze assets not yet in existence: *Roche v. Roche* (1981) 11 Fam. Law 243, C.A.

The party applying must give an undertaking as to damages, supported, if appropriate, by security or payment into court.

6–14   An order will only be granted if there is evidence that the respondent intends to part with assets: *Law Society v. Shanks* [1988] 1 FLR 504, CA—but compare *Shipman v. Shipman* [1991] 1 FLR 250 (Lincoln J.) on the balance of convenience continued a freezing order over the major part of the husband's expected severance pay holding that proof of intention was unnecessary.

Where such an application is made (particularly *ex parte*) the applicant must be extremely careful to be scrupulously candid in his affidavit to the court.

It is wrong in principle in a matrimonial case, before judgment, to grant a Mareva Injunction extending to all the assets of the other party: *Ghoth v. Ghoth* [1992] 2 FLR 300.

8. Company assets

Care must be taken to ensure that the order permits transactions in the ordinary 6–15 course of business and that there are no third party shareholders whose interests are effected. Subject to this, Mareva relief may be extended to freeze the company's bank accounts (*TSB Private Bank International v. Chabra* (1992)1 L.B.R 231).

9. Slip rule

Errors on the face of the record cannot be corrected under the slip rule since these 6–16 are orders which impose a fetter on civil liberties; *Langley v. Langley* [1994] 1 FLR 383.

Injunctive relief should not be used as an attempt to disturb the status quo or indulge in pre-emptive strikes prior to the ancillary relief dispute: *Poon v. Poon* [1994] 2 FLR 857; Thorpe J. (unthinkable that order should be given allowing wife to go ahead and emasculate husband's control of company. Judge further held that the Family Division did have jurisdiction over the family business which the family chose to incorporate. All current disputes within the family should be litigated in one court).

C. Procedure

1. When?

Application should be made *ex parte* in the first instance otherwise the assets may 6–17 be disposed of in anticipation of the hearing.

2. To whom?

Pursuant to FPR 1991, r.2.68 the application should be made in the first instance to the district judge and if necessary he can refer it to a judge: FPR, r.2.65

3. Documents

The application should be supported by an affidavit giving full details of the assets in question, the basis of the application and particulars of the financial position of the person against whom proceedings are brought.

4. Undertakings in lieu of injunctions

It is usual for any injunction which the court decides to make to continue until 6–18 the hearing of the claim for ancillary relief or until further order. The party against whom such injunction is made can always, by application to the court ask that the injunction be varied or discharged. When the party against whom the injunction is sought agrees, he may give an undertaking in the terms of the application. Such undertaking can be discharged or varied on application by either party. It may be that if the assets of the person against whom proceedings are brought are so large an injunction will be unnecessary.

5. If no suit pending under the 1973 Act

6–19   When no matrimonial suit is pending, questions between husband and wife as to ownership of property may be resolved by the court on an application under section 17 of the Married Women's Property Act 1882 (as extended and amended). A district judge may grant an injunction in those proceedings which is ancillary or incidental to any relief sought. Application should be made by summons or notice supported by an affidavit. Again, such application is usually made *ex parte* with a short return date.

D. Anton Piller/Mareva/Writ ne exeat regno

1. Anton Piller

6–20   An order may be made whereby the respondent is directed to permit the applicant's solicitor to enter that party's premises for the purpose of inspecting, photographing and taking possession of documents thereby to make copies: *Emanuel* [1982] 1 W.L.R. 669. But note *Burgess v. Burgess* (1996) Fam. Law 464, CA: it was held that the Anton Piller order is a rare weapon only to be used in extreme or exceptional cases. If ill judged application is made, this may result in an order for costs on an indemnity basis.

2. Mareva

6–21   An order which has the effect of freezing assets so as to preserve them for the benefit of creditors; but not to give a charge in favour of any particular creditor.

Anton Piller/Mareva

The conditions which must be fulfilled by the applicant are stringent (Practice Direction (*ex parte Mareva Injunctions* and *Anton Piller* Orders) [1994] 1 W.L.R. 1233.) *See also:* Civil Procedure Act 1997 (Act received Royal Assent on February 27, 1997 and places court's jurisdiction to make Anton Piller orders on a statutory footing).

3. Writ ne exeat regno

6–22   A party to matrimonial litigation may be prompted to flee the country—and if, for example, there are maintenance arrears the writ ne exeat regno followed up by an injunction to deliver up a passport may be an effective weapon in the hands of a wife in proceeding for a judgment debt in respect of those arrears: *Thaha v. Thaha* [1987] 2 F.L.R. 142. For further consideration see Goldrein, Wilkinson and Kershaw, *Commercial Litigation—Pre-emptive Remedies* (1996).

APPENDIX A

Case File

The following cases are digested in this Appendix

1. Horner v. Horner

[1982] Fam. 90

Held: Harassment of a party to a marriage by sending threatening postcards and A–01 making frequent telephone calls to her place of work was conduct which amounted to "molestation".

2. Johnson v. Walton

[1990] 1 FLR 350, CA

A–02 P and D had sexual relationship then fell out. P alleged that D had harassed her. D gave undertakings, inter alia, not to molest P nor cause nor encourage others to do so. The Court accepted the undertaking and explained consequences of breach. P applied to commit D for contempt of Court for breach of undertaking following photographs of P in partially nude state appearing in the national press. *Held:*

(a) The lower Court had been wrong to dismiss the application to commit on the ground that the undertaking should not have been accepted—that was not the issue:

"It cannot be too clearly stated that, when an injunctive order is made or when an undertaking is given, it operates until it is revoked on appeal or by the Court itself, and it has to be obeyed whether or not it should have been granted or accepted in the first place" (*per* Lord Donaldson MR p.352).

(b) If D had sent "the offending photograph" to the newspaper with the intent of causing distress to P, that could come within D's undertaking.

(c) Contempt proceedings are intended to "uphold the authority of the Court" and ensure that orders are obeyed. They are not intended to provide solace or compensation to P.

3. Smith v. Smith

[1988] 1 FLR 179, CA

A–03 *Held:* It should not be assumed that breach of an injunction order or undertaking automatically results in committal to prison—the Court should consider all the circumstances of the case. Further, the sentencing judge should not take into account any matters which had not either been proved by the plaintiff or admitted by the defendant.

4. Harrow LBC v. Johnstone

[1997] 1 W.L.R. 459, HL

A–04 *Facts:* H and W were joint tenants of council property. Following breakdown of their marriage W left the home and H obtained an injunction prohibiting W, *inter alia*, from excluding him from the property. W applied for rehousing and served notice to terminate the joint tenancy. H remained in the home and HLBC claimed possession. On HLBC's appeal against a decision upholding the dismissal of its claim for possession against H:

A–05 *Held:* Appeal allowed. W's notice to terminate the joint tenancy was effective. H's injunction was not a mandatory order requiring W to maintain rights in force created by the joint tenancy pending outcome of any matrimonial property proceedings. HLBC was entitled to possession, was carrying out its statutory housing duties and was not guilty of an abuse of process of the court.

5. Kinzler v. Kinzler

(1985) 15 Fam.Law 26, CA

Facts: The hotel had 22 bedrooms and was owned by H and W, and another couple, A–06 in equal shares. Until recently both men had had full time employment outside the hotel and had only been there every other week. Each couple had three children and self contained accommodation but shared the one kitchen for the whole hotel. It was submitted on behalf of H that the court had no jurisdiction to order him to vacate the public part of the hotel but only the private part as this alone constituted the matrimonial home.

Held: dismissing H's appeal, that whilst it was a question of fact and degree the A–07 whole hotel, in the instant case, was the matrimonial home since there was only one entrance and one kitchen and a child of the family slept in the private part (Collins [1960] 1 W.L.R. 660 distinguished.)

6. Re D(Minors) (Residence: Imposition of Condition)

The Times, April 11, 1996, CA

The lower Court made a residence order, stipulating that the mother must not A–08 permit contact between her children and W (with whom she had been living), nor could she allow him to live at her property.
Held: The condition amounted to an exclusion order against W, and interfered with the mother's freedom to choose how to live her life rather than focusing on the issue of the children's residence.

7. J v. J (A Minor) (Property Transfer)

[1993] 2 FLR 56, Eastham J.

Property transfer application—CA 1989, s.15 and Sched. 1. Applicant mother A–09 sought order requiring R to transfer his interest, to her for the benefit of her daughter, in the joint tenancy of their council home. A and R were not married but had cohabited for 10 years. R was not the father of A's child, though he had treated her as a child of the family.
Held: The application for property transfer could not succeed as R was not a "parent" within CA 1989, s.15(1), Sched. 1, para. 16(2). Had he fallen within the definition of "parent", a Local Authority tenancy is property within Sched. 1 para. 1(2)(e): *K v. K (Minors: Property Transfer)* [1992] 2 FLR 220.

8. F v. Cambridgeshire C.C.

[1995] 1 FLR 516, Stuart-White J

A–10 *Held:* A Local Authority cannot seek private law orders under CA 1989, s.8, and should not be joined as party to private law proceedings, as this is inconsistent with the scheme of the CA 1989 (despite discretion under FPC (CA 1989) Rules 1991, r.7)—there is little difference between applying for a residence etc order and inviting the Court to make a different section 8 order to the one proposed by the other parties.

9. Re S (Minors) (Inherent Jurisdiction—Ouster)

[1994] 1 FLR 623, Connell J.

A–11 *Held:* Local Authority able to invoke the inherent jurisdiction of the High Court to obtain an order ousting a parent from the family home where he presented a risk to the children—only possible if no other route was open under CA 1989. In the circumstances it was not appropriate to oust the father by making a "no contact" order under section 34 of the CA 1989.

10. Re J (Minors) (Ex Parte Orders)

[1997] 1 FCR 325, Hale J.

A–12 The court gave the following guidance re *ex parte* orders:

(a) there is potential for serious injustice, as courts are dealing with applications for orders without hearing both sides of the case; scrupulous care is required of those seeking *ex parte* orders both in relation to the application and to the implementation of any order made.

(b) solicitors are under a duty to be scrupulously accurate when describing the provisions of any order, not only to the person to whom it is addressed but also to others (*e.g.* process servers, police).

(c) the Police (who in the present case had accompanied the process server to serve the order) should always take care to understand whether (1) an order required them to do anything, and if so, what (*e.g.* recovery order); (2) circumstances required them to do anything (*e.g.* taking a child into police protection) or (3) their presence was necessary to prevent a breach of the peace: the police should make an independent assessment as to whether a breach of the peace was likely.

(d) counsel should not advise on the terms of an order made in their absence unless completely satisfied that they knew what it said, normally by seeing a copy.

11. Ansah v. Ansah

[1977] Fam. 138, CA

A–13 *Facts:* W filed a divorce petition containing serious allegations of violence which H denied. The case was then transferred to the High Court. H made an *ex parte* application in person to the county court and was granted an injunction to restrain

W from returning to the matrimonial home and molesting him "until further hearing of this application . . . . at the time and place to be notified." Neither W nor her solicitors had notice of the application. On several occasions W returned to the matrimonial home to care for her father who resided there. On the last occasion a row broke out and as a result of which H suffered minor injuries. H was granted a committal order in the High Court suspended on terms that W comply with the injunction but provided that it should be executed without further notice upon filing affidavit evidence that W had been served with the order and was in breach of it. W appealed against the grant of the injunction and the committal order.

Held: allowing the appeals, that (1) since the case had been transferred to the High A–14 Court the county court judge had no jurisdiction to grant the injunction; (2) H's evidence in support of the *ex parte* application did not disclose the urgent need for the order before a hearing *inter partes* could be arranged, therefore the injunction and the committal order would be discharged; and (3) the injunction should have been strictly limited to the shortest period before there could be an *inter partes* hearing.

12. Loseby v. Newman

[1995] 2 FLR 754, CA

P was assaulted by D, and obtained an *ex parte* non-molestation injunction which A–15 continued in force for 11 months "unless before then it is revoked by further order . . . . or until the trial of the action whichever is sooner". P brought committal proceedings for alleged breaches of the order, which were found proved. The suspended committal order was defective in various respects including failure to specify the order breached, which contempt the Court found proved and failure to properly specify the period of the suspension.
Held:

(a)   *ex parte* orders should not be made "more or less automatically" simply on the footing that "it is always open to the D to apply to discharge it" (*per* Hoffman L.J.)

(b)   It is particularly important that the seriousness of an order is explained to D—that is assisted by giving D the opportunity to attend an *inter partes* hearing.

(c)   The form of words adopted by the lower Court was undesirable in family disputes. *Ex parte* injunctions should not be granted for lengthy periods, and "should only be granted until a period when it is possible for the matter to come on before the Court *inter partes*". (*per* Balcombe L.J.)

(d)   An *ex parte* order should only be made when either there is no time to give the D notice to appear, or when there is reason to believe that the D, if given notice, would act to defeat the purpose of the order (*per* Hoffman L.J.).

13. Walters v. Whitelock

[1994] CLY 3762, CA

Process server told alleged contemnor (A) that he had documents for him and thrust A–16 the documents into A's clothing. A threw the documents to the floor.

Held: A had not accepted the documents but they were properly served—sufficient to bring to A's attention that they were legal documents which required his attention in connection with the proceedings.

14. Cleveland CC v. L

The Times, April 8, 1996, CA

A–17 L committed to prison for breach of restraint order made under CA 1989, s.100. He appealed on basis that

(a)   there was no penal notice on the order, and
(b)   he was not made aware of consequences of breach.

Held: Appeal allowed: RSC Ord. 45, r.7(4) provides that an order restraining a defendant from doing an act must carry a penal notice; however, such order may still be enforced without the penal notice if the defendant is present when the order is made or is informed of its contents: RSC Ord. 45, r.7(6). There was no evidence that L had been informed of the consequences of breach (*i.e.* that it would result in imprisonment)—the order would therefore be set aside.

15. Kumari v. Jalal

[1996] 4 All E.R. 65, CA

A–18 H was ordered to return specified items to W within seven days. H failed to comply with the order. At committal proceedings, H found to be in contempt of Court and sentenced to three months' imprisonment. H failed to return the items following his release from prison. W made second application for H's committal, for his continuing breach of the delivery order. H sentenced to a further six months' imprisonment for contempt.

Held: Allowing H's appeal, his failure to comply with the order within the time fixed was a single breach for which he had been committed to prison for three months; his continued failure to comply was not a new offence and he should not have been committed to prison a second time.

16. Roberts v. Roberts

[1990] 2 FLR 111, CA

A–19 H gave undertaking, *inter alia*, not to enter the part of the former matrimonial home where W was living. H moved into the "prohibited" part of the home after W had vacated the property. W applied to commit H for breach of his undertaking. H was committed to prison for 28 days suspended on condition that he vacate within 24 hours.

Held: Dismissing H's appeal, the judge was correct to refuse to hear argument on the merits of H's undertaking, and was right not to treat the application to commit as an application by H to discharge his undertaking on the merits.

> "He quite rightly refused to consider the merits as to whether or not the undertaking should be discharged when he had to deal with a much more fundamental and prior consideration as to what he should do about the admitted serious breach of the undertaking" (*per* Butler-Sloss L.J. at p. 114).

17. Holtom v. Holtom

(1981) 11 Fam.Law 249, CA

Facts: W had applied to the county court for an exclusion order against H from the A–20 matrimonial home. At the hearing before the deputy circuit judge W agreed to give an undertaking not to cohabit with another man at the home. He gave a cross-undertaking not to return save for the purposes of access. Subsequently, upon the hearing of H's application the county court judge found that W was in breach of the spirit of her undertaking. He ordered that she should be committed to prison for 14 days but that it should not be enforced without leave of the court.

Held: on W's appeal, that such an undertaking was bad and should never have been A–21 accepted by the court in the first place. As divorce proceedings had commenced but withdrawn the right thing was for H to issue a fresh petition based upon W's adultery. It was a total waste of time to hear the committal proceedings which were bound to be stayed.

18. Re De Cespedes

[1937] 2 All E.R. 572, CA

Bankruptcy Notice—application for order for substituted service. *Held:* Affidavit in A–22 support insufficient, as it did not state:

(a)   the fact that the debtor was not within the jurisdiction
(b)   that service within the jurisdiction by post would not reach him
(c)   that there was any reason to think that the house at which personal and postal service had been attempted was the place at which the debtor was known or expected to be found
(d)   any connection between the debtor and that particular address, or that the Notice would reach the mind/attention of the person to whom it was directed.

The order for substituted service could not be supported—all subsequent proceedings in the bankruptcy must fail.

19. Taylor v. Taylor

[1996] 2 CL 54

Contempt proceedings—R evaded service of notice to show cause—order made A–23 under CCR Ord. 7, 8 for substituted service. R failed to attend at committal hearing—alleged breaches proved in his absence—R committed to three months' imprisonment. R applied under CCR Ord. 37, r.2 to set aside committal order on the ground that he was unaware of the committal hearing date. Court heard oral evidence and found that R had deliberately chosen to stay away from the hearing.

Held: R had denied himself the opportunity of presenting his case to the Court—no danger of unfairness.

20. Lamb v. Lamb

(1984) 14 Fam.Law 60, CA

A–24 *Facts:* On July 25, 1983 W had been granted *inter alia*, non-molestation and ouster orders against H. On July 27, H was committed to prison, upon W's *ex parte* application for 14 days. Pursuant to that order H was arrested but on the judge's instructions brought before him on August 1. After hearing evidence, the judge decided to increase the sentence to one of three months.

Held: allowing H's appeal, that the making of the second order was wrong as H was being sentenced twice for the same offence. Save for some photographs of the damage which H had done there was no evidence of any further acts. Whilst the judge, having heard H's evidence, had thought it appropriate to impose a stiffer sentence he had no power to do so. The second order was therefore a nullity (*Church's Trustee v. Hubbard* [1902] 2 Ch. 784 applied).

21. Wellington v. Wellington

(1978) 122 S.J. 296

A–25 *Facts:* W was committed to prison for seven days for breach of an order not to return to the matrimonial home. On release, he again returned and was arrested. He was brought before the judge on a Sunday; he was committed for contempt but the order for committal was left blank and none of the requisites had been completed.

Held: W should be released immediately because of the defects.

22. Cinderby v. Cinderby: Pekesin v. Pekesin

(1978) 122 S.J. 436

A–26 *Facts:* H was ordered by Swansea County Court not to molest his wife or remain in or enter the matrimonial home; a power of arrest was attached. He remained in the home and was arrested for breach of that order; he was committed to prison for contempt without the limit of time being specified. W2 left the matrimonial home because of her husband's violence, and a month later the Court of Appeal ordered him to vacate the home and enable her to return. When she did so it was devoid of furniture and damaged. A county court judge committed H2 to prison "for a period of six months until further order".

Held: allowing appeals by the official solicitor in respect of both husbands, both A–27 committal orders were bad. Neither of them properly specified the duration of committal (*Wellington* (1978) 122 S.J. 297, CA applied) and they did not state the evidence, nor the particular contempt of which the husbands were guilty. No attempt should be made to remedy defects in a Court order without reference to a judge, and the slip rule could not be invoked in cases affecting the liberty of the subject.

23. Kavanagh v. Kavanagh

The Times, July 26, 1978, CA

Facts: H was ordered by Arnold J. on February 28, 1978 to vacate the former A–28 matrimonial home and not to return within 50 yards thereof, pursuant to an earlier order for sale on divorce proceedings. He failed to comply with the order and threatened prospective purchasers. On June 8, 1978 Lane J. heard evidence of H's breach of the earlier order in his absence and made a committal order. On June 28, 1978, the committal order was affirmed in H's presence. H appealed, contended insufficient particularity in the committal order.

Held: dismissed the appeal, H knew he was in breach of the February order, and there was no need to specify in a High Court order that he had not vacated the house. (*McIlraith v. Grady* [1968] 1 Q.B. 583 distinguished).

24. C v. G

The Times, October 14, 1996, CA

Contempt—sentence—Young father—frequent breaches of non-molestation order A–29 made in favour of the mother of his child—committed to prison for 13 months in lower court.

Held: on appeal: Manifestly too long—sentence reduced to eight months; the contemnor was

(a) a young man
(b) no previous convictions
(c) excessively fond of his child
(d) his breaches were a result of his distress rather than evil intent
(e) he had admitted his breaches and apologised

25. Re O (Contempt: Committal)

[1995] 2 FLR 767, CA

The defendants, the natural parents of two children, found out where the children's A–30 adoptive parents were living—they breached Court order by writing and sending six letters to different police stations which contained false allegations of abuse of their elder child by her adoptive father—the defendants falsely accused a social worker of writing the letter in an attempt to "frame" them.

Held: approving sentence of 12 months' imprisonment as "entirely appropriate", the Court took a serious view of the contempt in view of the following:

(a) the defendants had denied the breaches, had expressed no regret and made no promises not to repeat the breaches

(b) these were persistent and deliberate breaches of a Court order

(c) their conduct was calculated to cause distress to the adopters and disturb the adoption process

(d) their conduct amounted to an attempt to pervert the course of justice.

26. Sellars v. Sellars

May 1, 1984 (Ub. CAT No 1348) (unreported)

A–31 *Facts:* H appealed against a sentence of 28 days' imprisonment for contempt of court, eight days of which had been served before he was granted bail, for disregarding the terms of an injunction granted for W's protection. On appeal, W, who H had maintained had lied and was vindictively trying to put him into prison, took the view that H "may well have been brought to his senses" as a result of the eight days imprisonment he served before getting bail, although there was no apology for contempt by H himself.

A–32 *Held:* allowing the appeal, and reducing the sentence to eight days of imprisonment, that although there was no ground shown for criticising the decision that 28 days' imprisonment for H was the right and sensible course for the court to take, as this was a family case where the children were involved and having regard to the conciliatory approach of W, it was just possible that if the court acceded to W's request for mercy for H, that may play a useful part in the family relationships in the future bearing in mind that a divorce petition had now been filed and would be served tomorrow and H was going to make an application for interim access to the children.

27. Delaney v. Delaney

The Times, November 2, 1995, CA

A–33 D breached undertaking not to use violence against W—On October 5, court committed him to prison with a direction that his sentence would be further considered on October 20.

Held: Allowing D's appeal:

(a) the original sentence was bad and inconsistent with Contempt of Court Act 1981, s.14(1)—no power to consider sentence at a future date;

(b)   that part of the order allowing D to purge his contempt had been deleted—should not deprive D of such right;

(c)   by remanding D in custody before sentencing, D was effectively serving part of his sentence twice.

28. Vaughan v. Vaughan

[1973] 1 W.L.R. 1159

Facts: In October 1970 W obtained a decree nisi and, before it was made absolute,   A–34 obtained an injunction restraining H from molesting her. On four occasions between November 1970 and May 1971 H was committed to prison for breaches and periods varying from three weeks to two months. On each occasion he was released on giving an apology and a solemn undertaking to obey the terms of the injunction. He then served a period of imprisonment for burglary and did not contact W until April 1973 when he began pestering her by following her to and from her place of work although she repeatedly asked him not to do so and he knew that she was afraid of him. On May 10, 1973, a judge held that H was in serious breach of the injunction and guilty of contempt, committed him to prison for six months less one day and directed that he be not at liberty to apply for his release before the last day of that period.

Held: (On H's appeal) that the appeal be dismissed but that the order be varied by striking out the direction. (*Yager v. Musa* [1961] 2 Q.B. 214 applied.)

29. Blome v. Blome

(1976) 120 S.J. 315

Facts: H was ordered in 1975 by a registrar, after W had divorced him, to pay W a   A–35 lump sum of £25,000 and £200 a month and to pay £20 a week for each child. In December 1975 a deputy circuit judge granted him leave to appeal out of time, stayed the registrar's order, ordered H to pay £1,000 to W and £15 a week to W and £7.50 to each child. In January 1976 Dunn J. granted W an injunction restraining H from disposing of his assets. W applied under section 37 of the Matrimonial Causes Act 1973, and on January 26, Faulks J. continued the injunction and ordered production of documents. Those produced were unsatisfactory and late. W applied to commit H for breach of that order.

Held: (1) that there could be no committal order as there had been no personal   A–36 service of the mandatory injunction; (2) that the stay on the registrar's order be removed; (3) that the order granting H leave to appeal out of time be struck out (H was not taking any order of the court seriously) and H be debarred from defending W's section 37 application. (*Pearce* [1959] C.L.Y. 1451 not followed).

30. Masich v. Masich

(1977) 7 Fam.Law 245, CA

Facts: H appealed from an order excluding him from the matrimonial home by 6   A–37 p.m. on the day of the order which was served on H at 3.30 p.m. that day.

A–38 *Held:* allowing the appeal, that, violence not being alleged, there was nothing to justify turning H out of his home without hearing his side. Applications for injunctions requiring a spouse to leave the matrimonial home should be made on notice to the other side with both parties present at the hearing. Such applications should only be made *ex parte* in the most exceptional circumstances; otherwise they were an abuse of the process of the court and solicitors promoting them might themselves be liable to pay the costs.

31. Morgan v. Morgan

(1978) 9 Fam.Law 87 CA

A–39 *Facts*: On W's *ex parte* application (under the old 1976 Act) the judge granted a non-molestation injunction and attached a power of arrest. It was made to operate "until further order". At the *inter partes* hearing the injunction, as previously made, was continued and various other orders made.

Held: on appeal, that it was wholly unjustifiable and improper to make an injunction *ex parte* "until further order" (*Ansah* (1977) (above Case 11) applied).

32. Jacob v. Jacob

(1978) 9 Fam.Law 57 CA

A–40 *Facts*: W had petitioned for divorce and had issued proceedings for a non-molestation injunction. The documents were personally served upon H by enquiry agents since he was not legally represented at that stage. At court both parties were legally represented and H entered into the usual undertaking not to assault, molest or otherwise interfere with W. H later broke this undertaking and at the subsequent hearing gave a second undertaking to the judge in similar terms. The court order on this occasion was again served by enquiry agents. H broke this undertaking as well but on this occasion his solicitors refused to accept service claiming that they no longer had contact with H. The matter was finally adjourned generally when attempts to effect service were abandoned and it became apparent that H was now leaving W alone. On taxation of W's party and party bill for costs the [registrar] disallowed the costs of service by enquiry agents as being not reasonably incurred.

A–41 *Held*: allowing W's appeal, that when approaching the taxation of the costs of service in this type of case the [registrar] should always consider the merits of the individual case and the difficulties facing the petitioner's solicitors. Solicitors were under a particularly onerous duty to protect their client in the most efficient manner possible and should not be subjected to the risk of having costs reasonably incurred disallowed on some technical ground. Here service of proceedings and knowledge of them by H were of fundamental importance to the successful outcome of W's application for an injunction, or more so, her application to commit.

33. McConnell v. McConnell

(1980) Fam.Law 214, CA

Facts: W had applied for a non-molestation and ouster injunction against H. Having A–42
heard the evidence, the county court judge indicated that he was minded to grant an
injunction and invited H to give an undertaking instead without prejudice to his
right of appeal. H gave the undertaking and the judge ordered that W's application
be adjourned generally. The recital to the order stated "That having heard oral
evidence, the court making the declaration and determination that the petitioner is
entitled to an injunction in the terms of the undertaking hereinafter referred to
. . . ."

Held: dismissing H's appeal, that the Court of Appeal had no jurisdiction since it A–43
could only operate on orders. A declaration that a party is entitled to an injunction
was meaningless and pure surplusage. The course that should have been taken was
that application should have been made to the judge to release H from his
undertaking on the ground that he was no longer prepared to give it, in which case
the judge would no doubt have replaced it by an injunction. There really is not very
much point in taking undertakings from people where it is intended there should be
an injunction.

34. Galan v. Galan

[1985] FLR 905

Facts: There had been repeated ouster injunctions against H and various undertak- A–44
ings had been given by him. On two occasions he was committed to prison for being
in breach of court orders. A situation was established where it would constitute a
risk of violence and certain detriment to the family if H were permitted to return to
the matrimonial home. W was unable to present a petition for divorce until October
1986 and there was no likely chance of the parties' respective rights in the
matrimonial home being finally determined in the course of the following few
months either by negotiation or matrimonial proceedings. The judge made an
exclusion order which was unlimited in time.

Held: that normally an order unlimited in point of time or even expressed to endure A–45
"until further order" would not be appropriate. However, there was nothing in the
[DVMPA 1976] expressly to limit the discretion of the court as regards the duration
of the order and in exceptional cases an injunction [under section 1] limited to
endure "until further order," may be made if the circumstances were appropriate for
such an order. The facts of the present case were exceptional and the proper course
was to designate the exclusion order against H to endure "until further order."
(*Spencer v. Camacho* (1984) 12 H.L.R. 68 at 130 followed)

35. Chadda v. Chadda

The Times, January 3, 1981, CA

A–46 *Held:* Where it is found that a husband should vacate the home and it is apparent that he is earning a good wage in good employment and is able to find alternative accommodation within a comparatively short space of time it is appropriate to order him to vacate the matrimonial home within 14 days.

36. Nicholls v. Nicholls

(1997) 147 NLJ 61, CA

A–47 Lord Woolf M.R. gave the following guidance re setting aside defective committal orders:

(a) the relevant rules must be complied with in view of seriousness of committal orders. The judge signing the committal order must ensure it is properly drawn up;

(b) where there are technical defects in the order, it should only be set aside where it was in the interests of justice; it would not be set aside where the defendant had been fairly tried and the order made on valid grounds;

(c) justice does not require the order to be set aside for technical defects where the defendant has not suffered prejudice or injustice by the errors; the order may be amended

(d) in determining whether to set aside an order, the Court should consider the interests of any other party and the authority/credibility of the court system;

(e) where the defect has caused injustice the Court should consider ordering a new trial unless it would be unjust to do so.

37. Constanza

(1997) 4 *Archbold News* 3

A–48 *Facts:* the complainant suffered clinical depression and anxiety caused by the Defendant's actions, which included numerous silent phone calls to the Complainant at home and work, and sending over 800 letters. Defendant conceded his behaviour amounted to actual bodily harm but denied any assault. He asserted that:

(a) a person cannot be in fear of immediate violence unless s/he can see the perpetrator, and

(b) words alone cannot amount to an assault.

Held: Rejecting the appeal, it is sufficient if "the Crown had proved a fear of violence at some time not excluding the immediate future . . . how it got there, whether by seeing an action or hearing a threat and whether that threat was conveyed verbally through words spoken either directly in the presence of the Complainant or over the telephone or whether the fear was aroused through something written whether it be a letter or a fax seems to us wholly irrelevant" (*per* Schiemann L.J.).

APPENDIX B

Rules of Court

High court

County court

Family proceedings rules 1991

High Court Rules

Order 2

Effect of Non-Compliance

Non-compliance with rules (0.2, r.1)

1.—(1) Where, in beginning or purporting to begin any proceedings or at any **B–04** stage in the course of or in connection with any proceedings, there has, by reason of any thing done or left undone, been a failure to comply with the requirements of these rules, whether in respect of time, place, manner, form or content or in any other respect, the failure shall be treated as an irregularity and shall not nullify the proceedings, any step taken in the proceedings, or any document, judgment or order therein.

(2) Subject to paragraph (3) the Court may, on the ground that there has been such a failure as is mentioned in paragraph (1) and on such terms as to costs or

otherwise as it thinks just, set aside either wholly or in part the proceedings in which the failure occurred, any step taken in those proceedings or any document, judgment or order therein or exercise its powers under these rules to allow such amendments (if any) to be made and to make such order (if any) dealing with the proceedings generally as it thinks fit.

(3) The Court shall not wholly set aside any proceedings or the writ or other originating process by which they were begun on the ground that the proceedings were required by any of these rules to be begun by an originating process other than the one employed.

Application to set aside for irregularity (0.2, r.2)

B–05   2.—(1) An application to set aside for irregularity any proceedings, any step taken in any proceedings or any document, judgment or order therein shall not be allowed unless it is made within a reasonable time and before the party applying has taken any fresh step after becoming aware of the irregularity.

(2) An application under this rule may be made by summons or motion and the grounds of objection must be stated in the summons or notice of motion.

Order 20

Amendment

Amendment of judgment and orders (O.20, r.11)

B–06   11. Clerical mistakes in judgments or orders, or errors arising therein from any accidental slip or omission, may at any time be corrected by the Court on motion or summons without an appeal.

Order 29

Interlocutory Injunctions, Interim Preservation of Property, Interim Payments, etc.
I. Interlocutory Injunctions, Interim Preservation of Property, etc.

Application for Injunction (O.29, r.1)

B–07   1.—(1) An application for the grant of an injunction may be made by any party to a cause or matter before or after the trial of the cause or matter, whether or not a claim for the injunction was included in that party's writ, originating summons, counterclaim or third party notice, as the case may be.

(2) Where the case is one of urgency such application may be made *ex parte* on affidavit but, except as aforesaid, such application must be made by motion or summons.

(3) The plaintiff may not make such an application before the issue of the writ or originating summons by which the cause or matter is to be begun except where the case is one of urgency, and in that case the injunction applied for may be granted on terms providing for the issue of the writ or summons and such other terms, if any, as the Court thinks fit.

Note: The requirement formerly in r.1(2) that "the applicant is the plaintiff" was deleted by the Rule of the Supreme Court (Amendment) 1995, S.I. No. 2206(L9).

Order 41

Affidavits

Form of affidavit (O.41, r.1)

1.—(1) Subject to paragraphs (2) and (3) every affidavit sworn in a cause or **B–08** matter must be entitled in that cause or matter.

(2) Where a cause or matter is entitled in more than one matter, it shall be sufficient to state the first matter followed by the words "and other matters," and where a cause or matter is entitled in a matter or matters and between parties, that part of the title which consists of the matter or matters may be omitted.

(3) Where there are more plaintiffs than one, it shall be sufficient to state the full name of the first followed by the words "and others," and similarly with respect to defendants.

(4) Every affidavit must be expressed in the first person and, unless the Court otherwise directs, must state the place of residence of the deponent and his occupation or, if he has none, his description, and if he is, or is employed by, a party to the cause or matter in which the affidavit is sworn, the affidavit must state that fact.

In the case of a deponent who is giving evidence in a professional, business or other occupational capacity the affidavit may, instead of stating the deponent's place of residence, state the address at which he works, the position he holds and the name of his firm or employer, if any.

(5) Every affidavit must be bound in book form, and, whether or not both sides of the paper are used, the printed, written or typed sides of the paper must be numbered consecutively.

(6) Every affidavit must be divided into paragraphs numbered consecutively, each paragraph being as far as possible confined to a distinct portion of the subject.

(7) Dates, sums and other numbers must be expressed in an affidavit in figures and not in words.

(8) Every affidavit must be signed by the deponent and the jurat must be completed and signed by the person before whom it is sworn.

Affidavit by two or more deponents (O.41, r.2)

B–09   2. Where an affidavit is made by two or more deponents, the names of the persons making the affidavit must be inserted in the jurat except that, if the affidavit is sworn by both or all the deponents at one time before the same person, it shall be sufficient to state that it was sworn by both (or all) of the "above named" deponents.

Affidavit by illiterate or blind person (O.41, r.3)

3. Where it appears to the person administering the oath that the deponent is illiterate or blind, he must certify in the jurat that—

(a)   the affidavit was read in his presence to the deponent,
(b)   the deponent seemed perfectly to understand it, and
(c)   the deponent made his signature or mark in his presence;

and the affidavit shall not be used in evidence without such a certificate unless the Court is otherwise satisfied that it was read to and appeared to be perfectly understood by the deponent.

Order 42

Judgments and Orders

Judgment, etc., requiring act to be done: time for doing it (O.42, r.2)

B–10   2.—(1) Subject to paragraph (2), a judgment or order which requires a person to do an act must specify the time after service of the judgment or order, or some other time, within which the act is to be done.

(2) Where the act which any person is required by any judgment or order to do is to pay money to some other person, give possession of any land or deliver any goods, a time within which the act is to be done need not be specified in the judgment or order by virtue of paragraph (1) but the foregoing provision shall not affect the power of the Court to specify such a time and to adjudge or order accordingly.

Order 45

Enforcement of Judgments and Orders: General

Enforcement of judgment to do or abstain from doing any act (O.45, r.5)

5.—(1) Where—   B–11

(a) a person required by a judgment or order to do an act within a time specified in the judgment or order refuses or neglects to do it within that time or, as the case may be, within that time as extended or abridged under Order 3, rule 5, or

(b) a person disobeys a judgment or order requiring him to abstain from doing an act,

then, subject to the provisions of these rules, the judgment or order may be enforced by one or more of the following means, that is to say—

(i) with the leave of the Court, a writ of sequestration against the property of that person;

(ii) where that person is a body corporate, with the leave of the Court, a writ of sequestration against the property of any director or other officer of the body;

(iii) subject to the provisions of the Debtors Act 1869 and 1878, an order of committal against that person or, where that person is a body corporate, against any such officer.

(2) Where a judgment or order requires a person to do an act within a time therein specified and an order is subsequently made under rule 6 requiring the act to be done within some other time, references in paragraph (1) of this rule to a judgment or order shall be construed as references to the order made under rule 6.

(3) Where under any judgment or order requiring the delivery of any goods the person liable to execution has the alternative of paying the assessed value of the goods, the judgment or order shall not be enforceable by order of committal under paragraph (1), but the Court may, on the application of the person entitled to enforce the judgment or order, make an order requiring the first mentioned person to deliver the goods to the applicant within a time specified in the order, and that order may be so enforced.

Judgment, etc. requiring act to be done: order fixing time for doing it (O.45, r.6)

6.—(1) Notwithstanding that a judgment or order requiring a person to do an B–12
act specifies a time within which the act is to be done, the Court shall, without prejudice to Order 3, rule 5, have power to make an order requiring the act to be done within another time, being such time after service of that order, or such other time, as may be specified therein.

(2) Where, notwithstanding Order 42, rule 2(1) or by reason of Order 42, rule 2(2) a judgment or order requiring a person to do an act does not specify a time within which the act is to be done, the Court shall have power subsequently to make an order requiring the act to be done within such time after service of that order, or such other time, as may be specified therein.

(3) An application for an order under this rule must be made by summons and the summons must, notwithstanding anything in Order 65, rule 9, be served on the person required to do the act in question.

Service of copy of judgment, etc., prerequisite to enforcement under r.5 (O.45, r.7)

7–(1) In this rule references to an order shall be construed as including references to a judgment.

(2) Subject to Order 24, rule 16(3), Order 26, rule 6(3), and paragraphs (6) and (7) of this rule, an order shall not be enforced under rule 5 unless—

(a)   a copy of the order has been served personally on the person required to do or abstain from doing the act in question, and

(b)   in the case of an order requiring a person to do an act, the copy has been so served before the expiration of the time within which he was required to do the act.

(3) Subject as aforesaid, an order requiring a body corporate to do or abstain from doing an act shall not be enforced as mentioned in rule 5(1) (ii) or (iii) unless—

(a)   a copy of the order has also been served personally on the officer against whose property leave is sought to issue a writ of sequestration or against whom an order of committal is sought, and

(b)   in the case of an order requiring the body corporate to do an act, the copy has been so served before the expiration of the time within which the body was required to do the act.

(4) There must be prominently displayed on the front of the copy of an order served under this rule a warning to the person on whom the copy is served that disobedience to the order would be a contempt of court punishable by imprisonment, or (in the case of an order requiring a body corporate to do or abstain from doing an act) punishable by sequestration of the assets of the body corporate and by imprisonment of any individual responsible.

(5) With the copy of an order required to be served under this rule, being an order requiring a person to do an act, there must also be served a copy of any order made under Order 3, rule 5, extending or abridging the time for doing the act and, where the first-mentioned order was made under rule 5(3) or 6 of this Order, a copy of the previous order requiring the act to be done.

(6) An order requiring a person to abstain from doing an act may be enforced under rule 5 notwithstanding that service of a copy of the order has not been effected in accordance with this rule if the Court is satisfied that pending such

service, the person against whom or against whose property is sought to enforce the order has had notice thereof either—

(a)   by being present when the order was made, or

(b)   by being notified of the terms of the order, whether by telephone, telegram or otherwise.

(7) Without prejudice to its powers under Order 65, rule 4, the Court may dispense with service of a copy of an order under this rule if it thinks it just to do so.

Order 52

Committal

Committal for contempt of court (O.52, r.1)

1.—(1) The power of the High Court or Court of Appeal to punish for contempt **B–13** of court may be exercised by an order of committal.

(2) Where contempt of court—

(a)   is committed in connection with—

(i) any proceedings before a Divisional Court of the Queen's Bench Division, or

(ii) criminal proceedings, except where the contempt is committed in the face of the court or consists of disobedience to an order of the court or a breach of an undertaking to the court, or

(iii) proceedings in an inferior court, or

(b)   is committed otherwise than in connection with any proceedings, then, subject to paragraph (4), an order of committal may be made only by a Divisional Court of the Queen's Bench Division.

This paragraph shall not apply in relation to contempt of the Court of Appeal.

(3) Where contempt of court is committed in connection with any proceedings in the High Court, then, subject to paragraph (2), an order of committal may be made by a single judge of the Queen's Bench Division except where the proceedings were assigned or subsequently transferred to some other Division, in which case the order may be made only by a single judge of that other Division.

The reference in this paragraph to a single judge of the Queen's Bench Division shall, in relation to proceedings in any court the judge or judges of which are, when exercising the jurisdiction of that court, deemed by virtue of any enactment to constitute a court of the High Court, be construed as a reference to a judge of that court.

(4) Where by virtue of any enactment the High Court has power to punish or take steps for the punishment of any person charged with having done any thing in relation to a court, tribunal or person which would, if it had been done in relation to the High Court, have been a contempt of that Court, an order of committal may be made by a single judge of the Queen's Bench Division.

Application to Court other than Divisional Court (O.52, r.4)

B–14   4.—(1) Where an application for an order of committal may be made to a Court other than a Divisional Court, the application must be made by motion and be supported by an affidavit.

(2) Subject to paragraph (3) the notice of motion, stating the grounds of the application and accompanied by a copy of the affidavit in support of the application, must be served personally on the person sought to be committed.

(3) Without prejudice to its powers under Order 65, rule 4, the Court may dispense with service of the notice of motion under this rule if it thinks it just to do so.

(4) This rule does not apply to proceedings brought before a single judge by virtue of Order 64, rule 4.

Saving for power to commit without application for purpose (O.52, r.5)

5. Nothing in the foregoing provisions of this order shall be taken as affecting the power of the High Court or Court of Appeal to make an order of committal of its own motion against a person guilty of contempt of court.

Provisions as to hearing (O.52, r.6)

B–15   6.—(1) Subject to paragraph (2), the Court hearing an application for an order of committal may sit in private in the following cases, that is to say—

(a)   where the application arises out of proceedings relating to the wardship or adoption of an infant or wholly or mainly to the guardianship, custody, maintenance or upbringing of an infant, or rights of access to an infant;

(b)   where the application arises out of proceedings relating to a person suffering or appearing to be suffering from mental disorder within the meaning of the Mental Health Act 1983;

(c)   where the application arises out of proceedings in which a secret process, discovery or invention was in issue;

(d)   where it appears to the Court that in the interests of the administration of justice or for reasons of national security the application should be heard in private;

but, except as aforesaid, the application shall be heard in open court.

(2) If the Court hearing an application in private by virtue of paragraph (1) decides to make an order of committal against the person sought to be committed, it shall in open court state—

(a)   the name of that person,

(b)   in general terms the nature of the contempt of Court in respect of which the order of committal is being made, and

(c)   the length of the period of which he is being committed.

(3) Except with the leave of the Court hearing an application for an order of committal, no grounds shall be relied upon at the hearing except the grounds set out in the statement under rule 2 or, as the case may be, in the notice of motion under rule 4.

The foregoing provision is without prejudice to the powers of the Court under Order 20, rule 8.

(4) If on the hearing of the application the person sought to be committed expresses a wish to give oral evidence on his own behalf, he shall be entitled to do so.

Power to suspend execution of committal order (O.52, r.7)

7.—(1) The Court by whom an order of committal is made may by order direct B–16 that the execution of the order of committal shall be suspended for such period or on such terms or conditions as it may specify.

(2) Where execution of an order of committal is suspended by an order under paragraph (1), the applicant for the order of committal must, unless the Court otherwise directs, serve on the person against whom it was made a notice informing him of the making and terms of the order under that paragraph.

Discharge of person committed (O.52, r.8)

8.—(1) The Court may, on the application of any person committed to prison for B–17 any contempt of Court, discharge him.

(2) Where a person has been committed for failing to comply with a judgment or order requiring him to deliver any thing to some other person or to deposit it in Court or elsewhere, and a writ of sequestration has also been issued to enforce that judgment or order, then, if the thing is in the custody or power of the person committed, the commissioners appointed by the writ of sequestration may take possession of it as if it were the property of that person and, without prejudice to the generality of paragraph (1), the Court may discharge the person committed and may give such directions for dealing with the thing taken by the commissioners as it thinks fit.

Saving for other powers (O.52, r.9)

9. Nothing in the foregoing provisions of this Order shall be taken as affecting B–18 the power of the Court to make an order requiring a person guilty of contempt of court, or a person punishable by virtue of any enactment in like manner as if he had been guilty of contempt of the High Court, to pay a fine or to give security for his good behaviour, and those provisions, so far as applicable, and with the necessary modifications, shall apply in relation to an application for such an order as they apply in relation to an application for an order of committal.

Order 59

Appeals to the Court of Appeal

General powers of the Court (O.59, r.10)

B–19   10.—(1) In relation to an appeal the Court of Appeal shall have all the powers and duties as to amendment and otherwise of the High Court including, without prejudice to the generality of the foregoing words, the powers of the Court under Order 36 to refer any question or issue of fact for trial before, or inquiry and report by, an official referee.

In relation to a reference made to an official referee, any thing required or authorised under Order 36, rule 9, to be done by, to or before the Court shall be done by, to or before the Court of Appeal.

(2) The Court of Appeal shall have power to receive further evidence on questions of fact, either by oral examination in court, by affidavit, or by deposition taken before an examiner, but, in the case of an appeal from a judgment after trial or hearing of any cause or matter on the merits, no such further evidence (other than evidence as to matters which have occurred after the date of the trial or hearing) shall be admitted except on special grounds.

(3) The Court of Appeal shall have power to draw inferences of fact and to give any judgment and make any order which ought to have been given or made, and to make such further or other order as the case may require.

(4) The powers of the Court of Appeal under the foregoing provisions of this rule may be exercised notwithstanding that no notice of appeal of respondent's notice has been given in respect of any particular part of the decision of the court below or by any particular party to the proceedings in that court, or that any ground for allowing the appeal or for affirming or varying the decision of that court is not specified in such a notice; and the Court of Appeal may make any order, on such terms as the Court thinks just, to ensure the determination on the merits of the real question in controversy between the parties.

(5) The Court of Appeal may, in special circumstances, order that such security shall be given for the costs of an appeal as may be just.

(6) The powers of the Court of Appeal in respect of an appeal shall not be restricted by reason of any interlocutory order from which there has been no appeal.

(7) Documents impounded by order of the Court of Appeal shall not be delivered out of the custody of that Court except in compliance with an order of that Court:

Provided that where a Law Officer or the Director of Public Prosecutions makes a written request in that behalf, documents so impounded shall be delivered into his custody.

(8) Documents impounded by order of the Court of Appeal, while in the custody of that Court, shall not be inspected except by a person authorised to do so by an order of that Court.

(9) In any proceedings incidental to any cause or matter pending before the Court of Appeal, the powers conferred by this rule on the Court may be exercised by a single judge or the registrar.

Provided that the said powers of the Court of Appeal shall be exercisable only by that Court or a single judge in relation to

(a)   the grant, variation, discharge or enforcement of an injunction, or an undertaking given in lieu of an injunction; and

(b)   the grant or lifting of a stay of execution or proceedings.

Appeals in cases of contempt of court (O.59, r.20)

20.—(1) In the case of an appeal to the Court of Appeal under section 13 of the **B–20** Administration of Justice Act 1960, the notice of appeal must be served on the proper officer of the court from whose order or decision the appeal is brought as well as on the party or parties required to be served under rule 3.

This paragraph shall not apply in relation to an appeal to which rule 19 applies.

(2) Where, in the case of an appeal under the said section 13 to the Court of Appeal or to the House of Lords from the Court of Appeal, the appellant is in custody, the Court of Appeal may order his release on his giving security (whether by recognisance, with or without sureties, or otherwise and for such reasonable sum as that Court may fix) for his appearance within 10 days after the judgment of the Court of Appeal or, as the case may be, of the House of Lords on the appeal shall have been given, before the court from whose order or decision the appeal is brought unless the order or decision is reversed by that judgment.

(3) An application for the release of a person under paragraph (2) pending an appeal to the Court of Appeal or House of Lords under the said section 13 must be made by motion, and the notice of the motion must, at least 24 hours before the day named therein for the hearing, be served on the proper officer of the court from whose order or decision the appeal is brought and on all parties to the proceedings in that court who are directly affected by the appeal.

(4) Order 79, rule 9(6), (6A), (6B) and (8) shall apply in relation to the grant of bail under this rule by the Court of Appeal in a case of criminal contempt of court as they apply in relation to the grant of bail in criminal proceedings by the High Court, but with the substitution for references to a judge in chambers of references to the Court of Appeal and for references to the defendant of references to the appellant.

(5) When granting bail under this Rule in a case of civil contempt of court, the Court of Appeal may order that the recognisance or other security to be given by the appellant or the recognisance of any surety shall be given before any person authorised by virtue of section 119(1) of the Magistrates' Courts Act 1980 to take a recognisance where a magistrates' court having power to take it has, instead of taking it, fixed the amount in which the principal and his sureties, if any, are to be bound.

An order by the Court of Appeal granting bail as aforesaid must be in Form 98 in Appendix A with the necessary adaptations.

(6) Where in pursuance of an order of the Court of Appeal under paragraph (5) of this rule a recognisance is entered into or other security given before any person, it

shall be the duty of that person to cause the recognisance of the appellant or any surety or, as the case may be, a statement of the other security given, to be transmitted forthwith to the clerk of the court which committed the appellant; and a copy of such recognisance or statement shall at the same time be sent to the governor or keeper of the prison or other place of detention in which the appellant is detained, unless the recognisance or security was given before such governor or keeper.

(7) [*Revoked.*]

(8) The powers conferred on the Court of Appeal by paragraphs (2), (4), (5) and (6) of this rule may be exercised by a single judge.

Order 65

Service of Documents

Substituted service (O.65, r.4)

B–21   4.—(1) If, in the case of any document which by virtue of any provision of these rules is required to be served personally or is a document to which Order 10, rule 1, applies, it appears to the Court that it is impracticable for any reason to serve that document in the manner prescribed, the Court may make an order for substituted service of that document.

(2) An application for an order for substituted service may be made by an affidavit stating the facts on which the application is founded.

(3) Substituted service of a document, in relation to which an order is made under this rule, is effected by taking such steps as the Court may direct to bring the document to the notice of the person to be served.

Service of process on Sunday (O.65, r.10)

B–22   10.—(1) No process shall be served or executed within the jurisdiction on a Sunday except, in case of urgency, with the leave of the Court.

(2) For the purposes of this rule "process" includes a writ, judgment, notice, order, petition, originating or other summons or warrant.

Order 80

Disability

Person under disability must sue, etc., by next friend or guardian *ad litem* (O.80, r.2)

B–23   2.—(1) A person under disability may not bring, or make a claim, in any proceedings except by his next friend and may not acknowledge service, defend, make a counterclaim or intervene in any proceedings, or appear in any proceedings under a judgment or order notice of which has been served on him, except by his guardian *ad litem*.

(2) Subject to the provisions of these rules, anything which in the ordinary conduct of any proceedings is required or authorised by a provision of these rules to be done by a party to the proceedings shall or may, if the party is a person under disability, be done by his next friend or guardian *ad litem*.

(3) A next friend or guardian *ad litem* of a person under disability must act by a solicitor.

Order 89

Proceedings between Husband and Wife

Provisions as to actions in tort (O.89, r.2)

2.—(1) This rule applies to any action in tort brought by one of the parties to a marriage against the other during the subsistence of the marriage. **B–24**

(2) On the first application by summons or motion in an action to which this rule applies, the Court shall consider, if necessary of its own motion, whether the power to stay the action under section 1(2) of the Law Reform (Husband and Wife) Act 1962 should or should not be exercised.

(3) Notwithstanding anything in Order 13 or Order 19, judgment on failure to give notice of intention to defend or in default of defence shall not be entered in an action to which this rule applies except with the leave of the Court.

(4) An application for the grant of leave under paragraph (3) must be made by summons and the summons must, notwithstanding anything in Order 65, rule 9, be served on the defendant.

(5) If the summons is for leave to enter judgment on failure to give notice of intention to defend, the summons shall not be issued until after the time limited for acknowledging service of the writ.

County Court

Order 1

Citation, Application and Interpretation

Computation of time (O.1, r.9)

9.—(1) Any period of time fixed by these rules or by a judgment, order or direction for doing any act shall be reckoned in accordance with the following provisions of this rule. **B–25**

(2) Where the act is required to be done not less than a specified period before a specified date, the period starts immediately after the date on which the act is done and ends immediately before the specified date.

(3) Where the act is required to be done within a specified period after or from a specified date, the period starts immediately after that date.

(4) Where, apart from this paragraph, the period in question being a period of 3 days or less would include a day on which the court office is closed, that day shall be excluded.

(5) Where the time so fixed for doing an act in the court office expires on a day on which the office is closed, and for that reason the act cannot be done on that day, the act shall be in time if done on the next day on which the office is open.

Order 3

Commencement of Proceedings

Proceedings by action (O.3, r.1)

B–26   1. Subject to the provisions of any Act or rule, all proceedings authorised to be brought in a county court; where the object of the proceedings is to obtain relief against any person or to compel any person to do or abstain from doing any act, shall be brought by action and commenced by plaint.

Classes of action (O.3, r.2)

2.—(1)An action in which a claim is made for any relief other than the payment of money shall be a fixed date action.

(2) Except as otherwise provided by these rules, every other action shall be a default action.

(3) Nothing in this rule applies to an Admiralty action.

Commencement of action (O.3, r.3)

B–27   3.—(1) Subject to paragraphs (1A) and (1B) a plaintiff desiring to commence a default or fixed date action shall file a request for the issue of a summons, together with the particulars of claim and copies required by Order 6.

(1A) If the plaintiff so desires and the proper officer so allows, the summons may be prepared by the plaintiff and in that event the summons with a copy for each defendant shall be filed by the plaintiff with the documents mentioned in paragraph (1) and, where service is to be effected otherwise than by an officer of the court, a copy of the summons shall be filed for the court instead of a request.

(1B) Without prejudice to paragraph (1A), the summons in an action for recovery of land, including one in which the mortgagee under a mortgage of land claims possession of the mortgaged land, shall be prepared by the plaintiff and in that event the summons with a copy for each defendant shall be filed by the plaintiff with the documents mentioned in paragraph (1) and, where service is to be effected otherwise than by an officer of the court, a copy of the summons shall be filed for the court instead of a request.

(2) On the filing of the documents mentioned in paragraph (1) or paragraph (1A) the proper officer shall—

(a) enter a plaint in the records of the court and in the case of a fixed date action to which Order 17, rule 11 does not apply fix the return day;

(b) if necessary, prepare a summons;

(bb) issue the summons and make any necessary copies;

(c) annex to, or incorporate in, the summons and every copy so made a copy of the particulars of claim and also annex to every copy of the summons for service a copy of any documents filed under Order 6, rule 1(5) and form of admission, defence and counterclaim, and

(d) deliver to the plaintiff—

(i) a plaint note and

(ii) if the summons is to be served otherwise than by an officer of the court, the summons and all necessary copies, with any documents required to be annexed thereto, for service in accordance with Order 7.

(3) In the case of a fixed date action to which Order 17, rule 11 does not apply, the return day shall, unless the court otherwise directs or paragraph (4) applies, be a day fixed for the pre-trial review.

(4) Paragraph (3) shall not apply to an action for the recovery of land unless a claim is joined for some relief other than the payment of mesne profits or arrears of rent or for money secured by a mortgage or charge.

(5) Where a summons is to be served out of England and Wales, the plaintiff shall certify in his request for the issue of the summons that the conditions of paragraph (6) are satisfied.

(6) No summons shall be served out of England and Wales unless

(a) each claim made in the particulars of claim is either—

(i) one which by virtue of the Civil Jurisdiction and Judgments Act 1982 the court has power to hear and determine, or

(ii) one which by virtue of any other enactment a county court has power to hear and determine notwithstanding that the person against whom the claim is made is not within England and Wales or that the wrongful act, neglect or default giving rise to the claim did not take place within England and Wales; or

(b) leave to serve the summons out of England and Wales is given under Order 8.

(7) Where a claim made in the particulars of claim is one which the court has power to hear and determine by virtue of the Civil Jurisdiction and Judgments Act 1982, the particulars shall contain a statement that the court has power under the Act to hear and determine the claim, and that no proceedings involving the same cause of action are pending between the parties in Scotland, Northern Ireland or another Convention territory.

(8) For the purposes of this rule "Convention Territory" means the territory or territories of any Contracting state, as defined by section 1(3) of the Civil Jurisdiction and Judgments Act 1982, to which the Brussels Convention or the Lugano Convention as defined in section 1(1) of that Act apply.

General provisions as to actions (O.4, r.2)

B–28 2.—(1) An action may be commenced—

(a)   in the court for the district in which the defendant or one of the defendants resides or carries on business,

(b)   in the court for the district in which the cause of action wholly or in part arose, or

(c)   in the case of a default action, in any county court.

(2) Where the plaintiff sues as assignee, the action shall be commenced only in a court in which the assignor might have commenced the action but for the assignment.

(3) [*Omitted.*]

(4) [*Omitted.*]

Order 6

Particulars of Claim

General requirements (O.6, r.1)

B–29 1.—(1) Subject to the provisions of this rule, a plaintiff shall, at the time of commencing an action, file particulars of his claim specifying his cause of action and the relief or remedy which he seeks and stating briefly the material facts on which he relies.

(1A) In an action for an unliquidated sum the value of the plaintiff's claim shall, for the purposes of Order 21, rule 5(1), be treated as limited to the sum for the time being specified in sub-paragraph (b) of that paragraph, unless—

(a)   the plaintiff states in his particulars of claim or otherwise that the value of his claim exceeds the said sum; or

(b)   the court orders otherwise;

and, where a statement is made under sub-paragraph (a), the plaintiff shall forthwith file an amended statement whenever the value of his claim falls to the said sum or less.

(2) Where in an action for a debt the particulars of claim can conveniently be incorporated in the form of request for the issue of the summons, they may be incorporated in that form if the proper officer so allows.

(3) [*Omitted.*]

(4) Except where the particulars are incorporated in the request pursuant to paragraph (2), the plaintiff shall, when filing particulars of his claim, file a copy for each defendant to be served with the summons.

(5) Subject to paragraph (6), a plaintiff in an action for personal injuries shall file with his particulars of claim—

(a)   a medical report, and

(b)   a statement of the special damages claimed,

together with a copy of those documents for each defendant.

(6) Where the documents to which paragraph (5) applies are not filed with the particulars of claim, the Court—

(a)   may specify the period of time within which they are to be provided, in which case the plaintiff shall within the time so specified file a copy of them and serve further copies on each defendant; or

(b)   may make such other order as it thinks fit (including an order dispensing with the requirement of paragraph (5) or staying the proceedings).

(7) For the purposes of this rule,

"medical report" means a report substantiating all the personal injuries alleged in the particulars of claim which the plaintiff proposes to adduce in evidence as part of his case at the trial;

"a statement of the special damages claimed" means a statement giving full particulars of the special damages claimed for expenses and losses already incurred and an estimate of any future expenses and losses (including loss of earnings and of pension rights).

Personal service (O.7, r.2)

2. Where any document is required by an Act or rule to be served personally—   **B–30**

(a)   service shall be effected by leaving the document with the person to be served;

(b)   the document may be served by—

(i)   a bailiff of the court or, if the person to be served attends at the office of the court, any other officer of the court; or

(ii)   a party to the proceedings or some person acting as his agent, or

(iii)   the solicitor of a party or a solicitor acting as an agent for such solicitor or some person employed by either solicitor to serve the document;

but service shall not be effected by any person under the age of 16 years.
Prescribed form—O.7, r.2(b)-N68
■ R.S.C., O.65, rr.1 & 2.

Days on which no service permitted (O.7, r.3)

3. Without prejudice to Order 40, rule 5(5), no process shall be served or executed within England or Wales on a Sunday, Good Friday or Christmas Day except, in the case of urgency, with the leave of the court.

Violence or threats (O.7, r.5)

B–31   5. Where a bailiff is prevented by the violence or threats of the person to be served, or any other person acting in concert with him, from serving a document in manner prescribed by this Order, it shall be sufficient service to leave the document as near as practicable to the person to be served.

Proof of service or non-service (O.7, r.6)

6.—(1) Subject to paragraph (1A) person effecting service of any document shall—

(a)   if he is an officer of the court, make, sign and file a certificate showing the date, place and mode of service and any conduct money paid or tendered to the person served; and

(b)   if he is not an officer of the court, file an affidavit of service.

(1A) Where service is effected by the summons production centre established by Order 2, rule 7(1)—

(a)   the appropriate officer (within the meaning of Order 2, rule 6) on the day the document is issued shall be deemed to be the person effecting service; and

(b)   the mode of service need not be shown on the certificate.

(2) A bailiff who has failed to effect service of any document to be served by bailiff shall make, sign and file a certificate of non-service showing the reason why service has not been effected, and the proper officer of the bailiff's court shall send notice of non-service to the person at whose instance the document was issued.

Substituted service (O.7, r.8)

B–32   8.—(1) If it appears to the court that it is impracticable for any reason to serve a document in any manner prescribed by these rules for the service of that document, the court may, upon an affidavit showing grounds, make an order (in this rule called "an order for substituted service") giving leave for such steps to be taken as the court directs to bring the document to the notice of the person to be served.

(2) Where a document is to be served by bailiff, the proper officer of the bailiff's court shall, if so requested, take such steps as may be necessary to provide evidence on which an order for substituted service may be made.

Order 10

Persons under Disability

Person under disability to have next friend or guardian ad litem (O.10, r.1)

B–33   1.—(1) Except where a minor brings an action in his own name under section 47 of the Act, a person under disability may not bring or make a claim in any proceedings except by his next friend.

(2) A person under disability may not defend or make a counterclaim in any proceedings except by his guardian ad litem.

(3) Where a person is authorised under Part VII of the Mental Health Act 1983 (in this Order called "Part VII") to conduct legal proceedings in the name of a mental patient or on his behalf, that person shall be entitled to be the next friend or guardian ad litem, as the case may be, of the patient in any proceedings to which his authority extends, unless some other person is appointed by the court to be his next friend or guardian ad litem.

Order 13

Applications and Orders in the Course of Proceedings

General provisions (O.13, r.1)

1.—(1) Except as otherwise provided, the following paragraphs of this rule shall **B-34** have effect in relation to any application authorised by or under any Act or rule to be made in the course of an action or matter before or after judgment.

(2) Unless allowed or authorised to be made ex parte, the application shall be made on notice, which shall be filed and served on the opposite party not less than two days before the hearing of the application.

(3) Where the application is made ex parte, notice of the application shall be filed a reasonable time before the application is heard, unless the court otherwise directs.

(4) Unless allowed or authorised to be made otherwise, every application shall be heard in chambers.

(5) Where any party to the application fails to attend on the hearing the court may proceed in his absence if, having regard to the nature of the application, the court thinks it expedient to do so.

(6) The jurisdiction of the court to hear and determine the application may be exercised by the district judge and the applicant shall, unless the judge otherwise directs, make the application to the district judge in the first instance.

(7) Where the application is made to the district judge, he may refer to the judge any matter which he thinks should properly be decided by the judge, and the judge may either dispose of the matter or refer it back to the district judge with such directions as he thinks fit.

(8) The court may, as a condition of granting any application, impose such terms and conditions as it thinks fit, including a term or condition requiring any party to—

(a)   give security,

(b)   give an undertaking,

(c)   pay money into court,

(d)   pay all or any part of the costs of the proceedings, or

(e)   give a power of re-entry

(9) Unless the court otherwise directs, the costs of the application shall not be taxed until the general taxation of the costs of the action or matter and, where an

earlier taxation is directed, Order 38 shall apply as if the word "claimed" were substituted for the word "recovered" wherever it appears.

(10) An appeal shall lie to the judge from any order made by the district judge on the application and the appeal shall be disposed of in chambers unless the judge otherwise directs.

(11) An appeal under paragraph (10) shall be made on notice, which shall be filed and served on the opposite party within 5 days after the order appealed from or such further time as the judge may allow.

Extension or abridgment of time (O.13, r.4)

B–35   4.—(1) Except as otherwise provided, the period within which a person is required or authorised by these rules or by any judgment, order or direction to do any act in any proceedings may be extended or abridged by consent of all the parties or by the court on the application of any party.

(2) Any such period may be extended by the court although the application for extension is not made until after the expiration of the period.

■ R.S.C., O.3, r.5; see S.C.P., paras. 3/5/1 *et seq.* (abridging time, "unless" or conditional order to extend time, form of "unless" orders and other peremptory orders).

Application for injunction (O.13, r.6)

B–36   6.—(1) An application for the grant of an injunction may be made by any party to an action or matter before or after the trial or hearing, whether or not a claim for the injunction was included in that party's particulars of claim, originating application, petition, counterclaim or third party notice, as the case may be.

(2) Except where the district judge has power under Order 21, rule 5 or otherwise to hear and determine the proceedings in which the application is made, the application shall be made to the judge and rule 1(6) shall not apply.

(3) The application shall be made in the appropriate prescribed form and shall—

(a)   state the terms of the injunction applied for; and

(b)   be supported by an affidavit in which the grounds for making the application are set out,

and a copy of the affidavit and a copy of the application shall be served on the party against whom the injunction is sought not less than two days before the hearing of the application.

(3A) Where an order is sought ex parte before a copy of the application has been served on the other party, the affidavit shall explain why the application is so made and a copy of any order made ex parte shall be served with the application and affidavit in accordance with paragraph (3).

(4) An application may not be made before the issue of the summons, originating application or petition by which the action or matter is to be commenced except where the case is one of urgency, and in that case—

(a) the affidavit in support of the application shall show that the action or matter is one which the court to which the application is made has jurisdiction to hear and determine, and

(b) the injunction applied for shall, if granted, be on terms providing for the issue of the summons, originating application or petition in the court granting the application and on such other terms, if any, as the court thinks fit.

(4A) Paragraph (4)(a) and (b) shall apply, with the necessary modifications, where an application for an injunction is made by a defendant in a case of urgency before issuing a counterclaim or cross-application.

(5) Unless otherwise directed, every application not made ex parte shall be heard in open court.

(6) Except where the case is one of urgency, a draft of the injunction shall be prepared beforehand by the party making an application to the judge under paragraph (1) and, if the application is granted, the draft shall be submitted to the judge by whom the application was heard and shall be settled by him.

(7) The injunction, when settled, shall be forwarded to the proper officer for filing.

Order 15

Amendment

Clerical mistakes and errors (O.15, r.5)

5. Clerical mistakes in judgments or orders or errors arising therein from any **B–37** accidental slip or omission may at any time be corrected by the court.

Order 20

Evidence

Form and contents of affidavit (O.20, r.10)

10.—(1) Subject to the following paragraphs of this rule, the provision of the **B–38** R.S.C. with respect to—

(a) the form and contents of an affidavit;

(b) the making of an affidavit by two or more deponents or by a blind or illiterate deponent;

(c) the use of any affidavit which contains an interlineation, erasure or other alteration or is otherwise defective;

(d) the striking out of any matter which is scandalous, irrelevant or otherwise oppressive;

(e) the insufficiency of an affidavit sworn before any agent, partner or clerk of a party's solicitor; and

(f)   the making and marking of exhibits to an affidavit,

shall apply in relation to an affidavit for use in a county court as they apply in relation to an affidavit for use in the High Court.

(2) Before any affidavit is used in evidence it must be filed, but in an urgent case the court may make an order upon the undertaking of a party to file, within such time as the court may require, any affidavit used by him before it is filed.

(3) Every affidavit must be marked in the top right hand corner of the first page and in the top right hand corner of the back sheet with—

(a)   the party on whose behalf the affidavit is filed;
(b)   the initials and surname of the deponent;
(c)   the number of the affidavit in relation to the deponent;
(d)   the date on which it is sworn, and
(e)   the date on which it is filed.

(4) Unless the court otherwise orders, an affidavit may be used notwithstanding that it contains statements of information or belief.

(5) Every affidavit shall state which of the facts deposed to are within the deponent's knowledge and which are based on information or belief and shall give, in the former case, his means of knowledge and, in the latter case, the sources and grounds of the information or belief.

Order 21

Hearing of Action or Matter

District judge's jurisdiction (O.21, r.5)

B–39   5.—(1) The district judge shall have power to hear and determine—

(a)   any action or matter in which the defendant fails to appear at the hearing or admits the claim;
(b)   any action or matter the value of which does not exceed £5,000;
(c)   any action for recovery of land regardless of the value of any other claim which is brought in the same action and including one in which the mortgagee under a mortgage of land claims possession of the mortgaged land; and
(d)   by leave of the judge and with the consent of the parties, any other action or matter.

(2) In relation to an action brought to enforce a right to recover possession of goods, or to enforce such a right and to claim payment of a debt or other demand or damages, the value of the action or matter shall be construed as a reference to the aggregate amount claimed by the plaintiff, including the value of the goods or, in the case of goods let under a hire-purchase agreement, the unpaid balance of the total price.

(2A) In paragraph (1)(c) "mortgage" and "mortgagee" have the meanings assigned to them by section 21(7) of the Act.

(2B) Without prejudice to Order 50, rule 2, a district judge may, at any stage of an action or matter which he has power to hear and determine under paragraph (1) and subject to any right of appeal to the judge, exercise the same powers under section 38 of the Act as the court; but nothing in this paragraph shall authorise the district judge to commit any person to prison.

(3) Nothing in this rule shall prejudice any power conferred by any Act or rule on the district judge to hear and determine any other action or matter or authorise the district judge to exercise any jurisdiction conferred by any Act or rule on the judge alone.

Order 22

Time for Payment of Money Judgments

Time for complying with other judgments (O.22, r.3)

3. Every judgment or order requiring any person to do an act other than the payment of money shall state the time within which the act is to be done. **B–40**

Order 29

Committal for Breach of Order or Undertaking

Enforcement of judgment to do or abstain from doing any act (O.29, r.1)

1.—(1) Where a person required by a judgment or order to do an act refuses or **B–41** neglects to do it within the time fixed by the judgment or order or any subsequent order, or where a person disobeys a judgment or order requiring him to abstain from doing an act, then, subject to the Debtors Act 1869 and 1878 and to the provisions of these rules, the judgment or order may be enforced, by order of the judge, by a committal order against that person or, if that person is a body corporate, against any director or other officer of the body.

(2) Subject to paragraphs (6) and (7), a judgment or order shall not be enforced under paragraph (1) unless—

(a) a copy of the judgment or order has been served personally on the person required to do or abstain from doing the act in question and also, where that person is a body corporate, on the director or other officer of the body against whom a committal order is sought, and

(b) in the case of a judgment or order requiring a person to do an act, the copy has been so served before the expiration of the time within which he was required to do the act and was accompanied by a copy of any order, made between the date of the judgment or order and the date of service, fixing that time.

(3) Where a judgment or order enforceable by committal order under paragraph (1) has been given or made, the proper officer shall, if the judgment or order is in the nature of an injunction, at the time when the judgment or order is drawn up, and in any other case on the request of the judgment creditor, issue a copy of the judgment or order, indorsed with or incorporating a notice as to the consequences of disobedience, for service in accordance with paragraph (2).

(4) If the person served with the judgment or order fails to obey it, the proper officer shall, at the request of the judgment creditor, issue a notice warning him that an application will be made for him to be committed, and subject to paragraph (7) the notice shall be served on him personally.

(4A) The request for issue of the notice under paragraph (4) shall—

(a)   identify the provisions of the injunction or undertaking which it is alleged have been disobeyed or broken;

(b)   list the ways in which it is alleged that the injunction has been disobeyed or the undertaking has been broken,

(c)   be supported by an affidavit stating the grounds on which the application is made,

and, unless service is dispensed with under paragraph (7), a copy of the affidavit shall be served with the notice.

(5) If a committal order is made, the order shall be for the issue of a warrant of committal and, unless the judge otherwise orders—

(a)   a copy of the order shall be served on the person to be committed either before or at the time of the execution of the warrant; or

(b)   where the warrant has been signed by the judge, the order for issue of the warrant may be served on the person to be committed at any time within 36 hours after the execution of the warrant.

(6) A judgment or order requiring a person to abstain from doing an act may be enforced under paragraph (1) notwithstanding that service of a copy of the judgment or order has not been effected in accordance with paragraph (2) if the judge is satisfied that, pending such service, the person against whom it is sought to enforce the judgment or order has had notice thereof either—

(a)   by being present when the judgment or order was given or made, or

(b)   by being notified of the terms of the judgment or order whether by telephone, telegram or otherwise.

(7) Without prejudice to its powers under Order 7, rule 8, the court may dispense with service of a copy of a judgment or order under paragraph (2) or a notice under paragraph (4), if the court thinks it just to do so.

(8) Where service of a notice to show cause is dispensed with under paragraph (7) and a committal order is made, the judge may of his own motion fix a date and time when the person to be committed is to be brought before him or before the court.

Undertaking given by party (O.29, r.1A)

B–42   1A. Rule 1 (except paragraph (6)) shall apply to undertakings as it applies to orders with the necessary modifications and as if—

(a)   for paragraph (2) of that rule there were substituted the following—

"(2) A copy of the document recording the undertaking shall be delivered by the proper officer to the party giving the undertaking—

(a) by handing a copy of the document to him before he leaves the court building; or

(b) where his place of residence is known, by posting a copy to him at his place of residence; or

(c) through his solicitor,

and, where delivery cannot be effected in this way, the proper officer shall deliver a copy of the document to the party for whose benefit the undertaking is given and that party shall cause it to be served personally as soon as is practicable.";

(b)   in paragraph (7), the words from "a copy of" to "paragraph (2) or" were omitted.

Solicitor's undertaking (O.29, r.2)

2.—(1) An undertaking given by a solicitor in relation to any proceeding in a **B–43** county court may be enforced, by order of the judge of that court, by committal order against the solicitor.

(2) Where it appears to the judge that a solicitor has failed to carry out any such undertaking, he may of his own motion direct the proper officer to issue a notice calling on the solicitor to show cause why he should not be committed to prison.

(3) Where any party to the proceedings desires to have the undertaking enforced by committal order, the proper officer shall, on the application of the party supported by an affidavit setting out the facts on which the application is based, issue such a notice as is referred to in paragraph (2).

(4) A notice to show cause issued under paragraph (2) and (3) shall be served on the solicitor personally, together with a copy of any affidavit filed under paragraph (3), but rule 1(5) and (7) shall apply in relation to the notice as they apply in relation to a notice to show cause issued under rule 1(4).

Discharge of person in custody (O.29, r.3)

3.—(1) Where a person in custody under a warrant or order, other than a **B–44** warrant of committal to which Order 27, rule 8, or Order 28, rule 4 or 14, relates, desires to apply to the court for his discharge, he shall make his application in writing attested by the governor of the prison (or any other officer of the prison not below the rank of principal officer) showing that he has purged or is desirous of purging his contempt and shall, not less than one day before the application is made, serve notice of it on the party, if any, at whose instance the warrant or order was issued.

(2) If the committal order—

(a) does not direct that any application for discharge shall be made to a judge; or

(b) was made by the district judge under section 118 of the Act,

any application for discharge may be made to the district judge.

(3) Nothing in paragraph (1) shall apply to an application made by the Official Solicitor in his official capacity for the discharge of a person in custody.

Order 37

Rehearing, Setting Aside and Appeal from District Judge

Rehearing (O.37, r.1)

B–45   1.—(1) In any proceedings tried without a jury the judge shall have power on application to order a rehearing where no error of the court at the hearing is alleged.

(2) Unless the court otherwise orders, any application under paragraph (1) shall be made to the judge by whom the proceedings were tried.

(3) A rehearing may be ordered on any question without interfering with the finding or decision on any other question.

(4) Where the proceedings were tried by the district judge, the powers conferred on the judge by paragraphs (1) and (3) shall be exercisable by the district judge and paragraph (2) shall not apply.

(5) Any application for a rehearing under this rule shall be made on notice stating the grounds of the application and the notice shall be served on the opposite party not more than 14 days after the day of the trial and not less than 7 days before the day fixed for the hearing of the application.

(6) On receipt of the notice, the proper officer shall, unless the court otherwise orders, retain any money in court until the application had been heard.

Setting aside judgment given in party's absence (O.37, r.2)

2.—(1) Any judgment or order obtained against a party in his absence at the hearing may be set aside by the court on application by that party on notice.

(2) The application shall be made to the judge if the judgment or order was given or made by the judge and in any other case shall be made to the district judge.

Setting aside on failure of postal service (O.37, r.3)

B–46   3.—(1) Where in an action or matter the originating process has been sent to the defendant or inserted in his letter-box in accordance with Order 7, rule 10(1)(b) or (4)(a) or 13(1)(b) or (4) and after judgment has been entered or given or an order has been made it appears to the court that the process did not come to the knowledge of the defendant in due time, the court may of its own motion set aside the judgment or order and may give any such directions as the court thinks fit.

(2) The proper officer shall give notice to the plaintiff of the setting aside of any judgment or order under this rule.

Setting aside default judgment (O.37, r.4)

4.—(1) Without prejudice to rule 3, the court may, on application or of its own **B—47** motion, set aside, vary or confirm any judgment entered in a default action pursuant to Order 9, rule 6.

(2) An application under paragraph (1) shall be made on notice and, where such an application is made in a default action for a liquidated sum, the proceedings shall be automatically transferred to the defendant's home court if the judgment or order was not given or made in that court.

Non-compliance with rules (O.37, r.5)

5.—(1) Where there has been a failure to comply with any requirement of these **B—48** rules, the failure shall be treated as an irregularity and shall not nullify the proceedings, but the court may set aside the proceedings wholly or in part or exercise its powers under these rules to allow any such amendments and to give any such directions as it thinks fit.

(2) No application to set aside any proceedings for irregularity shall be granted unless made within a reasonable time, nor if the party applying has taken any step in the proceedings after knowledge of the irregularity.

(3) Where any such application is made, the grounds of objection shall be stated in the notice.

(4) The expression "proceedings" in paragraph (1), and where it first occurs in paragraph (2), includes any step taken in the proceedings and any document, judgment or order therein.

Appeal from district judge (O.37, r.6)

6.—(1) Any party affected by a judgment or final order of the district judge may, **B—49** except where he has consented to the terms thereof, appeal from the judgment or order to the judge, who may, upon such terms as he thinks fit,—

(a) set aside or vary the judgment or order or any part thereof, or
(b) give any other judgment or make any other order in substitution for the judgment or order appealed from, or
(c) remit the action or matter or any question therein to the district judge for rehearing or further consideration, or

(d) order a new trial to take place before himself or another judge of the court on a day to be fixed.

(2) The appeal shall be made on notice, which shall state the grounds of the appeal and be served within 14 days after the day on which judgment or order appealed from was given or made.

Imposition of terms and stay of execution (O.37, r.8)

B–50 8.—(1) An application to the judge or district judge under any of the foregoing rules may be granted on such terms as he thinks reasonable.

(2) Notice of any such application shall not of itself operate as a stay of execution on the judgment or order to which it relates but the court may order a stay of execution pending the hearing of the application or any rehearing or new trial ordered on the application.

(3) If a judgment or order is set aside under any of the foregoing rules, any execution issued on the judgment or order shall cease to have effect unless the court otherwise orders.

Family Proceedings Rules 1991

Rule 4.21A

Attachment of penal notice to section 8 order

B–51 4.21A —CCR Order 29, rule 1 (committal for breach of order or undertaking) shall apply to section 8 orders as if for paragraph (3) of that rule there were substituted the following:—

"(3) In the case of a section 8 order (within the meaning of section 8(2) of the Children Act 1989) enforceable by committal order under paragraph (1), the judge or the district judge may, on the application of the person entitled to enforce the order, direct that the proper officer issue a copy of the order, indorsed with or incorporating a notice as to the consequences of disobedience, for service in accordance with paragraph (2); and no copy of the order shall be issued with any such notice indorsed or incorporated save in accordance with such a direction."

Added by Family Proceedings (Amendment No. 2) Rules 1992 (S.I. 1992 No.2607).
See *Re N (A Minor) (Access: Penal Notice)* [1992] 1 F.L.R. 134, C.A.
See also *Re O (A Minor) (Contact: Imposition of Conditions)*, *The Times*, March 17, 1995, C.A.

Rule 7.2

Committal and injunction

B–52 7.2—(1) Subject to RSC Order 52, rule 6 (which, except in certain cases, requires an application for an order of committal to be heard in open court) an application for an order of committal in family proceedings pending in the High Court shall be made by summons.

(2) Where no judge is conveniently available to hear the application, then, without prejudice to CCR Order 29, rule 3(2) (which in certain circumstances gives jurisdiction to a district judge) an application for—

(a)   the discharge of any person committed, or

(b)   the discharge by consent of an injunction granted by a judge,

may be made to the district judge who may, if satisfied of the urgency of the matter and that it is expedient to do so, make any order on the application which a judge could have made.

(3) Where an order or warrant for the committal of any person to prison has been made or issued in family proceedings pending in the principal registry which are treated as pending in a divorce county court, that person shall, wherever he may be, be treated for the purposes of section 122 of the County Courts Act 1984 as being out of the jurisdiction of the principal registry; but if the committal is for failure to comply with the terms of an injunction, the order or warrant may, if a judge so directs, be executed by the tipstaff within any county court district.

(4) For the purposes of section 118 of the County Courts Act 1984 in its application to the hearing of family proceedings at the Royal Courts of Justice, the tipstaff shall be deemed to be an officer of the court.

Note—A committal order can be made against a party who has not been served with the summons (*Gilbert v. Gilbert* (1961) 105 S.J. 107) even if he is abroad (*O'Donovan v. O'Donovan* [1955] 1 W.L.R. 1086) but personal service should only be dispensed with where the matter is grave, the need for relief is urgent and it is shown that he has knowledge of the application (*Spooner v. Spooner* (1962) 106 S.J. 1034). The court is not justified in discharging a person who continues to disobey its order (*Corcoran v. Corcoran* [1950] 1 All E.R. 495) and will not hear an appeal or other application in the proceedings by a person disobeying an order of the court until he has purged his contempt (*Hadkinson v. Hadkinson* [1952] P. 285). Contempt in one suit is no bar to proceedings in another suit (*Bettinson v. Bettinson* [1965] Ch. 465). Committal for breach of a mandatory injunction will lie only if the order has been served, but in the case of a prohibitory injunction committal for breach will lie if the person restrained has notice of the injunction (*Husson v. Husson* [1962] 1 W.L.R. 1434; [1962] 3 All E.R. 1056). A committal order may be made for breach of an undertaking (*Hipgrave v. Hipgrave* [1962] P. 91). See *Hussain v. Hussain* [1986] Fam. 134, C.A. as to procedural requirements for committal for breach of undertaking and *Symmons v. Symmons* [1993] 2 F.L.R. 247.

Rule 9.2

Person under disability must sue by next friend etc.

9.2—(1) Except where rule 9.2A or any other rule otherwise provides, a person B–53 under disability may begin and prosecute any family proceedings by his next friend and may defend any such proceedings only by his guardian ad litem and, except as otherwise provided by this rule, it shall not be necessary for a guardian ad litem to be appointed by the court.

(2) No person's name shall be used in any proceedings as next friend of a person under disability unless he is the Official Solicitor or the documents mentioned in paragraph (7) have been filed.

(3) Where a person is authorised under Part VII to conduct legal proceedings in the name of a patient or on his behalf, that person shall, subject to paragraph (2), be entitled to be next friend or guardian ad litem of the patient in any family proceedings to which his authority extends.

(4) Where a person entitled to defend any family proceedings is a patient and there is no person authorised under Part VII to defend the proceedings in his name or on his behalf, then—

(a)   the Official Solicitor shall, if he consents, be the patient's guardian ad litem, but at any stage of the proceedings an application may be made on not less than four days' notice to the Official Solicitor, for the appointment of some other person as guardian;

(b)   in any other case, an application may be made on behalf of the patient for the appointment of a guardian ad litem;

and there shall be filed in support of any application under this paragraph the documents mentioned in paragraph (7).

(5) Where a petition, answer, originating application or originating summons has been served on a person whom there is reasonable ground for believing to be a person under disability and no notice of intention to defend has been given, or answer or affidavit in answer filed, on his behalf, the party at whose instance the document was served shall, before taking any further steps in the proceedings, apply to a district judge for directions as to whether a guardian ad litem should be appointed to act for that person in the cause, and on any such application the district judge may, if he considers it necessary in order to protect the interests of the person served, order that some proper person be appointed his guardian ad litem.

(6) Except where a minor is prosecuting or defending proceedings under rule 9.2A, no notice of intention to defend shall be given, or answer or affidavit in answer filed, by or on behalf of a person under disability unless the person giving the notice or filing the answer of affidavit—

(a)   is the Official Solicitor or, in a case to which paragraph (4) applies, is the Official Solicitor or has been appointed by the court to be guardian ad litem; or

(b)   in any other case, has filed the documents mentioned in paragraph (7).

(7) The documents referred to in paragraphs (2), (4) and (6) are—

(a)   a written consent to act by the proposed next friend or guardian ad litem;

(b)   where the person under disability is a patient and the proposed next friend or guardian ad litem is authorised under Part VII to conduct the proceedings in his name or on his behalf, an office copy, sealed with the seal of the Court of Protection, of the order or other authorisation made or given under Part VII; and

(c)   except where the proposed next friend or guardian ad litem is authorised as mentioned in sub-paragraph (b), a certificate by the solicitor acting for the person under disability—

    (i) that he knows or believes that the person to whom the certificate relates is a minor or patient, stating (in the case of a patient) the grounds of his knowledge or belief and, where the person under disability is a patient, that there is no person authorised as aforesaid, and

(ii) that the person named in the certificate as next friend or guardian ad litem has no interest in the cause or matter in question adverse to that of the person under disability and that he is a proper person to be next friend or guardian.

Amended by Family Proceedings (Amendment) Rules 1992 (S.I. 1992 No.456).

Rule 9.2A

Certain minors may sue without next friend etc.

9.2A—(1) Where a person entitled to begin, prosecute or defend any proceedings **B–54** to which this rule applies, is a minor to whom this Part applies, he may, subject to paragraph (4), begin, prosecute or defend, as the case may be, such proceedings without a next friend or guardian ad litem—

(a) where he has obtained the leave of the court for that purpose; or

(b) where a solicitor—

(i) considers that the minor is able, having regard to his understanding, to give instructions in relation to the proceedings; and

(ii) has accepted instructions from the minor to act for him in the proceedings and, where the proceedings have begun, is so acting.

(2) A minor shall be entitled to apply for the leave of the court under paragraph (1)(a) without a next friend or guardian ad litem either—

(a) by filing a written request for leave setting out the reasons for the application, or

(b) by making an oral request for leave at any hearing in the proceedings.

(3) On considering a request for leave filed under paragraph (2)(a), the court shall either—

(a) grant the request, whereupon the proper officer shall communicate the decision to the minor and, where the leave relates to the prosecution or defence of existing proceedings, to the other parties to those proceedings, or

(b) direct that the request be heard ex parte, whereupon the proper officer shall fix a date for such a hearing and give to the minor making the request such notice of the date so fixed as the court may direct.

(4) Where a minor has a next friend or guardian ad litem in proceedings and the minor wishes to prosecute or defend the remaining stages of the proceedings without a next friend or guardian ad litem, the minor may apply to the court for leave for that purpose and for the removal of the next friend or guardian ad litem; and paragraph (2) shall apply to the application as if it were an application under paragraph (1)(a).

(5) On considering a request filed under paragraph (2) by virtue of paragraph (4), the court shall either—

(a) grant the request, whereupon the proper officer shall communicate the decision to the minor and next friend or guardian ad litem concerned and to all other parties to the proceedings, or

(b)   direct that the request be heard, whereupon the proper officer shall fix a date for such a hearing and give to the minor and next friend or guardian ad litem concerned such notice of the date so fixed as the court may direct;

provided that the court may act under sub-paragraph (a) only if it is satisfied that the next friend or guardian ad litem does not oppose the request.

(6) Where the court is considering whether to

(a)   grant leave under paragraph (1)(a), or
(b)   grant leave under paragraph (4) and remove a next friend or guardian ad litem,

it shall grant the leave sought and, as the case may be, remove the next friend or guardian ad litem if it considers that the minor concerned has sufficient understanding to participate as a party in the proceedings concerned or proposed without a next friend or guardian ad litem.

(7) Where a request for leave is granted at a hearing fixed under paragraph (3)(b) (in relation to the prosecution or defence of proceedings already begun) or (5)(b), the proper officer shall forthwith communicate the decision to the other parties to the proceedings.

(8) The court may revoke any leave granted under paragraph (1)(a) where it considers that the child does not have sufficient understanding to participate as a party in the proceedings concerned without a next friend or guardian ad litem.

(9) Without prejudice to any requirement of CCR Order 50, rule 5 or RSC Order 67, where a solicitor is acting for a minor in proceedings which the minor is prosecuting or defending without a next friend or guardian ad litem by virtue of paragraph (1)(b) and either of the conditions specified in paragraph (1)(b)(i) and (ii) cease to be fulfilled, he shall forthwith so inform the court.

(10) Where—

(a)   the court revokes any leave under paragraph (8), or
(b)   either of the conditions specified in paragraph (1)(b)(i) and (ii) is no longer fulfilled,

the court may, if it considers it necessary in order to protect the interests of the minor concerned, order that some proper person be appointed his next friend or guardian ad litem.

(11) Where a minor is of sufficient understanding to begin, prosecute or defend proceedings without a next friend or guardian ad litem—

(a)   he may nevertheless begin, prosecute or defend them by his next friend or guardian ad litem; and
(b)   where he is prosecuting or defending proceedings by his next friend or guardian ad litem, the respective powers and duties of the minor and next friend or guardian ad litem, except those conferred or imposed by this rule, shall not be affected by the minor's ability to dispense with a next friend or guardian ad litem under the provisions of this rule.

Rule 9.3

Service on person under disability

9.3—(1) Where a document to which rule 2.9 applies is required to be served on **B–55** a person under disability, it shall be served—

(a) in the case of a minor who is not also a patient, on his father or guardian or, if he has no father or guardian, on the person with whom he resides or in whose care he is;

(b) in the case of a patient—

(i) on the person (if any) who is authorised under Part VII to conduct in the name of the patient or on his behalf the proceedings in connection with which the document is to be served, or

(ii) if there is no person so authorised, on the Official Solicitor if he has consented under rule 9.2(4) to be the guardian ad litem of the patient, or

(iii) in any other case, on the person with whom the patient resides or in whose care he is:

Provided that the court may order that a document which has been, or is to be, served on the person under disability or on a person other than one mentioned in sub-paragraph (a) or (b) shall be deemed to be duly served on the person under disability.

(2) Where a document is served in accordance with paragraph (1) it shall be indorsed with a notice in Form M24; and after service has been effected the person at whose instance the document was served shall, unless the Official Solicitor is the guardian ad litem of the person under disability or the court otherwise directs, file an affidavit by the person on whom the document was served stating whether the contents of the document were, or its purport was, communicated to the person under disability and, if not, the reasons for not doing so.

Amended by Family Proceedings (Amendment No.2) Rules 1992 (S.I. 1992 No.2067).

APPENDIX C

Practice Directions

---

13. Minor: Preventing Removal Abroad [1986] 1 W.L.R. 475

14. Disclosure of Addresses: [1989] Fam.Law 166

15. Issue of Passports: May 15, 1987 (unrep.)

16. Wardship: Visit Abroad [1973] 1 W.L.R. 690

17. Ward: Removal from Jurisdiction [1984] 1 W.L.R. 855

18. Ward: Removal from Jurisdiction: May 15, 1987 (unrep.)

19. Wards of Court: Taking out of England and Wales [1989] 3 All E.R. 89

20. Practice Direction (Article 177 Procedure) [1997] 1 C.M.L.R. 78, ECJ

1. Registrar's Direction: Filing Affidavits

Husband and Wife—Affidavit—Principal Registry—Fixed date of hearing—Filing affidavits and documents

C–02   1. Where in any cause or matter proceeding in the Principal Registry, a party wishes to file an affidavit or other document in connection with an application for which a hearing date has been fixed, the affidavit or other document must be lodged in the Principal Registry *not less than 14 clear days* before the appointed hearing date.

2. Where insufficient time remains before the hearing date to lodge the affidavit or other document as required by 1 above, it should, in case of an application before the judge, be lodged in Room 775 (Summons Clerk, Clerk of the Rules Department) at the Royal Courts of Justice as soon as possible *before* the hearing: where the application is before the registrar, it should be handed to the clerk to that registrar immediately before the hearing. Service should be effected upon the opposing party in the normal way.

3. The registrar's direction of January 12, 1981, *Practice Direction (Family Division: Filing Affidavits)* [1981] 1 W.L.R. 106, except paragraph 3, is cancelled.

B. P. Tickle
Senior Registrar

February 7 1984.

2. Filing of Affidavits in cases proceeding in the Principal Registry

C–03   *Affidavit—Filing—Practice—Family Division—Time for filing—Late filing—Effect— Effect on costs and consideration of affidavit.*

Difficulties are being experienced because of the late filing of affidavits in cases proceeding in the Principal Registry.

The President and judges of the Family Division require the attention of practitioners to be drawn to the practice set out in the Registrar's Direction of February 7, 1984 ([1984] 1 All E.R. 684, [1984] 1 W.L.R. 306). Failure to comply with this practice may result in costs being disallowed or being ordered to be paid by the solicitor personally. Affidavits which are lodged in the Principal Registry within 14 days before the hearing date instead of being lodged in the Clerk of the Rules' Department or with the clerk to the registrar may not be considered at all by the judge or the registrar as the case may be.

B P Tickle
Senior Registrar

February 20, 1987

3. Evidence: Documents

Practice—Documents—Form—Marking, numbering and binding of documents—Marking of exhibits—R.S.C., Ord, 41

This practice direction applies to the Court of Appeal and to all divisions of the C–04 High Court. Any affidavit, exhibit or bundle of documents which does not comply with R.S.C., Ord. 41 and this direction may be rejected by the court or made the subject for an order for costs.

Affidavits

1. *Marking*

At the top right hand corner of the first page of every affidavit, and also on the backsheet, there must be written in clear permanent dark blue or black marking: (i) the party on whose behalf it is filed; (ii) the initials and surname of the deponent; (iii) the number of the affidavit in relation to the deponent; and (iv) the date when sworn.

For example: 2nd Dft: E. W. Jones: 3rd: 24.7.82."

2. *Binding*

Affidavits must not be bound with thick plastic strips or anything else which would hamper filing.

Exhibits

3. *Markings generally*

Where space allows, the directions under paragraph 1 above apply to the first page of every exhibit.

4. *Documents other than letters*

(i) Clearly legible photographic copies of original documents may be exhibited instead of the originals provided the originals are made available for inspection by the other parties before the hearing and by the judge at the hearing.

(ii) Any document which the court is being asked to construe or enforce, or the trusts of which it is being asked to vary, should be separately exhibited, and should not be included in a bundle with other documents. Any such document should bear the exhibit mark directly, and not on a flysheet attached to it.

(iii) Court documents, such as probates, letters of administration, orders, affidavits or pleadings, should never be exhibited. Office copies of such documents prove themselves.

(iv) Where a number of documents are contained in one exhibit, a front page must be attached, setting out a list of the documents, with dates, which the exhibit contains, and the bundle must be securely fastened. The traditional method of securing is by tape, with the knot sealed (under the modern practice) by means of wafers; but any means of securing the bundle (except by staples) is acceptable, provided that it does not interfere with the perusal of the documents and it cannot readily be undone.

(v) This direction does not affect the current practice in relation to scripts in probate matters, or to an affidavit of due execution of a will.

5. *Letters*

C–05   (i) Copies of individual letters should not be made separate exhibits, but they should be collected together and exhibited in a bundle or bundles. The letters must be arranged in correct sequence with the earliest at the top, and properly paged in accordance with paragraph 6 below. They must be firmly secured together in the manner indicated in paragraph 4 above.

(ii) When original letters, or original letters and copies of replies, are exhibited as one bundle, the exhibit must have a front page attached, stating that the bundle consists of so many original letters and so many copies. As before, the letters and copies must be arranged in correct sequence and properly paged.

6. *Paging of documentary exhibits*

Any exhibit containing several pages must be paged consecutively at centre bottom.

7. *Copies of documents generally*

It is the responsibility of the solicitor by whom any affidavit is filed to ensure that every page of every exhibit is fully and easily legible. In many cases photocopies of documents, particularly of telex messages, are not. In all cases of difficulty, typed copies of the illegible document (paged with "a" numbers) should be included.

8. *Exhibits bound up with affidavit*

Exhibits must not be bound up with, or otherwise attached to, the affidavit itself.

9. *Exhibits other than documents*

C–06   The principles are as follows. (i) The exhibit must be clearly marked with the exhibit mark in such a manner that there is no likelihood of the contents being separated; and (ii) where the exhibit itself consists of more than one item (*e.g.*, a cassette in a plastic box), each and every separate part of the exhibit must similarly be separately marked with at least enough of the usual exhibit mark to ensure precise identification.

This is particularly important in cases where there are a number of similar exhibits which fall to be compared. Accordingly:

(a) The formal exhibit marking should, so far as practicable, be written on the article itself in an appropriate manner (*e.g.*, many fabrics can be directly marked with an indelible pen), or, if this is not possible, on a separate slip which is securely attached to the article in such a manner that it is not easily removable. (N.B. Items attached by Sellotape or similar means are readily removable). If the article is then enclosed in a container, the number of the exhibit should appear on the outside of the container unless it is transparent and the number is readily visible. Alternatively, the formal exhibit marking may be written on the container, or, if this is not possible, on a separate slip securely attached to the container. If this is done, then either—(i) the number of the exhibit and, if there is room, the short name and number of the case, the name of the deponent and the date of the affidavit must be written on the exhibit itself and on each separate part thereof; or (ii) all these particulars must appear on a slip securely attached to the article itself and to each separate part thereof.

(b) If the article, or part of the article, is too small to be marked in accordance with the foregoing provisions, it must be enclosed in a sealed transparent container of such a nature that it could not be reconstituted once opened, and the relevant slip containing the exhibit mark must be inserted in such container so as to be plainly visible. An enlarged photograph or photographs showing the relevant characteristics of each such exhibit will usually be required to be separately exhibited.

10. *Numbering*

Where a deponent deposes to more than one affidavit to which there are exhibits C–07 in any one matter, the numbering of such exhibits should run consecutively throughout, and not begin again with each affidavit.

11. *Reference to documents already forming part of an exhibit*

Where a deponent wishes to refer to a document already exhibited to some other deponent's affidavit, he should not also exhibit it to his own affidavit.

12. *Multiplicity of documents*

Where, by the time of the hearing, exhibits or affidavits have become numerous, they should be put in a consolidated bundle, or file or files, and be paged consecutively throughout in the top right hand corner, affidavits and exhibits being in separate bundles or files.

Bundles of documents generally

13. The directions under 5, 6 and 7 above apply to all bundles of documents. Accordingly they must be (i) firmly secured together, (ii) arranged in chronological order, beginning with the earliest, (iii) paged consecutively at centre bottom, and (iv) fully and easily legible.

14. Transcripts of judgments and evidence must not be bound up with any other documents, but must be kept separate.

15. In cases for trial where the parties will seek to place before the trial judge bundles of documents (apart from pleadings) comprising more than 100 pages, it is the responsibility of the solicitors for all parties to prepare and agree one single additional bundle containing the principal documents to which the parties will refer (including in particular the documents referred to in the pleadings) and to lodge such bundle with the court at least two working days before the date fixed for the hearing.

LORD LANE C.J.

July 21, 1983.

4. Evidence: Documents

Practice—Documents—Form—Marking of exhibits to affidavits—R.S.C. Ord. 41

C–08   Paragraph 1 of *Practice Direction (Evidence: Documents)* [1983] 1 W.L.R. 922 of July 21, 1983 shall be amended as follows: by adding a new requirement (iv) namely "the identifying initials and number of each exhibit to the affidavit;" by renumbering requirement (iv) as (v) and adding "EWJ 3, 4 and 5" to the end of the example given.

In all other respects *Practice Direction (Evidence: Documents)* [1983] 1 W.L.R. 922 is affirmed.

LORD TAYLOR OF GOSFORTH C.J.

March 23, 1995

5. Family Division: Hearing Duration

Husband and Wife—Practice—Royal Courts of Justice—Length of hearing—Summonses and applications for hearing before judge—Procedure on estimating length of hearing—Form of notice

C–09   1. Recent experience has shown that in some cases the estimated length of hearing of Family Division summonses and applications for hearing before a judge at the Royal Courts of Justice has been inaccurate, with a resultant waste of time for all concerned with litigation and a needless increase in costs. In order to remedy this situation the following procedure will apply with effect from the date of this registrar's direction.

2. On the issue of a summons or application (including restoring an adjourned summons or application or one referred to a judge) which is expected to last in excess of one day, the form of notice of estimate set out in the appendix to this registrar's direction, duly completed, must be lodged with the Clerk of the Rules. The form should be signed by counsel, if already instructed, or by the solicitor acting for the party.

3. A copy of the completed notice must be served at once on every other party. Upon receipt by the solicitor he, or counsel if instructed, must consider the estimate and if he disagrees with it adopt the procedure in paragraph 6 as soon as possible.

4. A copy of the completed notice or any revised notice must be included in every set of instructions or brief sent to counsel.

5. It is the continuing resonsibility of all solicitors and counsel when dealing with the case to consider whether or not the latest estimate recorded on the notice is accurate.

6. If any solicitor or counsel considers that the estimate needs revising either way a copy of the notice of estimate should be made, completed at box 5 with proposed revised estimate and served on the other parties and the Clerk of the Rules. The revised estimate should, whenever possible, be agreed with all other parties and signed jointly before being sent to the Clerk of the Rules. In the event of disagreement reference should be made to the Clerk of the Rules.

7. If an additional summons or a cross-summons is issued returnable on the same date, a separate notice of estimate should only be filed if the latest estimate is affected.

8. If within seven days of the date fixed for hearing it becomes apparent that the estimate requires revision, the Clerk of the Rules should be notified at once by telephone.

9. This registrar's direction does not apply to a party acting in person, but if the respondent(s) is represented by counsel or solicitor and he estimates that the matter will last in excess of one day he must immediately complete a notice of estimate and send it to the Clerk of the Rules.

10. The procedure relating to registrar's hearings, at the Divorce Registry Somerset House, is not affected by this direction.

11. Copies of the form of notice of estimate, D208, are available from the Clerk of the Rules Department at the Royal Courts of Justice and Room G39 of the Divorce Registry in Somerset House.

B. P. TICKLE
Senior Registrar

March 1, 1984

6. President's Direction: Hearings before High Court Judge: Time Estimates

Practice—Family Division—Proceedings relating to children—Estimated length of hearing— C–10
Duty of parties to give time estimate—Revision of time estimate—Children Act 1989.

1. As from the date of this direction, parties to proceedings under the Children Act 1989 or under the inherent jurisdiction of the High Court relating to children, which are pending in the High Court in London and in other centres and which are to be heard by a judge, will be required to provide an estimate of length of the hearing (a "time estimate") in accordance with the procedure set out in the following paragraphs. This procedure is intended to enable the court and the parties to be kept fully informed of any changes in time estimates so as to facilitate the listing and disposal of cases in the most effective manner.

2. When any hearing which is expected to last *one day or more* is fixed, whether upon application or at a directions hearing or on any other occasion, the party applying for the hearing ("the applicant") and such other parties as may then be before the court shall give a time estimate. Unless otherwise directed, this shall be in writing and shall be signed by the solicitor and by counsel, if instructed. A suitable form will be available from the court.

3. If any party to the proceedings is not before the court when the hearing is fixed, the applicant shall serve that party forthwith with a copy of the time estimate.

4. Any party served with a time estimate shall acknowledge receipt and shall inform the applicant and the court forthwith whether they agree or disagree with the estimate and in the latter case shall also give their own time estimate.

5. If at any time after a time estimate has been given any party considers that the time estimate should be revised, that party shall forthwith provide the court with a further time estimate and shall serve a copy on the other parties. It is the duty of solicitors to keep counsel informed of the time estimates given in the case and it is

the duty of both solicitors and counsel to keep the length of the hearing under review and to inform the court promptly of any change in the time estimate.

6. In cases where a hearing has been fixed for *less than a day*, if any party considers that it is likely to last for one day or more, then a time estimate shall be given by that party to the court and served on the other parties. If an additional application or cross-application is issued returnable on the same date, a further time estimate will only be required if the latest time estimate is affected.

7. A party shall provide a time estimate if so required by the court.

8. If, in the light of the information provided, the court considers that further directions are necessary or if any of the parties fail to provided the requisite information, a directions hearing will be fixed and notice of the appointment given to all parties by the court. In the event of a party failing to provide information when requested or if default is otherwise made in the provision of time estimates, liability for any wasted costs may arise for consideration.

9. This direction does not apply to parties in person. Where the applicant is a party in person, the other parties to the proceedings, if represented by a solicitor, must provide a time estimate to the court immediately upon being notified of the hearing.

10. This direction is not to be read as affecting the right of any party to apply to the court for directions at any time in relation to the listing of any application or for any other purpose.

11. The direction dated March 1 1984 ([1984] 1 All E.R. 783, [1984] 1 W.L.R. 475) shall continue to apply to proceedings other than proceedings under the Children Act 1989 or the inherent jurisdiction of the court relating to children.

12. Issued with the concurrence of the Lord Chancellor.

Novermber 22, 1993

STEPHEN BROWN P.

7. Family Proceedings: Case Management

Practice—Family proceedings—Case management—Court's control over preparation for and conduct of hearings—Practitioners' failure to conduct cases economically to be penalised in costs—Pretrial review and skeleton arguments

C–11   1. The importance of reducing the cost and delay of civil litigation makes it necessary for the court to assert greater control over the preparation for and conduct of hearings than has hitherto been customary. Failure by practitioners to conduct cases economically will be visited by appropriate orders for costs, including wasted costs orders.

2. The court will accordingly exercise its discretion to limit—(a) discovery; (b) the length of opening and closing oral submissions; (c) the time allowed for the examination and cross-examination of witnesses; (d) the issues on which it wishes to be addressed; (e) reading aloud from documents and authorities.

3. Unless otherwise ordered, every witness statement or affidavit shall stand as the evidence in chief of the witness concerned. The substance of the evidence which a party intends to adduce at the hearing must be sufficiently detailed, but without prolixity; it must be confined to material matters of fact, not (except in the case of

the evidence of professional witnesses) of opinion; and if hearsay evidence is to be adduced, the source of the information must be declared or good reason given for not doing so.

4. It is a duty owed to the court both by the parties and by their legal representatives to give full and frank disclosure in ancillary relief applications and also in all matters in respect of children. The parties and their advisers must also use their best endeavours: (a) to confine the issues and the evidence called to what is reasonably considered to be essential for the proper presentation of their case; (b) to reduce or eliminate issues for expert evidence; (c) in advance of the hearing to agree which are the issues or the main issues.

5. Unless the nature of the hearing makes it unnecessary and in the absence of specific directions, bundles should be agreed and prepared for use by the court, the parties and the witnesses and shall be in A4 format where possible, suitably secured. The bundles for use by the court shall be lodged with the court (the Clerk of the Rules in matters in the Royal Courts of Justice, London) at least two clear days before the hearing. Each bundle should be paginated, indexed, wholly legible, and arranged chronologically. Where documents are copied unnecessarily or bundled incompetently the cost will be disallowed.

6. In cases estimated to last for five days or more and in which no pre-trial review has been ordered, application should be made for a pre-trial review. It should when practicable be listed at least three weeks before the hearing and be conducted by the judge or district judge before whom the case is to be heard and should be attended by the advocates who are to represent the parties at the hearing. Whenever possible, all statements of evidence and all reports should be filed before the date of the review and in good time for them to have been considered by all parties.

7. Whenever practicable and in any matter estimated to last five days or more, each party should, not less than two clear days before the hearing, lodge with the court, or the Clerk of the Rules in matters in the Royal Courts of Justice in London, and deliver to other parties, a chronology and a skeleton argument concisely summarising that party's submissions in relation to each of the issues, and citing the main authorities relied upon. It is important that skeleton arguments should be brief.

8. In advance of the hearing upon request, and otherwise in course of their opening, parties should be prepared to furnish the court, if there is no core bundle, with a list of documents essential for a proper understanding of the case.

9. The opening speech should be succinct. At its conclusion other parties may be invited briefly to amplify their skeleton arguments. In a heavy case the court may in conjunction with final speeches require written submissions, including the findings of fact for which each party contends.

10. This practice direction which follows *Practice Direction (Civil Litigation: Case Management)* [1995] 1 W.L.R. 262 handed down by Lord Taylor of Gosforth C.J. and Sir Richard Scott V.-C. to apply in the Queen's Bench and Chancery Divisions, shall apply to all family proceedings in the High Court and in all care centres, family hearing centres and divorce county courts.

11. Issued with the concurrence of the Lord Chancellor.

Sir Stephen Brown P.

January 31, 1995

8. Family Division: Children Act 1989: Applications by Children

C-12   *Family proceedings—Orders in family proceedings—Application for order—Application by child concerned—Application to be determined in High Court—Application to be transferred to High Court for hearing—Children Act 1989, ss. 8, 10—Family Proceedings Rules 1991, r.4.3—Family Proceedings Courts (Children Act 1989) Rules 1991, r.3.*

Under section 10 of the Children Act 1989 the prior leave of the court is required in respect of applications by the child concerned for section 8 orders (contact, prohibited steps, residence and specific issue orders). Rule 4.3 of the Family Proceedings Rules 1991, S.I. 1991/1247, and r.3 of the Family Proceedings Courts (Children Act 1989) Rules 1991, S.I. 1991/1395, set out the procedure to be followed when applying for leave.

Such applications raise issues which are more appropriate for determination in the High Court and should be transferred there for hearing.

Issued with the concurrence of the Lord Chancellor.

STEPHEN BROWN P

February 22, 1993

9. Family Division: Distribution of Business

Practice—Family Division—Transfer of business—Distribution of business between the High Court and county court—Factors to be considered before transferring proceedings—Matrimonial and Family Proceedings Act 1984 (c. 42), ss. 38, 39

C-13   1. These directions are given under section 37 of the Matrimonial and Family Proceedings Act 1984 by the President of the Family Division, with the concurrence of the Lord Chancellor, and apply to all family proceedings which are transferrable between the High Court and county courts under sections 38 and 39 of that Act. They supersede *Practice Direction (Family Division: Business: Distribution)* [1988] 1 W.L.R. 558 given on 6 April 1988, save in respect of family proceedings concerning children pending immediately before October 14, 1991. They do not apply to

(a)   proceedings under the Children Act 1989 or under the Adoption Act 1976, which are governed by the Children (Allocation of Proceedings) Order 1991;

(b)   an application that a minor be made or cease to be a ward of court, or to proceedings under Part III of the Matrimonial and Family Proceedings Act 1984, which may be heard and determined in the High Court alone.

2. (1) Family proceedings to which these directions apply (including interlocutory proceedings) shall be dealt with in the High Court where it appears to the court seised of the case that by reason of the complexity, difficulty or gravity of the issues they ought to be tried in the High Court.

(2) Without prejudice to the generality of sub-paragraph (1), the following proceedings shall be dealt with in the High Court unless the nature of the issues of fact or law raised in the case makes them more suitable for trial in a county court than in the High Court:

C-14 (a)   petitions under section 1(2)(e) of the Matrimonial Causes Act 1973 which are opposed pursuant to section 5 of that Act;

(b) petitions for presumption of death and dissolution of marriage under section 19 of the Matrimonial Causes Act 1973;

(c) proceedings involving a contested issue of domicile;

(d) applications under section 5(6) of the Domicile and Matrimonial Proceedings Act 1973;

(e) applications to restrain a respondent from taking or continuing with foreign proceedings;

(f) suits in which the Queen's Proctor intervenes or shows cause and elects trial in the High Court;

(g) proceedings in relation to a ward of court—(i) in which the Official Solicitor is or becomes the guardian ad litem of the ward or of a party to the proceedings; (ii) in which a local authority is or becomes a party; (iii) in which an application for blood tests is made; (iv) in which an application is opposed on the grounds of want of jurisdiction; (v) in which there is a substantial foreign element; (vi) in which there is an opposed application for leave to take the child permanently out of the jurisdiction or where there is an application for temporary removal of a child from the jurisdiction and it is opposed on the ground that the child may not be duly returned;

(h) interlocutory applications involving—(i) *Mareva* injunctions; (ii) directions as to dealing with assets out of the jurisdiction;

(i) petitions in respect of declarations under Part III of the Family Law Act 1986.

3. (1) Proceedings in the county court for an order within sub-paragraph (2) shall be heard and determined in the High Court where either the county court or any party to the proceedings considers that any such orders, if made, should be recognised and enforced in Scotland or Northern Ireland under Part I of the Family Law Act 1986.

(2) The orders referred to in sub-paragraph (1) are those made by the county court in the exercise of its jurisdiction relating to wardship so far as it determines the living arrangements of a child or provides for the education of, or contact with, a child.

4. In proceedings where periodical payments, a lump sum or property are in issue the court shall have regard in particular to the following factors when considering in accordance with paragraph 2(1) above whether the complexity, difficulty or gravity of the issues are such that they ought to be tried in the High Court:

(a) the capital values of the assets involved and the extent to which they are available for, or susceptible to, distribution or adjustment;

(b) any substantial allegations of fraud or deception or non-disclosure;

(c) any substantial contested allegations of conduct.

An appeal in such proceedings from a district judge in a county court shall be transferred to the High Court where it appears to the district judge, whether on application by a party or otherwise, that the appeal raises a difficult or important question, whether of law or otherwise.

5. Subject to the foregoing, family proceedings may be dealt with in a county court.

6. Proceedings in the High Court which under the foregoing criteria fall to be dealt with in a county court or a divorce county court, as the case may be, and

proceedings in a county court which likewise fall to be dealt with in the High Court shall be transferred accordingly, in accordance with rules of court, unless to do so would cause undue delay or hardship to any party or other person involved.

SIR STEPHEN BROWN P.

June 5, 1992

10. County Court: Circuit Judge and District Judges Listing

C–15 *County court—Practice—Concurrent jurisdiction of circuit judges and district judges— Listing—Complex or important cases to be reserved to circuit judges—Identification of complex or important cases—Indication to be given by litigants.*
1. In general, to achieve maximum flexibility, business falling into the concurrent jurisdiction is to be listed before either a circuit judge or a district judge according to availability.

Special listing requirements
2. If a case appears to contain issues of particular importance or complexity it should, where possible, be reserved for a circuit judge. Where difficulty in listing arises, the listing officer should consult with the senior circuit judge at the court who has overall responsibility for the allocation and listing of work.
3. To assist listing officers to identify complex or important cases, litigants should, when giving a time estimate, also be asked to give a further indication in the following manner:

> "Cases in which the value of the claim is between £1,000 or £5,000 will normally be listed before either a circuit judge or a district judge according to the availability of judicial time. Are there any special reasons why you wish the case to be heard before a circuit judge?"

WATKINS L.J.
Deputy Chief Justice.

July 1, 1991

11. Family Division—Contempt of Court

C–16 *Husband and Wife—Practice—Contempt of court—Committal for contempt—Application by contemnor for release—Contemnor to be present in court.*
The President has directed that on applications for the release of a contemnor from prison the contemnor should be present in court to hear the outcome of the application.

The only exception to this practice is in those cases in which the provisions of the Mental Health Act 1959 [see now Mental Health Act 1983] apply and it is considered by the solicitor conducting the application that in the particular circumstances it would not be desirable for the contemnor to attend.

Issued with the concurrence of the Lord Chancellor.

B.P. TICKLE
Senior Registrar.

July 25, 1983

12. Family Division—Minor: Removal outside jurisdiction: Advice

Minor—Removal outside jurisdiction—Removal in defiance of court order—Advice on C–17
recovery of custody.

It sometimes happens that, without leave of the court or in contravention of an order of the court, a child is removed from the jurisdiction.

Where the child has been taken abroad, the Foreign and Commonwealth Office Consular Department can offer practical (but not legal) advice on the recovery of custody. This advice will be intended to supplement that given by the aggrieved person's legal representative.

Inquiries for assistance in tracing missing abducted children should be referred directly to the FCO Consular Department, Clive House, Petty France, London SW1H 9HD.

B. P. TICKLE
Senior Registrar.

October 16, 1984

13. Minor: Preventing Removal Abroad

Minor—Abduction—Removal from jurisdiction—Police acting to prevent minor being taken abroad—Information necessary before police institute port-alert—Notice to prevent issue of passport—Child Abduction Act 1984 (c. 37), ss. 1, 2

The Child Abduction Act 1984 came into force in October 1984. Section 1 of the Act C–18 which relates to England and Wales provides that in relation to a child under 16 (and subject to certain exceptions) an offence is committed by (a) a parent or guardian of the child, or (b) a person to whom custody has been awarded by a court in England and Wales, or (c) if the child is illegitimate, a person in respect of whom there are reasonable grounds for believing that he is the father, if that person takes or sends the child out of the United Kingdom (i) without the consent of each person who is a parent or guardian or to whom sole or joint custody has been awarded by a court in England and Wales, or (ii) if the child is the subject of a custody order, without the leave of the court which made the order, or (iii) without leave of the court having been obtained under the Guardianship of Minors Acts 1971 and 1973. For the purposes of the Act of 1984, the term "custody" includes "care and control."

Under section 2 of the Act, an offence is also committed in relation to a child under the age of 16 by any person who is not a parent or guardian or a person to whom custody has been granted if without lawful authority or reasonable excuse he takes or detains the child (a) so as to remove him from the lawful control of any person having such lawful control or (b) so as to keep him out of the lawful control of any person entitled thereto.

With effect from May 2, 1986 ports will be informed directly by the police (instead of the Home Office) when there is a real threat that a child is about to be removed unlawfully from the country. The police will provide a 24 hour service and will liaise with immigration officers at the ports in an attempt to identify children at risk of removal. It is not necessary first to obtain a court order in respect of a child under 16 before police assistance is sought. If an order has been obtained, however, it should be produced to them. Where the child is between the ages of 16 and 18, it will be an essential prerequisite that an order is obtained which restricts or restrains removal, or confers custody.

No ward, however, may be removed from the jurisdiction without the leave of the court. Evidence will need to be produced to the police that the child is a ward. This may either be an order confirming wardship, an injunction, or if no such order has been made, in cases of urgency, a sealed copy of the originating summons.

C-19   Any application for assistance to prevent a child's removal from the jurisdiction must be made by the applicant or his legal representative to a police station. This should normally be the applicant's local police station. However, in urgent cases, or where the wardship originating summons has just issued or where the court has just made the order relied on, contact may be made with any police station. If it is considered appropriate by the police, they will institute the "port-alert" system to try to prevent removal from the jurisdiction.

Where the police are asked to institute a "port-alert", they will need first to be satisfied that the danger of removal is *real* and *imminent*. "Imminent" means within 24 to 48 hours and "real" means that the port-alert is not being sought by or on behalf of the applicant merely by way of insurance.

The request for assistance should be accompanied by as much of the following information as possible.

The child: names, sex, date of birth, description, nationality, passport number (if known).

The person likely to remove: names, age, description, nationality, passport number (if known), relationship to child and whether child likely to assist him or her.

Person applying for a port-alert: names, relationship to child, nationality, telephone number (and solicitor's name and number if appropriate).

Likely destination

Likely time of travel and port of embarkation

Grounds for port-alert (as appropriate): 1. Suspected offence under section 1 of Child Abduction Act 1984; 2. Child subject to court order.

Details of person to whom the child should be returned if intercepted

If the police decide that the case is one in which the port-alert system should be used, the child's name will remain on the stop list for four weeks. After that time, it will be removed automatically unless a further application for a port stop is made.

Another measure which an interested party may take is to give notice in writing to the Passport Department, Home Office, that passport facilities should not be provided in respect of the minor either without leave of the court, or in cases other than wardship, the consent of the other parent, guardian, or person to whom custody or care and control has been granted, or the consent of the mother in the case of an illegitimate child.

The practice directions of July 15, 1963, *Practice Direction (Taking Child Out of Jurisdiction)* [1963] 1 W.L.R. 947, of July 18, 1973, *Practice Direction (Child: Preventing Removal Abroad)* [1973] 1 W.L.R. 1014, and of July 20, 1977, *Practice Direction (Ward: Removal from Jurisdiction)* [1977] 1 W.L.R. 1018, are hereby cancelled.

Issued with the approval of the President and the concurrence of the Lord Chancellor.

B. P. TICKLE
Senior Registrar

April 14, 1986.

14. Disclosure of addresses by Government Departments

The arrangements set out in the Registrar's Direction, *Disclosure of Addresses by* C–20
Government Departments, of April 26, 1988 ([1988] 2 FLR 183; [1988] Fam. Law
360; [1988] 2 All E.R. 573; [1988] 1 W.L.R. 648), whereby the court may request
the disclosure of addresses by government departments have been further extended.
These arrangements will now cover:

(a) tracing the address of a person in proceedings against whom another person is
seeking to obtain or enforce an order for financial provision either for himself
or herself or for the children of the former marriage; and,

(b) tracing the whereabouts of a child, or the person with whom the child is said
to be, in proceedings under the Child Abduction and Custody Act 1985 or in
which a custody order, as defined in Part I of the Family Law Act 1986, is
being sought or enforced.

Requests for such information will be made officially by the registrar. The
request, in addition to giving the information mentioned below, should certify:

(A) *In financial provision applications* either (a) that a financial provision order is in
existence, but cannot be enforced because the person against whom the order has
been made cannot be traced; or (b) that the applicant has filed or issued a notice,
petition or originating summons containing an application for financial provision
which cannot be served because the respondent cannot be traced.

A "financial provision order" means any order made under ss. 23, 24, 24A and
27 of the Matrimonial Causes Act 1973 or the variations of any order made under s.
31 of the 1973 Act, and any periodical payments or lump sum order made under
section 6 of the Family Law Reform Act 1969, the Guardianship of Minors Act
1971, s. 34 of the Children Act 1975, and any order registered in the High Court
under the Maintenance Orders (Facilities for Enforcement) Act 1920, the Maintenance Orders Act 1950 and the Maintenance Orders Act 1958, and any order made
under s. 17 of the Matrimonial and Family Proceedings Act 1984.

(B) *In wardship proceedings* that the child is the subject of wardship proceedings and C–21
cannot be traced and is believed to be with the person whose address is sought.
(C) *In custody proceedings* that the child is the subject of custody proceedings and
cannot be traced and is believed to be with the person whose address is sought.

The following notes set out the information required by those departments which
are likely to be of the greatest assistance to an applicant.

(1) Department of Social Security   C–22
The department most likely to be able to assist is the Department of Social Security,
whose records are the most comprehensive and complete. The possibility of

identifying one person amongst so many will depend on the particulars given. An address will not be supplied by the department unless it is satisfied from the particulars given that the record of the person has been reliably identified.

The applicant or his solicitor should therefore be asked to supply as much as possible of the following information about the person sought:

(i)   National Insurance number;

(ii)   surname;

(iii) forenames in full;

(iv) date of birth (or, if not known, approximate age);

(v)   last known address, with date when living there;

(vi) any other known address(es) with dates;

(vii) if the person sought is a war pensioner, his war pension and service particulars (if known);

and in applications for financial provision:

(viii) the exact date of the marriage and the wife's forenames.

Inquiries should be sent by the registrar to:

Department of Social Security
N1CB, Special Section A
Newcastle upon Tyne
NE98 1YU

The department will be prepared to search if given full particulars of the person's name and date of birth, but the chances of accurate identification are increased by the provision of more identifying information. Second requests for records to be searched, provided that a reasonable interval has elapsed, will be met by the Department of Social Security.

Supplementary Benefit/Income Support

C–23   Where, in the case of applications for financial provision, the wife is or has been in receipt of supplementary benefit/income support, it would be advisable in the first instance to make enquiries of the manager of the local Social Security office for the area in which she resides in order to avoid possible duplication of inquiries.

(2) Office of Population Censuses and Surveys National Health Service Central Register

The Office of Population Censuses and Surveys administers the National Health Service Central Register for the Department of Health. The records held in the Central Register include individuals' names, with dates of birth and National Health Service number, against a record of the Family Practitioner Committee area where the patient is currently registered with a National Health Service doctor. The Central Register does not hold individual patients' addresses, but can advise courts of the last Family Practitioner Committee area registration. Courts can then apply for information about addresses to the appropriate Family Practitioner Committee for independent action.

When application is made for the disclosure of Family Practitioner Committee area registrations from these records, the applicant or his solicitor should supply as much as possible of the following information about the person sought:

(i)   National Health Service number;
(ii)   surname;
(iii) forenames in full;
(iv)   date of birth (or, if not known, approximate age);
(v)   last known address;
(vi)   mother's maiden name.

Inquiries should be sent by the registrar to:

Office of Population Censuses and Surveys
National Health Service Central Register
Smedley Hydro, Trafalgar Road
Southport
Merseyside
PR8 2HH

(3) Passport Office

If all reasonable inquiries, including the aforesaid methods, have failed to reveal an   C-24
address, or if there are strong grounds for believing that the person sought may
have made a recent application for a passport, inquiries may be made to the Passport
Office. The applicant or his solicitor should provide as much of the following
information about the person as possible:

(i)   surname;
(ii)   forenames in full;
(iii) date of birth (or, if not known, approximate age);
(iv)   place of birth;
(v)   occupation;
(vi)   whether known to have travelled abroad, and, if so, the destination and dates;
(vii) last known address, with date living there;
(viii) any other known address(es), with dates.

The applicant or his solicitor must also undertake in writing that information
given in response to the inquiry will be used solely for the purpose for which it was
requested, i.e. to assist in tracing the husband in connection with the making or
enforcement of a financial provision order, or in tracing a child in connection with
custody or wardship proceedings, as the case may be.

Inquiries should be sent to:

The Chief Passport Officer
Passport Department
Home Office, Clive House
Petty France
London SW1H 9HD

(4) Ministry of Defence

In cases where the person sought is known to be serving, or to have recently served,
in any branch of H.M. Forces, the solicitor representing the applicant may obtain
the address for service of financial provision or custody and wardship proceedings
direct from the appropriate service department. In the case of army servicemen, the

solicitor can obtain a list of regiments and of the various manning and record offices from the Officer in Charge, Central Manning Support Office, Higher Barracks, Exeter EX4 4ND.

The solicitor's request should be accompanied by a written undertaking that the address will be used for the purpose of service of process in those proceedings and that, so far as is possible, the solicitor will disclose the address only to the court and not to the applicant or any other person, except in the normal course of the proceedings.

Alternatively, if the solicitor wishes to serve process on the person's commanding officer under the provisions contained in section 101 of the Naval Act 1957, s. 153 of the Army Act 1955, and s. 153 of the Air Force Act 1955 (all of which as amended by section 62 of the Armed Forces Act 1971), he may obtain that officer's address in the same way.

Where the applicant is acting in person, the appropriate service department is prepared to disclose the address of the person sought, or that of his commanding officer, to a registrar on receipt of an assurance that the applicant has given an undertaking that the information will be used solely for the purpose of serving process in the proceedings.

In all cases, the request should include details of the person's full name, service number, rank or rating, and his ship, arm or trade, corps regiment or unit or as much of this information as is available. The request should also include details of his date of birth, or, if not known, his age, his date of entry into the service and, if no longer serving, the date of discharge, and any other information, such as his last known address. Failure to quote the service number and the rank or rating may result in failure to identify the serviceman or, at least, in considerable delay.

Inquiries should be addressed as follows:

C–25

(a) Officers of Royal Navy and Women's Royal Naval Service

Ministry of Defence
(Naval Secretary)
Old Admiralty Building
Whitehall
London SW1A 2BD

Ratings in the Royal Navy
WRNS Ratings
QARNNS Ratings

The Commodore (Naval Drafting Division)
HMS Centurion
Grange Road
Gosport, Hants PO13 9XA

RN Medical and Dental Officers

Ministry of Defence
Medical Director
General (Naval)
First Avenue House
High Holborn
London WC1V 6HE

	Officers of Queen Alexandra's Royal Naval Nursing Service	Ministry of Defence The Matron-in-Chief QARNNS First Avenue House High Holborn London WC1V 6HE
	Naval Chaplains	Ministry of Defence Chaplain of the Fleet Lacon House Theobalds Road London WC1T 8RY
(b)	Royal Marine Officers	The Commandant-General Royal Marines (MS Branch) Old Admiralty Building Whitehall London SW1A 2BE
	Royal Marine Ranks	The Commodore (DRORM) HMS Centurion Grange Road Gosport, Hants PO13 9XA
(c)	Army Officers (Including WRAC and QARANC)	Ministry of Defence Army Officers' Documentation Office Government Buildings (F Block) Stanmore Middlesex HA7 4PZ
	Other Ranks, Army	The Manning & Record Office which is appropriate to the Regiment or Corps.
(d)	Royal Air Force and Women's Royal Air Force Officers (Including PMRAFNS)	Ministry of Defence AR&b (RAF) Eastern Avenue Barnwood Gloucester GL14 7PN
	Other Ranks, RAF and WRAF	Ministry of Defence RAF Personnel Management Centre RAF Innsworth Gloucester GL3 1EZ

General Notes

C–26 Records held by other departments are less likely to be of use, either because of their limited scope or because individual records cannot readily be identified. If, however, the circumstances suggest that the address may be known to another department, application may be made to it by the registrar, all relevant particulars available being given.

When any department is able to supply the address of the person sought to the registrar, it will be passed on by him to the applicant's solicitor (or, in proper cases, direct to the applicant if acting in person) on an understanding to use it only for the purpose of the proceedings.

Nothing in this practice direction affects the service in matrimonial causes of petitions which do not contain any application for financial provision, etc. The existing arrangements whereby the Department of Social Security will, at the request of the solicitor, forward a letter by ordinary post to a party's last known address remain in force in such cases.

The Registrar's Direction, *Disclosure of Addresses by Government Departments*, of April 26, 1988 is hereby revoked.

Issued with the concurrence of the Lord Chancellor.

February 13, 1989 **C.F. Turner**, *Senior Registrar*

15. Issue of Passports

C–27 It is the practice of the Passport Department of the Home Office to issue passports for wards in accordance with the Court's direction. This frequently results in passports being restricted to the holiday period specified in the order giving leave. It is the President's opinion that it is more convenient for wards' passports to be issued without such restriction.

The Passport Department has agreed to issue passports on this basis unless the Court otherwise directs. It will of course still be necessary for the leave of the Court to be obtained for the child's removal.

Issued with the concurrence of the Lord Chancellor.

B.P. TICKLE
Senior Registrar

16. Wardship: Visit Abroad

Infant—Ward of court—Removal from jurisdiction—General leave for ward to make temporary visits outside England and Wales—Conditions applicable to such leave

C–28 The following practice note has been issued by the President of the Family Division.

Where in wardship proceedings in the Family Division the court is satisfied that the ward should be able to leave England and Wales for temporary visits abroad without the necessity for special leave, an order may be made giving general leave for such visits, subject to compliance with the condition that the party obtaining the order (who will normally be the party having care and control of the ward) must lodge at the registry at which the matter is proceeding at least seven days before each proposed departure: (a) a written consent in unqualified terms by the other party or parties to the ward's leaving England and Wales for the period proposed; (b) a statement in writing giving the date on which it is proposed that the ward shall leave England and Wales, the period of absence and the whereabouts of the minor during such absence; and, unless otherwise directed, a written undertaking by the applicant to return the ward to England and Wales at the end of the proposed period of absence.

On compliance with these requirements a certificate, for production to the immigration authorities, stating that the conditions of the order have been complied with, may be obtained from the registry.

D. NEWTON
Senior Registrar

May 11, 1973.

17. Ward: Removal from jurisdiction

Minor—Ward of court—Removal from jurisdiction—Leave to remove minor—Applications in wardship and guardianship proceedings
The judges of the Family Division are of the opinion, and it is accordingly hereby C–29 directed, that an application for leave to remove a child out of England and Wales in wardship and guardianship cases shall be made to a judge except in the following cases when it shall be made to the registrar, namely, (a) where the application is unopposed, or (b) where the application is for the temporary removal of the child unless it is opposed on the ground that the child may not be duly returned.

The registrar may make such order on the application as he thinks fit or may refer it or any question arising thereon to a judge.

Issued with the approval of the President.

B. P. TICKLE
Senior Registrar

May 4, 1984.

Registrar's Direction
15 May 1987

18. Removal from jurisdiction

The President has directed that on application for leave to remove from the C–30 jurisdiction for holiday periods a ward of court who has been placed by a local authority with foster parents whose identity the Court considers should remain confidential, for example because they are prospective adopters, it is important that such foster parents should not be identified in the Court's order. In such cases the order should be expressed as giving leave to the local authority to arrange for the child to be removed from England and Wales for the purposes of holidays.

It is also considered permissible, where care and control has been given to a local authority, or to an individual, for the Court to give general leave to make such arrangements in suitable cases, thereby obviating the need to make application for leave each time it is desired to remove the child from the jurisdiction.

B.P. TICKLE
Senior Registrar

19. Wards of Court: Taking out of England and Wales

C–31 *Ward of court—Removal of ward from jurisdiction—Removal without leave of court— Temporary visits abroad—Holidays and educational journeys—Ward of court in local authority care and control—Conditions on which ward may proceed out of England and Wales without specific authority of court.*

The President has directed that where a local authority which is a party to wardship proceedings has obtained an order whereby a ward of court is in its care and control that local authority may arrange for or allow the ward to proceed out of England and Wales for holidays and educational journeys which it approves, without obtaining specific authority from the court, subject to the following conditions.

The conditions are: (i) that where the Official Solicitor acts as guardian ad litem of the ward or a party to the wardship proceedings his consent has been given; (ii) that other parties to the wardship proceedings have consented to the proposed holiday or journey or have been asked whether they have any objection and have not expressed any; this condition does not apply where the court has made an order authorising the placement of the ward with a view to adoption; (iii) that a written undertaking has been obtained from the person who will accompany the ward to return him at the end of the proposed holiday or journey or earlier if required to do so by the court.

Issued with the concurrence of the Lord Chancellor.

C.F. TURNER
Senior Registrar

July 21, 1989.

20. Guidance on References by National Courts for Preliminary Rulings

C–32 The development of the Community legal order is largely the result of co-operation between the Court of Justice of the European Communities and national courts and tribunals through the preliminary ruling procedure under **Article 177 E.C.** and the corresponding provisions of the ECSC and Euratom Treaties. (A preliminary ruling procedure is also provided for by protocols to several conventions concluded by the Member States, in particular the Brussels Convention on Jurisdiction and the Enforcement of Judgments in Civil and Commercial Matters.)

In order to make this co-operation more effective, and so enable the Court of Justice better to meet the requirements of national courts by providing helpful answers to preliminary questions, this Note for Guidance is addressed to all interested parties, in particular to all national courts and tribunals.

It must be emphasised that the Note is for guidance only and has no binding or interpretative effect in relation to the provisions governing the preliminary ruling procedure. It merely contains practical information which, in the light of experience in applying the preliminary ruling procedure, may help to prevent the kind of difficulties which the Court has sometimes encountered.

1. Any court or tribunal of a Member State may ask the Court of Justice to interpret a rule of Community law, whether contained in the Treaties or in acts of secondary law, if it considers that this is necessary for it to give judgment in a case pending before it.

Courts or tribunals against whose decisions there is no judicial remedy under national law must refer questions of interpretation arising before them to the Court of Justice, unless the Court has already ruled on the point or unless the correct application of the rule of Community law is obvious, (Case 283/81. Cilfit *v.* Ministry of Health [1982] E.C.R. 3415, [1983] 1 C.M.L.R. 472.)

2. The Court of Justice has jurisdiction to rule on the validity of acts of the Community institutions. National courts or tribunals may reject a plea challenging the validity of such an act. But where a national court (even one whose decision is still subject to appeal) intends to question the validity of a Community act, it must refer that question to the Court of Justice, (Case 314/85, Foto-Frost *v.* Hauptzollamt Lübeck-Ost [1987] E.C.R. 4199.)

Where, however, a national court or tribunal has serious doubts about the validity of a Community act on which a national measure is based, it may, in exceptional cases, temporarily suspend application of the latter measure or grant other interim relief with respect to it. It must then refer the question of validity to the Court of Justice, stating the reasons for which it considers that the Community act is not valid (Joined Cases C-143/88 and C-92/89, Zuckerfabrik Süderdithmarschen and Zuckerfabrik Soest [1991] 1 E.C.R. 415, [1993] 3 C.M.L.R. 1 and in Case C-465/93, Atlanta Fruchthandelsgesellschaft [1995] 1 E.C.R. 3761).

3. Questions referred for a preliminary ruling must be limited to the interpretation or validity of a provision of Community law, since the Court of Justice does not have jurisdiction to interpret national law or assess its validity. It is for the referring court or tribunal to apply the relevant rule of Community law in the specific case pending before it.

4. The order of the national court or tribunal referring a question to the Court of Justice for a preliminary ruling may be in any form allowed by national procedural law. Reference of a question or questions to the Court of Justice generally involves stay of the national proceedings until the Court has given its ruling, but the decision to stay proceedings is one which it is for the national court alone to take in accordance with its own national law.

5. The order for reference containing the question or questions referred to the Court will have to be translated by the Court's translators into the other official languages of the Community. Questions concerning the interpretation or validity of Community law are frequently of general interest and the Member States and Community institutions are entitled to submit observations. It is therefore desirable that the reference should be drafted as clearly and precisely as possible.

6. The order for reference should contain a statement of reasons which is succinct C–33 but sufficiently complete to give the Court, and those to whom it must be notified (the Member States, the Commission and in certain cases the Council and the

European Parliament), a clear understanding of the factual and legal context of the main proceedings, (Joined Cases C 320–322/90, TELEMARSICABRUZZO [1993] 1 E.C.R. 393. [1992] 2 C.M.L.R. 397.)

In particular, it should include:

— a statement of the facts which are essential to a full understanding of the legal significance of the main proceedings;
— an exposition of the national law which may be applicable;
— a statement of the reasons which have prompted the national court to refer the question or questions to the Court of Justice; and
— where appropriate, a summary of the arguments of the parties.

The aim should be to put the Court of Justice in a position to give the national court an answer which will be of assistance to it.

The order for reference should also be accompanied by copies of any documents needed for a proper understanding of the case, especially the text of the applicable national provisions. However, as the case-file or documents annexed to the order for reference itself includes all the relevant information.

C–34   7. A national court or tribunal may refer a question to the Court of Justice as soon as it finds that a ruling on the point or points of interpretation or validity is necessary to enable it to give judgment. It must be stressed, however, that it is not for the Court of Justice to decide issues of fact or to resolve disputes as to the interpretation or application of rules of national law. It is therefore desirable that a decision to refer should not be taken until the national proceedings have reached a stage where the national court is able to define, if only as a working hypothesis, the factual and legal context of the question; on any view, the administration of justice is likely to be best served if the reference is not made until both sides have been heard, (Case 70/77, SIMMENTHAL *v.* AMMINISTRAZIONE DELLE FINANZE DELLO STATO [1978] E.C.R. 1453, [1978] 3 C.M.L.R. 670.)

8. The order for reference and the relevant documents should be sent by the national court directly to the Court of Justice, by registered post, addressed to:

The Registry
Court of Justice of the European Communities
L-2925 Luxembourg
Telephone (352) 43031

The Court Registry will remain in contact with the national court until judgment is given, and will send copies of the various documents (written observations, Report for the Hearing, Opinion of the Advocate General). The Court will also send its judgment to the national court. The Court would appreciate being informed about the application of its judgment in the national proceedings and being sent a copy of the national court's final decision.

9. Proceedings for a preliminary ruling before the Court of Justice are free of charge. The Court does not rule on costs.

APPENDIX D

Statutes

189

4. County Courts Act 1984
    section 38
    section 76

5. Magistrates Courts Act 1980
    section 63
    section 65
    section 69
    section 128
    section 129

6. Law Reform (Husband and Wife) Act 1962
    section 1

7. Family Law Act 1986
    section 1(1) (a)–(d)
    section 34

8. Criminal Justice Act 1982
    section 9

9. Contempt of Court Act 1981
    section 14

10. Administration of Justice Act 1960
    section 1
    section 2
    section 13

11. Protection from Harrassment Act 1997
    section 1
    section 2
    section 3
    section 4
    section 5
    section 6
    section 7
    section 8
    section 9
    section 10
    section 11
    section 12
    section 13
    section 14
    section 15
    section 16

Family Law Act 1996

Part IV

Family Homes and Domestic Violence

Rights to occupy matrimonial home

30.—(1) This section applies if—   D–02

(a) one spouse is entitled to occupy a dwelling-house by virtue of—

  (i) a beneficial estate or interest or contract; or
  (ii) any enactment giving that spouse the right to remain in occupation; and

(b) the other spouse is not so entitled.

(2) Subject to the provisions of this Part, the spouse not so entitled has the following rights ("matrimonial home rights")—

(a) if in occupation, a right not to be evicted or excluded from the dwelling-house or any part of it by the other spouse except with the leave of the court given by an order under section 33;

(b) if not in occupation, a right with the leave of the court so given to enter into and occupy the dwelling-house.

(3) If a spouse is entitled under this section to occupy a dwelling-house or any part of a dwelling-house, any payment or tender made or other thing done by that spouse in or towards satisfaction of any liability of the other spouse in respect of rent, mortgage payments or other outgoings affecting the dwelling-house is, whether or not it is made or done in pursuance of an order under section 40, as good as if made or done by the other spouse.

(4) A spouse's occupation by virtue of this section—   D–03

(a) is to be treated, for the purposes of the Rent (Agriculture) Act 1976 and the Rent Act 1977 (other than Part V and sections 103 to 106 of that Act), as occupation by the other spouse as the other spouse's residence, and

(b) if the spouse occupies the dwelling-house as that spouse's only or principal home, is to be treated, for the purposes of the Housing Act 1985 [Part I of the Housing Act 1988 and Chapter I of Part V of the Housing Act 1996]* as occupation by the other spouse as the other spouse's only or principal home.

(5) If a spouse ("the first spouse")—

(a) is entitled under this section to occupy a dwelling-house or any part of a dwelling-house, and

---

* As amended by the Housing Act 1996 (Consequential Amendments) Order 1997, S.I. 1997 No. 74, art. 2, Sched. para. 10.

(b)   makes any payment in or towards satisfaction of any liability of the other spouse ("the second spouse") in respect of mortgage payments affecting the dwelling-house,

the person to whom the payment is made may treat it as having been made by the second spouse, but the fact that that person has treated any such payment as having been so made does not affect any claim of the first spouse against the second spouse to an interest in the dwelling-house by virtue of the payment.

D–04   (6) If a spouse is entitled under this section to occupy a dwelling-house or part of a dwelling-house by reason of an interest of the other spouse under a trust, all the provisions of subsections (3) to (5) apply in relation to the trustees as they apply in relation to the other spouse.

(7) This section does not apply to a dwelling-house which has at no time been, and which was at no time intended by the spouses to be, a matrimonial home of theirs.

(8) A spouse's matrimonial home rights continue—

(a)   only so long as the marriage subsists, except to the extent that an order under section 33(5) otherwise provides; and

(b)   only so long as the other spouse is entitled as mentioned in subsection (1) to occupy the dwelling-house, except where provision is made by section 31 for those rights to be a charge on an estate or interest in the dwelling-house.

(9) It is hereby declared that a spouse—

(a)   who has an equitable interest in a dwelling-house or in its proceeds of sale, but

(b)   is not a spouse in whom there is vested (whether solely or as joint tenant) a legal estate in fee simple or a legal term of years absolute in the dwelling-house,

is to be treated, only for the purpose of determining whether he has matrimonial home rights, as not being entitled to occupy the dwelling-house by virtue of that interest.

D–05   31.—(1) Subsections (2) and (3) apply if, at any time during a marriage, one spouse is entitled to occupy a dwelling-house by virtue of a beneficial estate or interest.

(2) The other spouse's matrimonial home rights are a charge on the estate or interest.

(3) The charge created by subsection (2) has the same priority as if it were an equitable interest created at whichever is the latest of the following dates—

(a)   the date on which the spouse so entitled acquires the estate or interest;

(b)   the date of the marriage; and

(c)   1st January 1968 (the commencement date of the Matrimonial Homes Act 1967).

(4) Subsections (5) and (6) apply if, at any time when a spouse's matrimonial home rights are a charge on an interest of the other spouse under a trust, there are, apart from either of the spouses, no persons, living or unborn, who are or could become beneficiaries under the trust.

(5) The rights are a charge also on the estate or interest of the trustees for the other spouse.

(6) The charge created by subsection (5) has the same priority as if it were an equitable interest created (under powers overriding the trusts) on the date when it arises.

(7) In determining for the purposes of subsection (4) whether there are any persons who are not, but could become, beneficiaries under the trust, there is to be disregarded any potential exercise of a general power of appointment exercisable by either or both of the spouses alone (whether or not the exercise of it requires the consent of another person).

(8) Even though a spouse's matrimonial home rights are a charge on an estate or interest in the dwelling-house, those rights are brought to an end by—

(a)   the death of the other spouse, or

(b)   the termination (otherwise than by death) of the marriage,

unless the court directs otherwise by an order made under section 33(5).

(9) If—

(a)   a spouse's matrimonial home rights are a charge on an estate or interest in the dwelling-house, and

(b)   that estate or interest is surrendered to merge in some other estate or interest expectant on it in such circumstances that, but for the merger, the person taking the estate or interest would be bound by the charge,

the surrender has effect subject to the charge and the persons thereafter entitled to the other estate or interest are, for so long as the estate or interest surrendered would have endured if not so surrendered, to be treated for all purposes of this Part as deriving title to the other estate or interest under the other spouse or, as the case may be, under the trustees for the other spouse, by virtue of the surrender.

D–06

(10) If the title to the legal estate by virtue of which a spouse is entitled to occupy a dwelling-house (including any legal estate held by trustees for that spouse) is registered under the Land Registration Act 1925 or any enactment replaced by that Act—

(a)   registration of a land charge affecting the dwelling-house by virtue of this Part is to be effected by registering a notice under that Act; and

(b)   a spouse's matrimonial home rights are not an overriding interest within the meaning of that Act affecting the dwelling-house even though the spouse is in actual occupation of the dwelling-house.

(11) A spouse's matrimonial home rights (whether or not constituting a charge) do not entitle that spouse to lodge a caution under section 54 of the Land Registration Act 1925.

(12) If—

(a)   a spouse's matrimonial home rights are a charge on the estate of the other spouse or of trustees of the other spouse, and

(b)   that estate is the subject of a mortgage,

then if, after the date of the creation of the mortgage ("the first mortgage"), the charge is registered under section 2 of the Land Charges Act 1972, the charge is, for the purposes of section 94 of the Law of Property Act 1925 (which regulates the rights of mortgagees to make further advances ranking in priority to subsequent mortgages), to be deemed to be a mortgage subsequent in date to the first mortgage.

(13) It is hereby declared that a charge under subsection (2) or (5) is not registrable under subsection (10) or under section 2 of the Land Charges Act 1972 unless it is a charge on a legal estate.

32. Schedule 4 re-enacts with consequential amendments and minor modifications provisions of the Matrimonial Homes Act 1983.

Occupation orders

D–07 **33.**—(1) If—

(a) a person ("the person entitled")—

(i) is entitled to occupy a dwelling-house by virtue of a beneficial estate or interest or contract or by virtue of any enactment giving him the right to remain in occupation, or

(ii) has matrimonial home rights in relation to a dwelling-house, and

(b) the dwelling-house—

(i) is or at any time has been the home of the person entitled and of another person with whom he is associated, or

(ii) was at any time intended by the person entitled and any such other person to be their home,

the person entitled may apply to the court for an order containing any of the provisions specified in subsections (3), (4) and (5).

(2) If an agreement to marry is terminated, no application under this section may be made by virtue of section 62(3)(e) by reference to that agreement after the end of the period of three years beginning with the day on which it is terminated.

(3) An order under this section may—

(a) enforce the applicant's entitlement to remain in occupation as against the other person ("the respondent");

(b) require the respondent to permit the applicant to enter and remain in the dwelling-house or part of the dwelling-house;

(c) regulate the occupation of the dwelling-house by either or both parties;

(d) if the respondent is entitled as mentioned in subsection (1)(a)(i), prohibit, suspend or restrict the exercise by him of his right to occupy the dwelling-house;

(e) if the respondent has matrimonial home rights in relation to the dwelling-house and the applicant is the other spouse, restrict or terminate those rights;

(f) require the respondent to leave the dwelling-house or part of the dwelling-house; or

(g)   exclude the respondent from a defined area in which the dwelling-house is
      included.

(4) An order under this section may declare that the applicant is entitled as
mentioned in subsection (1)(a)(i) or has matrimonial home rights.

(5) If the applicant has matrimonial home rights and the respondent is the other
spouse, an order under this section made during the marriage may provide that
those rights are not brought to an end by—

(a)   the death of the other spouse; or
(b)   the termination (otherwise than by death) of the marriage.

(6) In deciding whether to exercise its powers under subsection (3) and (if so) in
what manner, the court shall have regard to all the circumstances including—

(a)   the housing needs and housing resources of each of the parties and of any
      relevant child;
(b)   the financial resources of each of the parties;
(c)   the likely effect of any order, or of any decision by the court not to exercise its
      powers under subsection (3), on the health, safety or well-being of the parties
      and of any relevant child; and
(d)   the conduct of the parties in relation to each other and otherwise.

(7) If it appears to the court that the applicant or any relevant child is likely to
suffer significant harm attributable to conduct of the respondent if an order under
this section containing one or more of the provisions mentioned in subsection (3) is
not made, the court shall make the order unless it appears to it that—

(a)   the respondent or any relevant child is likely to suffer significant harm if the
      order is made; and
(b)   the harm likely to be suffered by the respondent or child in that event is as
      great as, or greater than, the harm attributable to conduct of the respondent
      which is likely to be suffered by the applicant or child if the order is not
      made.

(8) The court may exercise its powers under subsection (5) in any case where it
considers that in all the circumstances it is just and reasonable to do so.

(9) An order under this section—

(a)   may not be made after the death of either of the parties mentioned in
      subsection (1); and
(b)   except in the case of an order made by virtue of subsection (5)(a), ceases to
      have effect on the death of either party.

(10) An order under this section may, in so far as it has continuing effect, be
made for a specified period, until the occurrence of a specified event or until further
order.

34.—(1) If a spouse's matrimonial home rights are a charge on the estate or
interest of the other spouse or of trustees for the other spouse—

(a)   an order under section 33 against the other spouse has, except so far as a
      contrary intention appears, the same effect against persons deriving title
      under the other spouse or under the trustees and affected by the charge, and

(b)   sections 33(1), (3), (4) and (10) and 30(3) to (6) apply in relation to any person deriving title under the other spouse or under the trustees and affected by the charge as they apply in relation to the other spouse.

(2) The court may make an order under section 33 by virtue of subsection (1)(b) if it considers that in all the circumstances it is just and reasonable to do so.

D–08   **35.**—(1) This section applies if—

(a)   one former spouse is entitled to occupy a dwelling-house by virtue of a beneficial estate or interest or contract, or by virtue of any enactment giving him the right to remain in occupation;

(b)   the other former spouse is not so entitled; and

(c)   the dwelling-house was at any time their matrimonial home or was at any time intended by them to be their matrimonial home.

(2) The former spouse not so entitled may apply to the court for an order under this section against the other former spouse ("the respondent").

(3) If the applicant is in occupation, an order under this section must contain provision—

(a)   giving the applicant the right not to be evicted or excluded from the dwelling-house or any part of it by the respondent for the period specified in the order; and

(b)   prohibiting the respondent from evicting or excluding the applicant during that period.

(4) If the applicant is not in occupation, an order under this section must contain provision—

(a)   giving the applicant the right to enter into and occupy the dwelling-house for the period specified in the order; and

(b)   requiring the respondent to permit the exercise of that right.

(5) An order under this section may also—

(a)   regulate the occupation of the dwelling-house by either or both of the parties;

(b)   prohibit, suspend or restrict the exercise by the respondent of his right to occupy the dwelling-house;

(c)   require the respondent to leave the dwelling-house or part of the dwelling-house; or

(d)   exclude the respondent from a defined area in which the dwelling-house is included.

(6) In deciding whether to make an order under this section containing provision of the kind mentioned in subsection (3) or (4) and (if so) in what manner, the court shall have regard to all the circumstances including—

(a)   the housing needs and housing resources of each of the parties and of any relevant child;

(b)   the financial resources of each of the parties;

(c)   the likely effect of any order, or of any decision by the court not to exercise its powers under subsection (3) or (4), on the health, safety or well-being of the parties and of any relevant child;

(d)   the conduct of the parties in relation to each other and otherwise;

(e)   the length of time that has elapsed since the parties ceased to live together;

(f)   the length of time that has elapsed since the marriage was dissolved or annulled; and

(g)   the existence of any pending proceedings between the parties—

> (i) for an order under section 23A or 24 of the Matrimonial Causes Act 1973 (property adjustment orders in connection with divorce proceedings etc.);
>
> (ii) for an order under paragraph 1(2)(d) or (e) of Schedule 1 to the Children Act 1989 (orders for financial relief against parents); or
>
> (iii) relating to the legal or beneficial ownership of the dwelling-house.

(7) In deciding whether to exercise its power to include one or more of the D–09 provisions referred to in subsection (5) ("a subsection (5) provision") and (if so) in what manner, the court shall have regard to all the circumstances including the matters mentioned in subsection (6)(a) to (e).

(8) If the court decides to make an order under this section and it appears to it that, if the order does not include a subsection (5) provision, the applicant or any relevant child is likely to suffer significant harm attributable to conduct of the respondent, the court shall include the subsection (5) provision in the order unless it appears to the court that—

(a)   the respondent or any relevant child is likely to suffer significant harm if the provision is included in the order; and

(b)   the harm likely to be suffered by the respondent or child in that event is as great as or greater than the harm attributable to conduct of the respondent which is likely to be suffered by the applicant or child if the provision is not included.

(9) An order under this section—

(a)   may not be made after the death of either of the former spouses; and

(b)   ceases to have effect on the death of either of them.

(10) An order under this section must be limited so as to have effect for a specified period not exceeding six months, but may be extended on one or more occasions for a further specified period not exceeding six months.

(11) A former spouse who has an equitable interest in the dwelling-house or in the proceeds of sale of the dwelling-house but in whom there is not vested (whether solely or as joint tenant) a legal estate in fee simple or a legal term of years absolute in the dwelling-house is to be treated (but only for the purpose of determining whether he is eligible to apply under this section) as not being entitled to occupy the dwelling-house by virtue of that Interest.

(12) Subsection (11) does not prejudice any right of such a former spouse to apply for an order under section 33.

(13) So long as an order under this section remains in force, subsections (3) to (6) of section 30 apply in relation to the applicant—

(a)   as if he were the spouse entitled to occupy the dwelling-house by virtue of that section; and

(b)   as if the respondent were the other spouse.

D–10   36.—(1) This section applies if—

(a)   one cohabitant or former cohabitant is entitled to occupy a dwelling-house by virtue of a beneficial estate or interest or contract or by virtue of any enactment giving him the right to remain in occupation;

(b)   the other cohabitant or former cohabitant is not so entitled; and

(c)   that dwelling-house is the home in which they live together as husband and wife or a home in which they at any time so lived together or intended so to live together.

(2) The cohabitant or former cohabitant not so entitled may apply to the court for an order under this section against the other cohabitant or former cohabitant ("the respondent").

(3) If the applicant is in occupation, an order under this section must contain provision—

(a)   giving the applicant the right not to be evicted or excluded from the dwelling-house or any part of it by the respondent for the period specified in the order; and

(b)   prohibiting the respondent from evicting or excluding the applicant during that period.

(4) If the applicant is not in occupation, an order under this section must contain provision—

(a)   giving the applicant the right to enter into and occupy the dwelling-house for the period specified in the order; and

(b)   requiring the respondent to permit the exercise of that right.

(5) An order under this section may also—

(a)   regulate the occupation of the dwelling-house by either or both of the parties;

(b)   prohibit, suspend or restrict the exercise by the respondent of his right to occupy the dwelling-house;

(c)   require the respondent to leave the dwelling-house or part of the dwelling-house; or

(d)   exclude the respondent from a defined area in which the dwelling-house is included.

D–11   (6) In deciding whether to make an order under this section containing provision of the kind mentioned in subsection (3) or (4) and (if so) in what manner, the court shall have regard to all the circumstances including—

(a)   the housing needs and housing resources of each of the parties and of any relevant child;

(b)   the financial resources of each of the parties;

(c)   the likely effect of any order, or of any decision by the court not to exercise its powers under subsection (3) or (4), on the health, safety or well-being of the parties and of any relevant child;

(d)   the conduct of the parties in relation to each other and otherwise;

(e)   the nature of the parties' relationship;

(f)   the length of time during which they have lived together as husband and wife;

(g)   whether there are or have been any children who are children of both parties or for whom both parties have or have had parental responsibility;

(h)   the length of time that has elapsed since the parties ceased to live together; and

(i)   the existence of any pending proceedings between the parties—

      (i) for an order under paragraph 1(2)(d) or (e) of Schedule 1 to the Children Act 1989 (orders for financial relief against parents); or

      (ii) relating to the legal or beneficial ownership of the dwelling-house.

(7) In deciding whether to exercise its powers to include one or more of the **D–12** provisions referred to in subsection (5) ("a subsection (5) provision") and (if so) in what manner, the court shall have regard to all the circumstances including—

(a)   the matters mentioned in subsection (6)(a) to (d); and

(b)   the questions mentioned in subsection (8).

(8) The questions are—

(a)   whether the applicant or any relevant child is likely to suffer significant harm attributable to conduct of the respondent if the subsection (5) provision is not included in the order; and

(b)   whether the harm likely to be suffered by the respondent or child if the provision is included is as great as or greater than the harm attributable to conduct of the respondent which is likely to be suffered by the applicant or child if the provision is not included.

(9) An order under this section—

(a)   may not be made after the death of either of the parties; and

(b)   ceases to have effect on the death of either of them.

(10) An order under this section must be limited so as to have effect for a specified period not exceeding six months, but may be extended on one occasion for a further specified period not exceeding six months.

(11) A person who has an equitable interest in the dwelling-house or in the proceeds of sale of the dwelling-house but in whom there is not vested (whether solely or as joint tenant) a legal estate in fee simple or a legal term of years absolute in the dwelling-house is to be treated (but only for the purpose of determining whether he is eligible to apply under this section) as not being entitled to occupy the dwelling-house by virtue of that interest.

(12) Subsection (11) does not prejudice any right of such a person to apply for an order under section 33.

(13) So long as the order remains in force, subsections (3) to (6) of section 30 apply in relation to the applicant—

(a)   as if he were a spouse entitled to occupy the dwelling-house by virtue of that section; and

(b)   as if the respondent were the other spouse.

D–13   37.—(1) This section applies if—

(a)   one spouse or former spouse and the other spouse or former spouse occupy a dwelling-house which is or was the matrimonial home; but
(b)   neither of them is entitled to remain in occupation—

(i) by virtue of a beneficial estate or interest or contract; or
(ii) by virtue of any enactment giving him the right to remain in occupation.

(2) Either of the parties may apply to the court for an order against the other under this section.

(3) An order under this section may—

(a)   require the respondent to permit the applicant to enter and remain in the dwelling-house or part of the dwelling-house;
(b)   regulate the occupation of the dwelling-house by either or both of the spouses;
(c)   require the respondent to leave the dwelling-house or part of the dwelling-house; or
(d)   exclude the respondent from a defined area in which the dwelling-house is included.

(4) Subsections (6) and (7) of section 33 apply to the exercise by the court of its powers under this section as they apply to the exercise by the court of its powers under subsection (3) of that section.

(5) An order under this section must be limited so as to have effect for a specified period not exceeding six months, but may be extended on one or more occasions for a further specified period not exceeding six months.

D–14   38.—(1) This section applies if—

(a)   one cohabitant or former cohabitant and the other cohabitant or former cohabitant occupy a dwelling-house which is the home in which they live or lived together as husband and wife; but
(b)   neither of them is entitled to remain in occupation—

(i) by virtue of a beneficial estate or interest or contract; or
(ii) by virtue of any enactment giving him the right to remain in occupation.

(2) Either of the parties may apply to the court for an order against the other under this section.

(3) An order under this section may—

(a)   require the respondent to permit the applicant to enter and remain in the dwelling-house or part of the dwelling-house;
(b)   regulate the occupation of the dwelling-house by either or both of the parties;
(c)   require the respondent to leave the dwelling-house or part of the dwelling-house; or
(d)   exclude the respondent from a defined area in which the dwelling-house is included.

(4) In deciding whether to exercise its powers to include one or more of the provisions referred to in subsection (3) ("a subsection (3) provision") and (if so) in what manner, the court shall have regard to all the circumstances including—

(a)   the housing needs and housing resources of each of the parties and of any relevant child;

(b)   the financial resources of each of the parties;

(c)   the likely effect of any order, or of any decision by the court not to exercise its powers under subsection (3), on the health, safety or well-being of the parties and of any relevant child;

(d)   the conduct of the parties in relation to each other and otherwise; and

(e)   the questions mentioned in subsection (5).

(5) The questions are—

(a)   whether the applicant or any relevant child is likely to suffer significant harm attributable to conduct of the respondent if the subsection (3) provision is not included in the order; and

(b)   whether the harm likely to be suffered by the respondent or child if the provision is included is as great as or greater than the harm attributable to conduct of the respondent which is likely to be suffered by the applicant or child if the provision is not included.

(6) An order under this section shall be limited so as to have effect for a specified period not exceeding six months, but may be extended on one occasion for a further specified period not exceeding six months.

39.—(1) In this Part an "occupation order" means an order under section 33, 35,   D–15 36, 37 or 38.

(2) An application for an occupation order may be made in other family proceedings or without any other family proceedings being instituted.

(3) If—

(a)   an application for an occupation order is made under section 33, 35, 36, 37 or 38, and

(b)   the court considers that it has no power to make the order under the section concerned, but that it has power to make an order under one of the other sections,

the court may make an order under that other section.

(4) The fact that a person has applied for an occupation order under sections 35 to 38, or that an occupation order has been made, does not affect the right of any person to claim a legal or equitable interest in any property in any subsequent proceedings (including subsequent proceedings under this Part).

40.—(1) The court may on, or at any time after, making an occupation order   D–16 under section 33, 35 or 36—

(a)   impose on either party obligations as to—

(i) the repair and maintenance of the dwelling-house; or

(ii) the discharge of rent, mortgage payments or other outgoings affecting the dwelling-house;

(b)   order a party occupying the dwelling-house or any part of it (including a party who is entitled to do so by virtue of a beneficial estate or interest or contract or by virtue of any enactment giving him the right to remain in occupation) to make periodical payments to the other party in respect of the accommodation, if the other party would (but for the order) be entitled to occupy the dwelling-house by virtue of a beneficial estate or interest or contract or by virtue of any such enactment;

(c)   grant either party possession or use of furniture or other contents of the dwelling-house;

(d)   order either party to take reasonable care of any furniture or other contents of the dwelling-house;

(e)   order either party to take reasonable steps to keep the dwelling-house and any furniture or other contents secure.

(2) In deciding whether and, if so, how to exercise its powers under this section, the court shall have regard to all the circumstances of the case including—

(a)   the financial needs and financial resources of the parties; and

(b)   the financial obligations which they have, or are likely to have in the foreseeable future, including financial obligations to each other and to any relevant child.

(3) An order under this section ceases to have effect when the occupation order to which it relates ceases to have effect.

D–17   **41.**—(1) This section applies if the parties are cohabitants or former cohabitants.

(2) Where the court is required to consider the nature of the parties' relationship, it is to have regard to the fact that they have not given each other the commitment involved in marriage.

Non-molestation orders

42.—(1) In this Part a "non-molestation order" means an order containing either or both of the following provisions—

(a)   provision prohibiting a person ("the respondent") from molesting another person who is associated with the respondent;

(b)   provision prohibiting the respondent from molesting a relevant child.

(2) The court may make a non-molestation order—

(a)   if an application for the order has been made (whether in other family proceedings or without any other family proceedings being instituted) by a person who is associated with the respondent; or

(b)   if in any family proceedings to which the respondent is a party the court considers that the order should be made for the benefit of any other party to the proceedings or any relevant child even though no such application has been made.

(3) In subsection (2) "family proceedings" includes proceedings in which the court has made an emergency protection order under section 44 of the Children Act 1989 which includes an exclusion requirement (as defined in section 44A(3) of that Act).

(4) Where an agreement to marry is terminated, no application under subsection (2)(a) may be made by virtue of section 62(3)(e) by reference to that agreement after the end of the period of three years beginning with the day on which it is terminated.

(5) In deciding whether to exercise its powers under this section and, if so, in what manner, the court shall have regard to all the circumstances including the need to secure the health, safety and well-being—

(a)   of the applicant or, in a case falling within subsection (2)(b), the person for whose benefit the order would be made; and

(b)   of any relevant child.

(6) A non-molestation order may be expressed so as to refer to molestation in general, to particular acts of molestation, or to both.

(7) A non-molestation order may be made for a specified period or until further order.

(8) A non-molestation order which is made in other family proceedings ceases to have effect if those proceedings are withdrawn or dismissed.

Further provisions relating to occupation and non-molestation orders

43.—(1) A child under the age of sixteen may not apply for an occupation order D–18 or a non-molestation order except with the leave of the court.

(2) The court may grant leave for the purposes of subsection (1) only if it is satisfied that the child has sufficient understanding to make the proposed application for the occupation order or non-molestation order.

44.—(1) Subject to subsection (2), the court shall not make an order under D–19 section 33 or 42 by virtue of section 62(3)(e) unless there is produced to it evidence in writing of the existence of the agreement to marry.

(2) Subsection (1) does not apply if the court is satisfied that the agreement to marry was evidenced by—

(a)   the gift of an engagement ring by one party to the agreement to the other in contemplation of their marriage, or

(b)   a ceremony entered into by the parties in the presence of one or more other persons assembled for the purpose of witnessing the ceremony.

45.—(1) The court may, in any case where it considers that it is just and D–20 convenient to do so, make an occupation order or a non-molestation order even though the respondent has not been given such notice of the proceedings as would otherwise be required by rules of court.

(2) In determining whether to exercise its powers under subsection (1), the court shall have regard to all the circumstances including—

(a)   any risk of significant harm to the applicant or a relevant child, attributable to conduct of the respondent, if the order is not made immediately;

(b)   whether it is likely that the applicant will be deterred or prevented from pursuing the application if an order is not made immediately; and

(c)   whether there is reason to believe that the respondent is aware of the proceedings but is deliberately evading service and that the applicant or a relevant child will be seriously prejudiced by the delay involved—

(i) where the court is a magistrates' court, in effecting service of proceedings; or

(ii) in any other case, in effecting substituted service.

(3) If the court makes an order by virtue of subsection (1) it must afford the respondent an opportunity to make representations relating to the order as soon as just and convenient at a full hearing.

(4) If, at a full hearing, the court makes an occupation order ("the full order"), then—

(a) for the purposes of calculating the maximum period for which the full order may be made to have effect, the relevant section is to apply as if the period for which the full order will have effect began on the date on which the initial order first had effect; and

(b) the provisions of section 36(10) or 38(6) as to the extension of orders are to apply as if the full order and the initial order were a single order.

(5) In this section—

"full hearing" means a hearing of which notice has been given to all the parties in accordance with rules of court;

"initial order" means an occupation order made by virtue of subsection (1); and

"relevant section" means section 33(10), 35(10), 36(10), 37(5) or 38(6).

D–21   46.—(1) In any case where the court has power to make an occupation order or non-molestation order, the court may accept an undertaking from any party to the proceedings.

(2) No power of arrest may be attached to any undertaking given under subsection (1).

(3) The court shall not accept an undertaking under subsection (1) in any ease where apart from this section a power of arrest would be attached to the order.

(4) An undertaking given to a court under subsection (1) is enforceable as if it were an order of the court.

(5) This section has effect without prejudice to the powers of the High Court and the county court apart from this section.

D–22   47.—(1) In this section "a relevant order" means an occupation order or a non-molestation order.

(2) If—

(a) the court makes a relevant order; and

(b) it appears to the court that the respondent has used or threatened violence against the applicant or a relevant child,

it shall attach a power of arrest to one or more provisions of the order unless satisfied that in all the circumstances of the case the applicant or child will be adequately protected without such a power of arrest.

(3) Subsection (2) does not apply in any case where the relevant order is made by virtue of section 45(1), but in such a case the court may attach a power of arrest to one or more provisions of the order if it appears to it—

(a) that the respondent has used or threatened violence against the applicant or a relevant child; and

(b)   that there is a risk of significant harm to the applicant or child, attributable to conduct of the respondent, if the power of arrest is not attached to those provisions immediately.

(4) If, by virtue of subsection (3), the court attaches a power of arrest to any provisions of a relevant order, it may provide that the power of arrest is to have effect for a shorter period than the other provisions of the order.

(5) Any period specified for the purposes of subsection (4) may be extended by the court (on one or more occasions) on an application to vary or discharge the relevant order.

(6) If, by virtue of subsection (2) or (3), a power of arrest is attached to certain provisions of an order, a constable may arrest without warrant a person whom he has reasonable cause for suspecting to be in breach of any such provision.

(7) If a power of arrest is attached under subsection (2) or (3) to certain provisions of the order and the respondent is arrested under subsection (6)—

(a)   he must be brought before the relevant judicial authority within the period of 24 hours beginning at the time of his arrest; and
(b)   if the matter is not then disposed of forthwith, the relevant judicial authority before whom he is brought may remand him.

In reckoning for the purposes of this subsection any period of 24 hours, no account is to be taken of Christmas Day, Good Friday or any Sunday.

(8) If the court has made a relevant order but—

(a)   has not attached a power of arrest under subsection (2) or (3) to any provisions of the order, or
(b)   has attached that power only to certain provisions of the order,

then, if at any time the applicant considers that the respondent has failed to comply with the order, he may apply to the relevant judicial authority for the issue of a warrant for the arrest of the respondent.

(9) The relevant judicial authority shall not issue a warrant on an application under subsection (8) unless—

(a)   the application is substantiated on oath; and
(b)   the relevant judicial authority has reasonable grounds for believing that the respondent has failed to comply with the order.

(10) If a person is brought before a court by virtue of a warrant issued under subsection (9) and the court does not dispose of the matter forthwith, the court may remand him.

(11) Schedule 5 (which makes provision corresponding to that applying in magistrates' courts in civil cases under sections 128 and 129 of the Magistrates' Courts Act 1980) has effect in relation to the powers of the High Court and a county court to remand a person by virtue of this section.

(12) If a person remanded under this section is granted bail (whether in the High Court or a county court under Schedule 5 or in a magistrates' court under section 128 or 129 of the Magistrates' Courts Act 1980), he may be required by the relevant judicial authority to comply, before release on bail or later, with such

requirements as appear to that authority to be necessary to secure that he does not interfere with witnesses or otherwise obstruct the course of justice.

D–23   48.—(1) If the relevant judicial authority has reason to consider that a medical report will be required, any power to remand a person under section 47(7)(b) or (10) may be exercised for the purpose of enabling a medical examination and report to be made.

(2) If such a power is so exercised, the adjournment must not be for more than 4 weeks at a time unless the relevant judicial authority remands the accused in custody.

(3) If the relevant judicial authority so remands the accused, the adjournment must not be for more than 3 weeks at a time.

(4) If there is reason to suspect that a person who has been arrested—

(a)   under section 47(6), or

(b)   under a warrant issued on an application made under section 47(8),

is suffering from mental illness or severe mental impairment, the relevant judicial authority has the same power to make an order under section 35 of the Mental Health Act 1983 (remand for report on accused's mental condition) as the Crown Court has under section 35 of the Act of 1983 in the case of an accused person within the meaning of that section.

D–24   49.—(1) An occupation order or non-molestation order may be varied or discharged by the court on an application by—

(a)   the respondent, or

(b)   the person on whose application the order was made.

(2) In the case of a non-molestation order made by virtue of section 42(2)(b), the order may be varied or discharged by the court even though no such application has been made.

(3) If a spouse's matrimonial home rights are a charge on the estate or interest of the other spouse or of trustees for the other spouse, an order under section 33 against the other spouse may also be varied or discharged by the court on an application by any person deriving title under the other spouse or under the trustees and affected by the charge.

(4) If, by virtue of section 47(3), a power of arrest has been attached to certain provisions of an occupation order or non-molestation order, the court may vary or discharge the order under subsection (1) in so far as it confers a power of arrest (whether or not any application has been made to vary or discharge any other provision of the order).

Enforcement powers of magistrates' courts

D–25   50.—(1) If, under section 63(3) of the Magistrates' Courts Act 1980, a magistrates' court has power to commit a person to custody for breach of a relevant requirement, the court may by order direct that the execution of the order of committal is to be suspended for such period or on such terms and conditions as it may specify.

(2) In subsection (1) "a relevant requirement" means—

(a)   an occupation order or non-molestation order;

(b)   an exclusion requirement included by virtue of section 38A of the Children Act 1989 in an interim care order made under section 38 of that Act; or

(c)   an exclusion requirement included by virtue of section 44A of the Children Act 1989 in an emergency protection order under section 44 of that Act.

51.—(1) A magistrates' court has the same power to make a hospital order or guardianship order under section 37 of the Mental Health Act 1983 or an interim hospital order under section 38 of that Act in the case of a person suffering from mental illness or severe mental impairment who could otherwise be committed to custody for breach of a relevant requirement as a magistrates' court has under those sections in the case of a person convicted of an offence punishable on summary conviction with imprisonment.

(2) In subsection (1) "a relevant requirement" has the meaning given by section 50(2).

Interim care orders and emergency protection orders

52. Schedule 6 makes amendments of the provisions of the Children Act 1989 D–26 relating to interim care orders and emergency protection orders.

Transfer of tenancies

53. Schedule 7 makes provision in relation to the transfer of certain tenancies on divorce etc. or on separation of cohabitants.

Dwelling-house subject to mortgage

54.—(1) In determining for the purposes of this Part whether a person is entitled to occupy a dwelling-house by virtue of an estate or interest, any right to possession of the dwelling-house conferred on a mortgagee of the dwelling-house under or by virtue of his mortgage is to be disregarded.

(2) Subsection (1) applies whether or not the mortgagee is in possession.

(3) Where a person ("A") is entitled to occupy a dwelling-house by virtue of an estate or interest, a connected person does not by virtue of—

(a)   any matrimonial home rights conferred by section 30, or

(b)   any rights conferred by an order under section 35 or 36,

have any larger right against the mortgagee to occupy the dwelling-house than A has by virtue of his estate or interest and of any contract with the mortgagee.

(4) Subsection (3) does not apply, in the case of matrimonial home rights, if under section 31 those rights are a charge, affecting the mortgagee, on the estate or interest mortgaged.

(5) In this section "connected person", in relation to any person, means that person's spouse, former spouse, cohabitant or former cohabitant.

D–27 55.—(1) This section applies if a mortgagee of land which consists of or includes a dwelling-house brings an action in any court for the enforcement of his security.

(2) A connected person who is not already a party to the action is entitled to be made a party in the circumstances mentioned in subsection (3).

(3) The circumstances are that—

(a) the connected person is enabled by section 30(3) or (6) (or by section 30(3) or (6) as applied by section 35(13) or 36(13)), to meet the mortgagor's liabilities under the mortgage;

(b) he has applied to the court before the action is finally disposed of in that court; and

(c) the court sees no special reason against his being made a party to the action and is satisfied—

(i) that he may be expected to make such payments or do such other things in or towards satisfaction of the mortgagor's liabilities or obligations as might affect the outcome of the proceedings; or

(ii) that the expectation of it should be considered under section 36 of the Administration of Justice Act 1970.

(4) In this section "connected person" has the same meaning as in section 54.

D–28 56.—(1) This section applies if a mortgagee of land which consists, or substantially consists, of a dwelling-house brings an action for the enforcement of his security, and at the relevant time there is—

(a) in the case of unregistered land, a land charge of Class F registered against the person who is the estate owner at the relevant time or any person who, where the estate owner is a trustee, preceded him as trustee during the subsistence of the mortgage; or

(b) in the case of registered land, a subsisting registration of—

(i) a notice under section 31(10);

(ii) a notice under section 2(8) of the Matrimonial Homes Act 1983; or

(iii) a notice or caution under section 2(7) of the Matrimonial Homes Act 1967.

(2) If the person on whose behalf—

(a) the land charge is registered, or

(b) the notice or caution is entered,

is not a party to the action, the mortgagee must serve notice of the action on him.

(3) If—

(a) an official search has been made on behalf of the mortgagee which would disclose any land charge of Class F, notice or caution within subsection (1)(a) or (b),

(b) a certificate of the result of the search has been issued, and

(c) the action is commenced within the priority period,

the relevant time is the date of the certificate.

(4) In any other case the relevant time is the time when the action is commenced.

(5) The priority period is, for both registered and unregistered land, the period for which, in accordance with section 11(5) and (6) of the Land Charges Act 1972, a certificate on an official search operates in favour of a purchaser.

Jurisdiction and procedure etc.

57.—(1) For the purposes of this Part "the court" means the High Court, a   D–29 county court or a magistrates' court.

(2) Subsection (1) is subject to the provision made by or under the following provisions of this section, to section 59 and to any express provision as to the jurisdiction of any court made by any other provision of this Part.

(3) The Lord Chancellor may by order specify proceedings under this Part which may only be commenced in—

(a)   a specified level of court;

(b)   a court which falls within a specified class of court; or

(c)   a particular court determined in accordance with, or specified in, the order.

(4) The Lord Chancellor may by order specify circumstances in which specified proceedings under this Part may only be commenced in—

(a)   a specified level of court;

(b)   a court which falls within a specified class of court; or

(c)   a particular court determined in accordance with, or specified in, the order.

(5) The Lord Chancellor may by order provide that in specified circumstances the whole, or any specified part of any specified proceedings under this Part is to be transferred to—

(a)   a specified level of court;

(b)   a court which falls within a specified class of court; or

(c)   a particular court determined in accordance with, or specified in, the order.

(6) An order under subsection (5) may provide for the transfer to be made at any stage, or specified stage, of the proceedings and whether or not the proceedings, or any part of them, have already been transferred.

(7) An order under subsection (5) may make such provision as the Lord Chancellor thinks appropriate for excluding specified proceedings from the operation of section 38 or 39 of the Matrimonial and Family Proceedings Act 1984 (transfer of family proceedings) or any other enactment which would otherwise govern the transfer of those proceedings, or any part of them.

(8) For the purposes of subsections (3), (4) and (5), there are three levels of court—

(a)   the High Court;

(b)   any county court; and

(c)   any magistrates' court.

(9) The Lord Chancellor may by order make provision for the principal registry of the Family Division of the High Court to be treated as if it were a county court for specified purposes of this Part, or of any provision made under this Part.

(10) Any order under subsection (9) may make such provision as the Lord Chancellor thinks expedient for the purpose of applying (with or without modifications) provisions which apply in relation to the procedure in county courts to the principal registry when it acts as if it were a county court.

(11) In this section "specified" means specified by an order under this section.

D–30   **58.** The powers of the court in relation to contempt of court arising out of a person's failure to comply with an order under this Part may be exercised by the relevant judicial authority.

59.—(1) A magistrates' court shall not be competent to entertain any application, or make any order, involving any disputed question as to a party's entitlement to occupy any property by virtue of a beneficial estate or interest or contract or by virtue of any enactment giving him the right to remain in occupation, unless it is unnecessary to determine the question in order to deal with the application or make the order.

(2) A magistrates' court may decline jurisdiction in any proceedings under this Part if it considers that the case can more conveniently be dealt with by another court.

(3) The powers of a magistrates' court under section 63(2) of the Magistrates' Courts Act 1980 to suspend or rescind orders shall not apply in relation to any order made under this Part.

60.—(1) Rules of court may provide for a prescribed person, or any person in a prescribed category, ("a representative") to act on behalf of another in relation to proceedings to which this Part applies.

(2) Rules made under this section may, in particular, authorise a representative to apply for an occupation order or for a non-molestation order for which the person on whose behalf the representative is acting could have applied.

(3) Rules made under this section may prescribe—

(a)   conditions to be satisfied before a representative may make an application to the court on behalf of another; and

(b)   considerations to be taken into account by the court in determining whether, and if so how, to exercise any of its powers under this Part when a representative is acting on behalf of another.

(4) Any rules made under this section may be made so as to have effect for a specified period and may make consequential or transitional provision with respect to the expiry of the specified period.

(5) Any such rules may be replaced by further rules made under this section.

D–31   **61.**—(1) An appeal shall lie to the High Court against—

(a)   the making by a magistrates' court of any order under this Part, or

(b)   any refusal by a magistrates' court to make such an order,

but no appeal shall lie against any exercise by a magistrates' court of the power conferred by section 59(2).

(2) On an appeal under this section, the High Court may make such orders as may be necessary to give effect to its determination of the appeal.

(3) Where an order is made under subsection (2), the High Court may also make such incidental or consequential orders as appear to it to be just.

(4) Any order of the High Court made on an appeal under this section (other than one directing that an application be re-heard by a magistrates' court) shall, for the purposes—

(a)   of the enforcement of the order, and

(b)   of any power to vary, revive or discharge orders,

be treated as if it were an order of the magistrates' court from which the appeal was brought and not an order of the High Court.

(5) The Lord Chancellor may by order make provision as to the circumstances in which appeals may be made against decisions taken by courts on questions arising in connection with the transfer, or proposed transfer, of proceedings by virtue of any order under section 57(5).

(6) Except to the extent provided for in any order made under subsection (5), no appeal may be made against any decision of a kind mentioned in that subsection.

General

62.—(1) For the purposes of this Part—   D–32

(a)   "cohabitants" are a man and a woman who, although not married to each other, are living together as husband and wife; and

(b)   "former cohabitants" is to be read accordingly, but does not include cohabitants who have subsequently married each other.

(2) In this Part, "relevant child", in relation to any proceedings under this Part, means—

(a)   any child who is living with or might reasonably be expected to live with either party to the proceedings;

(b)   any child in relation to whom an order under the Adoption Act 1976 or the Children Act 1989 is in question in the proceedings; and

(c)   any other child whose interests the court considers relevant.

(3) For the purposes of this Part, a person is associated with another person if—

(a)   they are or have been married to each other;

(b)   they are cohabitants or former cohabitants;

(c)   they live or have lived in the same household, otherwise than merely by reason of one of them being the other's employee, tenant, lodger or boarder;

(d)   they are relatives;

(e)   they have agreed to marry one another (whether or not that agreement has been terminated);

(f)   in relation to any child, they are both persons falling within subsection (4); or

(g)   they are parties to the same family proceedings (other than proceedings under this Part).

(4) A person falls within this subsection in relation to a child if—

(a)   he is a parent of the child; or

(b)   he has or has had parental responsibility for the child.

(5) If a child has been adopted or has been freed for adoption by virtue of any of the enactments mentioned in section 16(1) of the Adoption Act 1976, two persons are also associated with each other for the purposes of this Part if—

(a)   one is a natural parent of the child or a parent of such a natural parent; and

(b)   the other is the child or any person—

    (i) who has become a parent of the child by virtue of an adoption order or has applied for an adoption order, or

    (ii) with whom the child has at any time been placed for adoption.

(6) A body corporate and another person are not, by virtue of subsection (3)(f) or (g), to be regarded for the purposes of this Part as associated with each other.

D–33   63.—(1) In this Part—

"adoption order" has the meaning given by section 72(1) of the Adoption Act 1976;

"associated", in relation to a person, is to be read with section 62(3) to (6);

"child" means a person under the age of eighteen years;

"cohabitant" and "former cohabitant" have the meaning given by section 62(1);

"the court" is to be read with section 57;

"development" means physical, intellectual, emotional, social or behavioural development;

"dwelling-house" includes (subject to subsection (4))—

(a)   any building or part of a building which is occupied as a dwelling,

(b)   any caravan, house-boat or structure which is occupied as a dwelling,

and any yard, garden, garage or outhouse belonging to it and occupied with it;

"family proceedings" means any proceedings—

(a)   under the inherent jurisdiction of the High Court in relation to children; or

(b)   under the enactments mentioned in subsection (2);

"harm"—

(a)   in relation to a person who has reached the age of eighteen years, means ill-treatment or the impairment of health; and

(b)   in relation to a child, means ill-treatment or the impairment of health or development;

"health" includes physical or mental health;

"ill-treatment" includes forms of ill-treatment which are not physical and, in relation to a child, includes sexual abuse;

"matrimonial home rights" has the meaning given by section 30;

"mortgage", "mortgagor" and "mortgagee" have the same meaning as in the Law of Property Act 1925;

"mortgage payments" includes any payments which, under the terms of the mortgage, the mortgagor is required to make to any person;

"non-molestation order" has the meaning given by section 42(1);

"occupation order" has the meaning given by section 39;

"parental responsibility" has the same meaning as in the Children Act 1989;

"relative", in relation to a person, means—

(a)   the father, mother, stepfather, stepmother, son, daughter, stepson, stepdaughter, grandmother, grandfather, grandson or granddaughter of that person or of that person's spouse or former spouse, or

(b)   the brother, sister, uncle, aunt, niece or nephew (whether of the full blood or of the half blood or by affinity) of that person or of that person's spouse or former spouse,

and includes, in relation to a person who is living or has lived with another person as husband and wife, any person who would fall within paragraph (a) or (b) if the parties were married to each other;

"relevant child", in relation to any proceedings under this Part, has the meaning given by section 62(2);

"the relevant judicial authority", in relation to any order under this Part, means—

(a)   where the order was made by the High Court, a judge of that court;

(b)   where the order was made by a county court, a judge or district judge of that or any other county court; or

(c)   where the order was made by a magistrates' court, any magistrates' court.

(2) The enactments referred to in the definition of "family proceedings" are—   D–34

(a)   Part II;

(b)   this Part;

(c)   the Matrimonial Causes Act 1973;

(d)   the Adoption Act 1976;

(e)   the Domestic Proceedings and Magistrates' Courts Act 1978;

(f)   Part III of the Matrimonial and Family Proceedings Act 1984;

(g)   Parts I, II and IV of the Children Act 1989;

(h)   section 30 of the Human Fertilisation and Embryology Act 1990.

(3) Where the question of whether harm suffered by a child is significant turns on the child's health or development, his health or development shall be compared with that which could reasonably be expected of a similar child.

(4) For the purposes of sections 31, 32, 53 and 54 and such other provisions of this Part (if any) as may be prescribed, this Part is to have effect as if paragraph (b) of the definition of "dwelling-house" were omitted.

(5) It is hereby declared that this Part applies as between the parties to a marriage even though either of them is, or has at any time during the marriage been, married to more than one person.

213

SCHEDULE 4

PROVISIONS SUPPLEMENTARY TO SECTIONS 30 AND 31

Interpretation

D–35   1.—(1) In this Schedule—

(a)   any reference to a solicitor includes a reference to a licensed conveyancer or a recognised body, and

(b)   any reference to a person's solicitor includes a reference to a licensed conveyancer or recognised body acting for that person.

(2) In sub-paragraph (1)—

"licensed conveyancer" has the meaning given by section 11(2) of the Administration of Justice Act 1985;

"recognised body" means a body corporate for the time being recognised under section 9 (incorporated practices) or section 32 (provision of conveyancing by recognised bodies) of that Act.

Restriction on registration where spouse entitled to more than one charge

2. Where one spouse is entitled by virtue of section 31 to a registrable charge in respect of each of two or more dwelling-houses, only one of the charges to which that spouse is so entitled shall be registered under section 31(10) or under section 2 of the Land Charges Act 1972 at any one time, and if any of those charges is registered under either of those provisions the Chief Land Registrar, on being satisfied that any other of them is so registered, shall cancel the registration of the charge first registered.

Contract for sale of house affected by registered charge to include term requiring cancellation of registration before completion

3.—(1) Where one spouse is entitled by virtue of section 31 to a charge on an estate in a dwelling-house and the charge is registered under section 31(10) or section 2 of the Land Charges Act 1972, it shall be a term of any contract for the sale of that estate whereby the vendor agrees to give vacant possession of the dwelling-house on completion of the contract that the vendor will before such completion procure the cancellation of the registration of the charge at his expense.

(2) Sub-paragraph (1) shall not apply to any such contract made by a vendor who is entitled to sell the estate in the dwelling-house freed from any such charge.

(3) If, on the completion of such a contract as is referred to in sub-paragraph (1), there is delivered to the purchaser or his solicitor an application by the spouse entitled to the charge for the cancellation of the registration of that charge, the term of the contract for which sub-paragraph (1) provides shall be deemed to have been performed.

(4) This paragraph applies only if and so far as a contrary intention is not expressed in the contract.

(5) This paragraph shall apply to a contract for exchange as it applies to a contract for sale.

(6) This paragraph shall, with the necessary modifications, apply to a contract for the grant of a lease or underlease of a dwelling-house as it applies to a contract for the sale of an estate in a dwelling-house.

Cancellation of registration after termination of marriage, etc.

4.—(1) Where a spouse's matrimonial home rights are a charge on an estate in **D–36** the dwelling-house and the charge is registered under section 31(10) or under section 2 of the Land Charges Act 1972, the Chief Land Registrar shall, subject to sub-paragraph (2), cancel the registration of the charge if he is satisfied—

(a) by the production of a certificate or other sufficient evidence, that either spouse is dead, or

(b) by the production of an official copy of a decree or order of a court, that the marriage in question has been terminated otherwise than by death, or

(c) by the production of an order of the court, that the spouse's matrimonial home rights constituting the charge have been terminated by the order.

(2) Where—

(a) the marriage in question has been terminated by the death of the spouse entitled to an estate in the dwelling-house or otherwise than by death, and

(b) an order affecting the charge of the spouse not so entitled had been made under section 33(5),

then if, after the making of the order, registration of the charge was renewed or the charge registered in pursuance of sub-paragraph (3), the Chief Land Registrar shall not cancel the registration of the charge in accordance with sub-paragraph (1) unless he is also satisfied that the order has ceased to have effect.

(3) Where such an order has been made, then, for the purposes of sub-paragraph (2), the spouse entitled to the charge affected by the order may—

(a) if before the date of the order the charge was registered under section 31(10) or under section 2 of the Land Charges Act 1972, renew the registration of the charge, and

(b) if before the said date the charge was not so registered, register the charge under section 31(10) or under section 2 of the Land Charges Act 1972.

(4) Renewal of the registration of a charge in pursuance of sub-paragraph (3) shall be effected in such manner as may be prescribed, and an application for such renewal or for registration of a charge in pursuance of that sub-paragraph shall contain such particulars of any order affecting the charge made under section 33(5) as may be prescribed.

(5) The renewal in pursuance of sub-paragraph (3) of the registration of a charge shall not affect the priority of the charge.

(6) In this paragraph "prescribed" means prescribed by rules made under section 16 of the Land Charges Act 1972 or section 144 of the Land Registration Act 1925, as the circumstances of the case require.

Release of matrimonial home rights

D–37   5.—(1) A spouse entitled to matrimonial home rights may by a release in writing release those rights or release them as respects part only of the dwelling-house affected by them.

(2) Where a contract is made for the sale of an estate or interest in a dwelling-house, or for the grant of a lease or underlease of a dwelling-house, being (in either case) a dwelling-house affected by a charge registered under section 31(10) or under section 2 of the Land Charges Act 1972, then, without prejudice to sub-paragraph (1), the matrimonial home rights constituting the charge shall be deemed to have been released on the happening of whichever of the following events first occurs—

(a)   the delivery to the purchaser or lessee, as the case may be, or his solicitor on completion of the contract of an application by the spouse entitled to the charge for the cancellation of the registration of the charge; or

(b)   the lodging of such an application at Her Majesty's Land Registry.

Postponement of priority of charge

6. A spouse entitled by virtue of section 31 to a charge on an estate or interest may agree in writing that any other charge on, or interest in, that estate or interest shall rank in priority to the charge to which that spouse is so entitled.

SCHEDULE 5

POWERS OF HIGH COURT AND COUNTY COURT TO REMAND

Interpretation

D–38   1. In this Schedule "the court" means the High Court or a county court and includes—

(a)   in relation to the High Court, a judge of that court, and

(b)   in relation to a county court, a judge or district judge of that court.

Remand in custody or on bail

2.—(1) Where a court has power to remand a person under section 47, the court may—

(a)   remand him in custody, that is to say, commit him to custody to be brought before the court at the end of the period of remand or at such earlier time as the court may require, or

(b)   remand him on bail—

   (i) by taking from him a recognizance (with or without sureties) conditioned as provided in sub-paragraph (3), or

   (ii) by fixing the amount of the recognizances with a view to their being taken subsequently in accordance with paragraph 4 and in the meantime committing the person to custody in accordance with paragraph (a).

(2) Where a person is brought before the court after remand, the court may further remand him.

(3) Where a person is remanded on bail under sub-paragraph (1), the court may direct that his recognizance be conditioned for his appearance—

(a) before that court at the end of the period of remand, or

(b) at every time and place to which during the course of the proceedings the hearing may from time to time be adjourned.

(4) Where a recognizance is conditioned for a person's appearance in accordance with sub-paragraph (1)(b), the fixing of any time for him next to appear shall be deemed to be a remand; but nothing in this sub-paragraph or sub-paragraph (3) shall deprive the court of power at any subsequent hearing to remand him afresh.

(5) Subject to paragraph 3, the court shall not remand a person under this paragraph for a period exceeding 8 clear days, except that—

(a) if the court remands him on bail, it may remand him for a longer period if he and the other party consent, and

(b) if the court adjourns a case under section 48(1), the court may remand him for the period of the adjournment.

(6) Where the court has power under this paragraph to remand a person in custody it may, if the remand is for a period not exceeding 3 clear days, commit him to the custody of a constable.

Further remand

3.—(1) If the court is satisfied that any person who has been remanded under D–39 paragraph 2 is unable by reason of illness or accident to appear or be brought before the court at the expiration of the period for which he was remanded, the court may, in his absence, remand him for a further time; and paragraph 2(5) shall not apply.

(2) Notwithstanding anything in paragraph 2(1), the power of the court under sub-paragraph (1) to remand a person on bail for a further time may be exercised by enlarging his recognizance and those of any sureties for him to a later time.

(3) Where a person remanded on bail under paragraph 2 is bound to appear before the court at any time and the court has no power to remand him under sub-paragraph (1), the court may in his absence enlarge his recognizance and those of any sureties for him to a later time; and the enlargement of his recognizance shall be deemed to be a further remand.

Postponement of taking of recognizance

4. Where under paragraph 2(1)(b)(ii) the court fixes the amount in which the principal and his sureties, if any, are to be bound, the recognizance may thereafter be taken by such person as may be prescribed by rules of court, and the same consequences shall follow as if it had been entered into before the court.

SCHEDULE 6

AMENDMENTS OF CHILDREN ACT 1989

1. After section 38 of the Children Act 1989 insert—

D–40

"38A.—(1) Where—

(a) on being satisfied that there are reasonable grounds for believing that the circumstances with respect to a child are as mentioned in section 31(2)(a) and (b)(i), the court makes an interim care order with respect to a child, and

(b) the conditions mentioned in subsection (2) are satisfied,

the court may include an exclusion requirement in the interim care order.

(2) The conditions are—

(a) that there is reasonable cause to believe that, if a person ("the relevant person") is excluded from a dwelling-house in which the child lives, the child will cease to suffer, or cease to be likely to suffer, significant harm, and

(b) that another person living in the dwelling-house (whether a parent of the child or some other person)—

(i) is able and willing to give to the child the care which it would be reasonable to expect a parent to give him, and

(ii) consents to the inclusion of the exclusion requirement.

(3) For the purposes of this section an exclusion requirement is any one or more of the following—

(a) a provision requiring the relevant person to leave a dwelling-house in which he is living with the child,

(b) a provision prohibiting the relevant person from entering a dwelling-house in which the child lives, and

(c) a provision excluding the relevant person from a defined area in which a dwelling-house in which the child lives is situated.

(4) The court may provide that the exclusion requirement is to have effect for a shorter period than the other provisions of the interim care order.

(5) Where the court makes an interim care order containing an exclusion requirement, the court may attach a power of arrest to the exclusion requirement.

(6) Where the court attaches a power of arrest to an exclusion requirement of an interim care order, it may provide that the power of arrest is to have effect for a shorter period than the exclusion requirement.

(7) Any period specified for the purposes of subsection (4) or (6) may be extended by the court (on one or more occasions) on an application to vary or discharge the interim care order.

(8) Where a power of arrest is attached to an exclusion requirement of an interim care order by virtue of subsection (5), a constable may arrest without warrant any person whom he has reasonable cause to believe to be in breach of the requirement.

(9) Sections 47(7), (11) and (12) and 48 of, and Schedule 5 to, the Family Law Act 1996 shall have effect in relation to a person arrested under subsection (8) of this section as they have effect in relation to a person arrested under section 47(6) of that Act.

(10) If, while an interim care order containing an exclusion requirement is in force, the local authority have removed the child from the dwelling-house from which the relevant person is excluded to other accommodation for a continuous

period of more than 24 hours, the interim care order shall cease to have effect in so far as it imposes the exclusion requirement.

38B.—(1) In any case where the court has power to include an exclusion **D–41** requirement in an interim care order, the court may accept an undertaking from the relevant person.

(2) No power of arrest may be attached to any undertaking given under subsection (1).

(3) An undertaking given to a court under subsection (1)—

(a) shall be enforceable as if it were an order of the court, and

(b) shall cease to have effect if, while it is in force, the local authority have removed the child from the dwelling-house from which the relevant person is excluded to other accommodation for a continuous period of more than 24 hours.

(4) This section has effect without prejudice to the powers of the High Court and county court apart from this section.

(5) In this section "exclusion requirement" and "relevant person" have the same meaning as in section 38A."

2. In section 39 of the Children Act 1989 (discharge and variation etc. of care orders and supervision orders) after subsection (3) insert—

"(3A) On the application of a person who is not entitled to apply for the order to be discharged, but who is a person to whom an exclusion requirement contained in the order applies, an interim care order may be varied or discharged by the court in so far as it imposes the exclusion requirement.

(3B) Where a power of arrest has been attached to an exclusion requirement of an interim care order, the court may, on the application of any person entitled to apply for the discharge of the order so far as it imposes the exclusion requirement, vary or discharge the order in so far as it confers a power of arrest (whether or not any application has been made to vary or discharge any other provision of the order)."

3. After section 44 of the Children Act 1989 insert—   **D–42**
"44A.—(1) Where—

(a) on being satisfied as mentioned in section 44(1)(a), (b) or (c), the court makes an emergency protection order with respect to a child, and

(b) the conditions mentioned in subsection (2) are satisfied,

the court may include an exclusion requirement in the emergency protection order.

(2) The conditions are—

(a) that there is reasonable cause to believe that, if a person ("the relevant person") is excluded from a dwelling-house in which the child lives, then—

(i) in the case of an order made on the ground mentioned in section 44(1)(a), the child will not be likely to suffer significant harm, even though the child is not removed as mentioned in section 44(1)(a)(i) or does not remain as mentioned in section 44(1)(a)(ii), or

(ii) in the case of an order made on the ground mentioned in paragraph (b) or (c) of section 44(1), the enquiries referred to in that paragraph will cease to be frustrated, and

(b) that another person living in the dwelling-house (whether a parent of the child or some other person)—

(i) is able and willing to give to the child the care which it would be reasonable to expect a parent to give him, and

(ii) consents to the inclusion of the exclusion requirement.

(3) For the purposes of this section an exclusion requirement is any one or more of the following—

(a) a provision requiring the relevant person to leave a dwelling-house in which he is living with the child,

(b) a provision prohibiting the relevant person from entering a dwelling-house in which the child lives, and

(c) a provision excluding the relevant person from a defined area in which a dwelling-house in which the child lives is situated.

(4) The court may provide that the exclusion requirement is to have effect for a shorter period than the other provisions of the order.

(5) Where the court makes an emergency protection order containing an exclusion requirement, the court may attach a power of arrest to the exclusion requirement.

(6) Where the court attaches a power of arrest to an exclusion requirement of an emergency protection order, it may provide that the power of arrest is to have effect for a shorter period than the exclusion requirement.

(7) Any period specified for the purposes of subsection (4) or (6) may be extended by the court (on one or more occasions) on an application to vary or discharge the emergency protection order.

(8) Where a power of arrest is attached to an exclusion requirement of an emergency protection order by virtue of subsection (5), a constable may arrest without warrant any person whom he has reasonable cause to believe to be in breach of the requirement.

(9) Sections 47(7), (11) and (12) and 48 of, and Schedule 5 to, the Family Law Act 1996 shall have effect in relation to a person arrested under subsection (8) of this section as they have effect in relation to a person arrested under section 47(6) of that Act.

(10) If, while an emergency protection order containing an exclusion requirement is in force, the applicant has removed the child from the dwelling-house from which the relevant person is excluded to other accommodation for a continuous period of more than 24 hours, the order shall cease to have effect in so far as it imposes the exclusion requirement.

D–43   44B.—(1) In any case where the court has power to include an exclusion requirement in an emergency protection order, the court may accept an undertaking from the relevant person.

220

(2) No power of arrest may be attached to any undertaking given under subsection (1).

(3) An undertaking given to a court under subsection (1)—

(a)   shall be enforceable as if it were an order of the court, and

(b)   shall cease to have effect if, while it is in force, the applicant has removed the child from the dwelling-house from which the relevant person is excluded to other accommodation for a continuous period of more than 24 hours.

(4) This section has effect without prejudice to the powers of the High Court and county court apart from this section.

(5) In this section "exclusion requirement" and "relevant person" have the same meaning as in section 44A.

4. In section 45 of the Children Act 1989 (duration of emergency protection orders and other supplemental provisions), insert after subsection (8)—

"(8A) On the application of a person who is not entitled to apply for the order to be discharged, but who is a person to whom an exclusion requirement contained in the order applies, an emergency protection order may be varied or discharged by the court in so far as it imposes the exclusion requirement.

(8B) Where a power of arrest has been attached to an exclusion requirement of an emergency protection order, the court may, on the application of any person entitled to apply for the discharge of the order so far as it imposes the exclusion requirement, vary or discharge the order in so far as it confers a power of arrest (whether or not any application has been made to vary or discharge any other provision of the order)."

5. In section 105(1) of the Children Act 1989 (interpretation), after the definition of "domestic premises", insert—

"dwelling-house" includes—

(a)   any building or part of a building which is occupied as a dwelling;

(b)   any caravan, house-boat or structure which is occupied as a dwelling;

and any yard, garden, garage or outhouse belonging to it and occupied with it;".

SCHEDULE 7

Transfer of Certain Tenancies on Divorce etc. or on Separation of Cohabitants

Part I

General

Interpretation

1. In this Schedule—   D–44

"cohabitant", except in paragraph 3, includes (where the context requires) former cohabitant;

"the court" does not include a magistrates' court,

"landlord" includes—

(a) any person from time to time deriving title under the original landlord; and

(b) in relation to any dwelling-house, any person other than the tenant who is, or (but for Part VII of the Rent Act 1977 or Part II of the Rent (Agriculture) Act 1976) would be, entitled to possession of the dwelling-house;

"Part II order" means an order under Part II of this Schedule;

"a relevant tenancy" means—

(a) a protected tenancy or statutory tenancy within the meaning of the Rent Act 1977;

(b) a statutory tenancy within the meaning of the Rent (Agriculture) Act 1976;

(c) a secure tenancy within the meaning of section 79 of the Housing Act 1985;

(d) an assured tenancy or assured agricultural occupancy within the meaning of Part I of the Housing Act 1988; or

[(e) an introductory tenancy within the meaning of Chapter I of Part V of the Housing Act 1996;]*

"spouse", except in paragraph 2, includes (where the context requires) former spouse; and

"tenancy" includes sub-tenancy.

*Material within square brackets omitted or substituted by the Housing Act 1996 (Consequential Amendments) Order 1997, S.I. 1997 No. 74, art 2, Sched. para. 10

Cases in which the court may make an order

2.—(1) This paragraph applies if one spouse is entitled, either in his own right or jointly with the other spouse, to occupy a dwelling-house by virtue of a relevant tenancy.

(2) At any time when it has power to make a property adjustment order under section 23A (divorce or separation) or 24 (nullity) of the Matrimonial Causes Act 1973 with respect to the marriage, the court may make a Part II order.

3.—(1) This paragraph applies if one cohabitant is entitled, either in his own right or jointly with the other cohabitant, to occupy a dwelling-house by virtue of a relevant tenancy.

(2) If the cohabitants cease to live together as husband and wife, the court may make a Part II order.

4. The court shall not make a Part II order unless the dwelling-house is or was—

(a) in the case of spouses, a matrimonial home; or

(b) in the case of cohabitants, a home in which they lived together as husband and wife.

Matters to which the court must have regard

5. In determining whether to exercise its powers under Part II of this Schedule and, if so, in what manner, the court shall have regard to all the circumstances of the case including—

(a)   the circumstances in which the tenancy was granted to either or both of the spouses or cohabitants or, as the case requires, the circumstances in which either or both of them became tenant under the tenancy;

(b)   the matters mentioned in section 33(6)(a), (b) and (c) and, where the parties are cohabitants and only one of them is entitled to occupy the dwelling-house by virtue of the relevant tenancy, the further matters mentioned in section 36(6)(e), (f), (g) and (h); and

(c)   the suitability of the parties as tenants.

PART II

ORDERS THAT MAY BE MADE

References to entitlement to occupy

6. References in this Part of this Schedule to a spouse or a cohabitant being **D–45** entitled to occupy a dwelling-house by virtue of a relevant tenancy apply whether that entitlement is in his own right or jointly with the other spouse or cohabitant.

Protected, secure or assured tenancy or assured agricultural occupancy

7.—(1) If a spouse or cohabitant is entitled to occupy the dwelling-house by virtue of a protected tenancy within the meaning of the Rent Act 1977, a secure tenancy within the meaning of the Housing Act 1985 [an assured tenancy] or assured agricultural occupancy within the meaning of Part I of the Housing Act 1988 [or an introductory tenancy within the meaning of Chapter I of Part V of the Housing Act 1996], the court may by order direct that, as from such date as may be specified in the order, there shall, by virtue of the order and without further assurance, be transferred to, and vested in, the other spouse or cohabitant—

(a)   the estate or interest which the spouse or cohabitant so entitled had in the dwelling-house immediately before that date by virtue of the lease or agreement creating the tenancy and any assignment of that lease or agreement, with all rights, privileges and appurtenances attaching to that estate or interest but subject to all covenants, obligations, liabilities and incumbrances to which it is subject; and

(b)   where the spouse or cohabitant so entitled is an assignee of such lease or agreement, the liability of that spouse or cohabitant under any covenant of indemnity by the assignee express or implied in the assignment of the lease or agreement to that spouse or cohabitant.

(2) If an order is made under this paragraph, any liability or obligation to which the spouse or cohabitant so entitled is subject under any covenant having reference to the dwelling-house in the lease or agreement, being a liability or obligation falling due to be discharged or performed on or after the date so specified, shall not be enforceable against that spouse or cohabitant.

(3) If the spouse so entitled is a successor within the meaning of Part IV of the Housing Act 1985, his former spouse or former cohabitant (or, if a separation order

is in force, his spouse) shall be deemed also to be a successor within the meaning of that Part.

[(3A) If the spouse or cohabitant so entitled is a successor within the meaning of section 132 of the Housing Act 1996, his former spouse or former cohabitant (or, if a separation order is in force, his spouse) shall be deemed also to be a successor within the meaning of that section].

(4) If the spouse or cohabitant so entitled is for the purpose of section 17 of the Housing Act 1988 a successor in relation to the tenancy or occupancy, his former spouse or former cohabitant (or, if a separation order is in force, his spouse) is to be deemed to be a successor in relation to the tenancy or occupancy for the purposes of that section.

(5) If the transfer under sub-paragraph (1) is of an assured agricultural occupancy, then, for the purposes of Chapter III of Part I of the Housing Act 1988—

(a)   the agricultural worker condition is fulfilled with respect to the dwelling-house while the spouse or cohabitant to whom the assured agricultural occupancy is transferred continues to be the occupier under that occupancy, and

(b)   that condition is to be treated as so fulfilled by virtue of the same paragraph of Schedule 3 to the Housing Act 1988 as was applicable before the transfer.

(6) In this paragraph, references to a separation order being in force include references to there being a judicial separation in force.

N.B. Material in square brackets added by the Housing Act 1996 (Consequential Amendments) Order 1997 S.I. 1997 No. 74, art. 2, Sched. para. 10

Statutory tenancy within the meaning of the Rent Act 1977

D–46   8.—(1) This paragraph applies if the spouse or cohabitant is entitled to occupy the dwelling-house by virtue of a statutory tenancy within the meaning of the Rent Act 1977.

(2) The court may by order direct that, as from the date specified in the order—

(a)   that spouse or cohabitant is to cease to be entitled to occupy the dwelling-house; and

(b)   the other spouse or cohabitant is to be deemed to be the tenant or, as the case may be, the sole tenant under that statutory tenancy.

(3) The question whether the provisions of paragraphs 1 to 3, or (as the case may be) paragraphs 5 to 7 of Schedule 1 to the Rent Act 1977, as to the succession by the surviving spouse of a deceased tenant, or by a member of the deceased tenant's family, to the right to retain possession are capable of having effect in the event of the death of the person deemed by an order under this paragraph to be the tenant or sole tenant under the statutory tenancy is to be determined according as those provisions have or have not already had effect in relation to the statutory tenancy.

Statutory tenancy within the meaning of the Rent (Agriculture) Act 1976

9.—(1) This paragraph applies if the spouse or cohabitant is entitled to occupy the dwelling-house by virtue of a statutory tenancy within the meaning of the Rent (Agriculture) Act 1976.

(2) The court may by order direct that, as from such date as may be specified in the order—

(a) that spouse or cohabitant is to cease to be entitled to occupy the dwelling-house; and

(b) the other spouse or cohabitant is to be deemed to be the tenant or, as the case may be, the sole tenant under that statutory tenancy.

(3) A spouse or cohabitant who is deemed under this paragraph to be the tenant under a statutory tenancy is (within the meaning of that Act) a statutory tenant in his own right, or a statutory tenant by succession, according as the other spouse or cohabitant was a statutory tenant in his own right or a statutory tenant by succession.

PART III

SUPPLEMENTARY PROVISIONS

Compensation

10.—(1) If the court makes a Part II order, it may by the order direct the making D–47 of a payment by the spouse or cohabitant to whom the tenancy is transferred ("the transferee") to the other spouse or cohabitant ("the transferor").

(2) Without prejudice to that, the court may, on making an order by virtue of sub-paragraph (1) for the payment of a sum—

(a) direct that payment of that sum or any part of it is to be deferred until a specified date or until the occurrence of a specified event, or

(b) direct that that sum or any part of it is to be paid by instalments.

(3) Where an order has been made by virtue of sub-paragraph (1), the court may, on the application of the transferee or the transferor—

(a) exercise its powers under sub-paragraph (2), or

(b) vary any direction previously given under that sub-paragraph,

at any time before the sum whose payment is required by the order is paid in full.

(4) In deciding whether to exercise its powers under this paragraph and, if so, in what manner, the court shall have regard to all the circumstances including—

(a) the financial loss that would otherwise be suffered by the transferor as a result of the order;

(b) the financial needs and financial resources of the parties; and

(c) the financial obligations which the parties have, or are likely to have in the foreseeable future, including financial obligations to each other and to any relevant child.

(5) The court shall not give any direction under sub-paragraph (2) unless it appears to it that immediate payment of the sum required by the order would cause

the transferee financial hardship which is greater than any financial hardship that would be caused to the transferor if the direction were given.

Liabilities and obligations in respect of the dwelling-house

D–48   11.—(1) If the court makes a Part II order, it may by the order direct that both spouses or cohabitants are to be jointly and severally liable to discharge or perform any or all of the liabilities and obligations in respect of the dwelling-house (whether arising under the tenancy or otherwise) which—

(a)   have at the date of the order fallen due to be discharged or performed by one only of them; or

(b)   but for the direction, would before the date specified as the date on which the order is to take effect fall due to be discharged or performed by one only of them.

(2) If the court gives such a direction, it may further direct that either spouse or cohabitant is to be liable to indemnify the other in whole or in part against any payment made or expenses incurred by the other in discharging or performing any such liability or obligation.

Date when order made between spouses is to take effect

12.—(1) In the case of a decree of nullity of marriage, the date specified in a Part II order as the date on which the order is to take effect must not be earlier than the date on which the decree is made absolute.

(2) In the case of divorce proceedings or separation proceedings, the date specified in a Part II order as the date on which the order is to take effect is to be determined as if the court were making a property adjustment order under section 23A of the Matrimonial Causes Act 1973 (regard being had to the restrictions imposed by section 23B of that Act).

Remarriage of either spouse

D–49   13.—(1) If after the making of a divorce order or the grant of a decree annulling a marriage either spouse remarries, that spouse is not entitled to apply, by reference to the making of that order or the grant of that decree, for a Part II order.

(2) For the avoidance of doubt it is hereby declared that the reference in sub-paragraph (1) to remarriage includes a reference to a marriage which is by law void or voidable.

Rules of court

14.—(1) Rules of court shall be made requiring the court, before it makes an order under this Schedule, to give the landlord of the dwelling-house to which the order will relate an opportunity of being heard.

(2) Rules of court may provide that an application for a Part II order by reference to an order or decree may not, without the leave of the court by which that order

was made or decree was granted, be made after the expiration of such period from the order or grant as may be prescribed by the rules.

Saving for other provisions of Act

15.—(1) If a spouse is entitled to occupy a dwelling-house by virtue of a tenancy, this Schedule does not affect the operation of sections 30 and 31 in relation to the other spouse's matrimonial home rights.

(2) If a spouse or cohabitant is entitled to occupy a dwelling-house by virtue of a tenancy, the court's powers to make orders under this Schedule are additional to those conferred by sections 33, 35 and 36.

SCHEDULE 8

PART III

AMENDMENTS CONNECTED WITH PART IV

The Land Registration Act 1925 (c.21)

45. In section 64 of the Land Registration Act 1925 (certificates to be produced D–50 and noted on dealings) in subsection (5) for "section 2(8) of the Matrimonial Homes Act 1983" substitute "section 31(10) of the Family Law Act 1996" and for "rights of occupation" substitute "matrimonial home rights".

The Land Charges Act 1972 (c.61)

46. In section 1(6A) of the Land Charges Act 1972 (cases where county court has jurisdiction to vacate registration) in paragraph (d)—

(a) after "section 1 of the Matrimonial Homes Act 1983" insert "or section 33 of the Family Law Act 1996"; and
(b) for "that section" substitute "either of those sections".

47. In section 2(7) of that Act (Class F land charge) for "Matrimonial Homes Act 1983" substitute "Part IV of the Family Law Act 1996".

The Land Compensation Act 1973 (c. 26)

48.—(1) Section 29A of the Land Compensation Act 1973 (spouses having statutory rights of occupation) is amended as follows.

(2) In subsection (1), for "rights of occupation (within the meaning of the Matrimonial Homes Act 1983)" substitute "matrimonial home rights (within the meaning of Part IV of the Family Law Act 1996)".

(3) In subsection (2)(a), for "rights of occupation" substitute "matrimonial home rights".

The Magistrates' Courts Act 1980 (c. 43)

D–51   49. In section 65(1) of the Magistrates' Courts Act 1980 (meaning of family proceedings) after paragraph (o) insert—

"(p) Part IV of the Family Law Act 1996;".

The Contempt of Court Act 1981 (c. 49)

50. In Schedule 3 to the Contempt of Court Act 1981 (application of Magistrates' Courts Act 1980 to civil contempt proceedings), in paragraph 3 for the words from "or, having been arrested" onwards substitute—

"or, having been arrested under section 47 of the Family Law Act 1996 in connection with the matter of the complaint, is at large after being remanded under subsection (7)(b) or (10) of that section."

The Supreme Court Act 1981 (c. 51)

51. In Schedule 1 to the Supreme Court Act 1981 (distribution of business in High Court), in paragraph 3 (Family Division)—

(a)   in paragraph (d), after "matrimonial proceedings" insert "or proceedings under Part IV of the Family Law Act 1996", and

(b)   in paragraph (f)(i), for "Domestic Violence and Matrimonial Proceedings Act 1976" substitute "Part IV of the Family Law Act 1996".

The Matrimonial and Family Proceedings Act 1984 (c. 42)

D–52   52. For section 22 of the Matrimonial and Family Proceedings Act 1984 substitute—

"22.—(1) This section applies if—

(a)   an application is made by a party to a marriage for an order for financial relief; and

(b)   one of the parties is entitled, either in his own right or jointly with the other party, to occupy a dwelling-house situated in England or Wales by virtue of a tenancy which is a relevant tenancy within the meaning of Schedule 7 to the Family Law Act 1996 (certain statutory tenancies).

(2) The court may make in relation to that dwelling-house any order which it could make under Part II of that Schedule if—

(a)   a divorce order,

(b)   a separation order, or

(c)   a decree of nullity of marriage,

had been made or granted in England and Wales in respect of the marriage.

(3) The provisions of paragraphs 10, 11 and 14(1) in Part III of that Schedule apply in relation to any order under this section as they apply to any order under Part II of that Schedule."

The Housing Act 1985 (c. 68)

53.—(1) Section 85 of the Housing Act 1985 (extended discretion of court in **D–53** certain proceedings for possession) is amended as follows.

(2) In subsection (5)—

(a)   in paragraph (a), for "rights of occupation under the Matrimonial Homes Act 1983" substitute "matrimonial home rights under Part IV of the Family Law Act 1996"; and

(b)   for "those rights of occupation" substitute "those matrimonial home rights".

(3) After subsection (5) insert—

"(5A) If proceedings are brought for possession of a dwelling-house which is let under a secure tenancy and—

(a)   an order is in force under section 35 of the Family Law Act 1996 conferring rights on the former spouse of the tenant or an order is in force under section 36 of that Act conferring rights on a cohabitant or former cohabitant (within the meaning of that Act) of the tenant,

(b)   the former spouse, cohabitant or former cohabitant is then in occupation of the dwelling-house, and

(c)   the tenancy is terminated as a result of those proceedings,

the former spouse, cohabitant or former cohabitant shall, so long as he or she remains in occupation, have the same rights in relation to, or in connection with, any adjournment, stay, suspension or postponement in pursuance of this section as he or she would have if the rights conferred by the order referred to in paragraph (a) were not affected by the termination of the tenancy."

54. In section 99B of that Act (persons qualifying for compensation for improvements) in subsection (2) for paragraph (f) substitute—

"(f) a spouse, former spouse, cohabitant or former cohabitant of the improving tenant to whom the tenancy has been transferred by an order made under Schedule 1 to the Matrimonial Homes Act 1983 or Schedule 7 to the Family Law Act 1996."

55. In section 101 of that Act (rent not to be increased on account of tenant's **D–54** improvements) in subsection (3) for paragraph (d) substitute—

"(d) a spouse, former spouse, cohabitant or former cohabitant of the tenant to whom the tenancy has been transferred by an order made under Schedule 1 to the Matrimonial Homes Act 1983 or Schedule 7 to the Family Law Act 1996."

56. In section 171B of that Act (extent of preserved right to buy: qualifying persons and dwelling-houses) in subsection (4)(b)(ii) after "Schedule 1 to the Matrimonial Homes Act 1983" insert "or Schedule 7 to the Family Law Act 1996".

The Insolvency Act 1986 (c. 45)

57.—(1) Section 336 of the Insolvency Act 1986 (rights of occupation etc. of bankrupt's spouse) is amended as follows.

(2) In subsection (1), for "rights of occupation under the Matrimonial Homes Act 1983" substitute "matrimonial home rights under Part IV of the Family Law Act 1996".

(3) In subsection (2)—

(a)　for "rights of occupation under the Act of 1983" substitute "matrimonial home rights under the Act of 1996", and

(b)　in paragraph (b), for "under section 1 of that Act" substitute "under section 33 of that Act".

(4) In subsection (4), for "section 1 of the Act of 1983" substitute "section 33 of the Act of 1996".

58.—(1) Section 337 of that Act is amended as follows.

D–55　(2) In subsection (2), for "rights of occupation under the Matrimonial Homes Act 1983" substitute "matrimonial home rights under Part IV of the Family Law Act 1996".

(3) For subsection (3) substitute—

"(3) The Act of 1996 has effect, with the necessary modifications, as if—

(a)　the rights conferred by paragraph (a) of subsection (2) were matrimonial home rights under that Act,

(b)　any application for such leave as is mentioned in that paragraph were an application for an order under section 33 of that Act, and

(c)　any charge under paragraph (b) of that subsection on the estate or interest of the trustee were a charge under that Act on the estate or interest of a spouse."

(4) In subsections (4) and (5) for "section 1 of the Act of 1983" substitute "section 33 of the Act of 1996".

The Housing Act 1988 (c. 50)

D–56　59.—(1) Section 9 of the Housing Act 1988 (extended discretion of court in possession claims) is amended as follows.

(2) In subsection (5)—

(a)　In paragraph (a), for "rights of occupation under the Matrimonial Homes Act 1983" substitute "matrimonial home rights under Part IV of the Family Law Act 1996", and

(b)　for "those rights of occupation" substitute "those matrimonial home rights".

(3) After subsection (5) insert—

"(5A) In any case where—

(a)　at a time when proceedings are brought for possession of a dwelling-house let on an assured tenancy—

(i) an order is in force under section 35 of the Family Law Act 1996 conferring rights on the former spouse of the tenant, or

(ii) an order is in force under section 36 of that Act conferring rights on a cohabitant or former cohabitant (within the meaning of that Act) of the tenant,

(b)   that cohabitant, former cohabitant or former spouse is then in occupation of the dwelling-house, and

(c)   the assured tenancy is terminated as a result of those proceedings,

the cohabitant, former cohabitant or former spouse shall have the same rights in relation to, or in connection with, any such adjournment as is referred to in subsection (1) above or any such stay, suspension or postponement as is referred to in subsection (2) above as he or she would have if the rights conferred by the order referred to in paragraph (a) above were not affected by the termination of the tenancy."

The Children Act 1989 (c. 41)

60.—(1) In section 8(4) of the Children Act 1989 (meaning of "family **D–57** proceedings" for purposes of that Act), omit paragraphs (c) and (f) and after paragraph (g) insert—

"(h)   the Family Law Act 1996."

(2) In Schedule 11 to that Act, in paragraph 6(a) (amendment of the Domestic Proceedings and Magistrates' Courts Act 1978), for "sections 16(5)(c) and" substitute "section".

The Courts and Legal Services Act 1990 (c. 41)

61. In section 58 of the Courts and Legal Services Act 1990 (conditional fee agreements) in subsection (10), omit paragraphs (b) and (e) and immediately before the "or" following paragraph (g) insert—

"(gg)   Part IV of the Family Law Act 1996".

SCHEDULE 9

MODIFICATIONS, SAVING AND TRANSITIONAL

Pending applications for orders relating to occupation and molestation

8.—(1) In this paragraph and paragraph 10 "the existing enactments" means— **D–58**

(a)   the Domestic Violence and Matrimonial Proceedings Act 1976;

(b)   sections 16 to 18 of the Domestic Proceedings and Magistrates' Courts Act 1978; and

(c)   sections 1 and 9 of the 1983 Act.

(2) Nothing in Part IV, Part III of Schedule 8 or Schedule 10 affects any application for an order or injunction under any of the existing enactments which is pending immediately before the commencement of the repeal of that enactment.

Pending applications under Schedule 1 to the Matrimonial Homes Act 1983

9. Nothing in Part IV, Part III of Schedule 8 or Schedule 10 affects any application for an order under Schedule 1 to the 1983 Act which is pending immediately before the commencement of the repeal of that Schedule.

Existing orders relating to occupation and molestation

10.—(1) In this paragraph "an existing order" means any order or injunction under any of the existing enactments which—

(a)   is in force immediately before the commencement of the repeal of that enactment; or

(b)   was made or granted after that commencement in proceedings brought before that commencement.

(2) Subject to sub-paragraphs (3) and (4), nothing in Part IV, Part III of Schedule 8 or Schedule 10—

(a)   prevents an existing order from remaining in force; or

(b)   affects the enforcement of an existing order.

(3) Nothing in Part IV, Part III of Schedule 8 or Schedule 10 affects any application to extend, vary or discharge an existing order, but the court may, if it thinks it just and reasonable to do so, treat the application as an application for an order under Part IV.

(4) The making of an order under Part IV between parties with respect to whom an existing order is in force discharges the existing order.

Matrimonial home rights

D–59   11.—(1) Any reference (however expressed) in any enactment, instrument or document (whether passed or made before or after the passing of this Act) to rights of occupation under, or within the meaning of, the 1983 Act shall be construed, so far as is required for continuing the effect of the instrument or document, as being or as the case requires including a reference to matrimonial home rights under, or within the meaning of, Part IV.

(2) Any reference (however expressed) in this Act or in any other enactment, instrument or document (including any enactment amended by Schedule 8) to matrimonial home rights under, or within the meaning of, Part IV shall be construed as including, in relation to times, circumstances and purposes before the commencement of sections 30 to 32, a reference to rights of occupation under, or within the meaning of, the 1983 Act.

12.—(1) Any reference (however expressed) in any enactment, instrument or document (whether passed or made before or after the passing of this Act) to registration under section 2(8) of the 1983 Act shall, in relation to any time after the commencement of sections 30 to 32, be construed as being or as the case requires including a reference to registration under section 31(10).

(2) Any reference (however expressed) in this Act or in any other enactment, instrument or document (including any enactment amended by Schedule 8) to registration under section 31(10) shall be construed as including a reference to—

(a)   registration under section 2(7) of the Matrimonial Homes Act 1967 or section 2(8) of the 1983 Act, and

(b)   registration by caution duly lodged under section 2(7) of the Matrimonial Homes Act 1967 before 14th February 1983 (the date of the commencement of section 4(2) of the Matrimonial Homes and Property Act 1981).

13. In sections 30 and 31 and Schedule 4—   D–60

(a)   any reference to an order made under section 33 shall be construed as
including a reference to an order made under section 1 of the 1983 Act, and

(b)   any reference to an order made under section 33(5) shall be construed as
including a reference to an order made under section 1 of the 1983 Act by
virtue of section 2(4) of that Act.

14. Neither section 31(11) nor the repeal by the Matrimonial Homes and
Property Act 1981 of the words "or caution" in section 2(7) of the Matrimonial
Homes Act 1967, affects any caution duly lodged as respects any estate or interest
before 14th February 1983.

15. Nothing in this Schedule is to be taken to prejudice the operation of sections
16 and 17 of the Interpretation Act 1978 (which relate to the effect of repeals).

SCHEDULE 10

REPEALS

D–61

Chapter	Short title	Extent of repeal
1968 c. 63.	The Domestic and Appellate Proceedings (Restriction of Publicity) Act 1968.	Section 2(1)(b).
1973 c. 18.	The Matrimonial Causes Act 1973.	Sections 1 to 7.
		In section 8(1)(b), the words "or before the decree nisi is made absolute".
		Sections 9 and 10.
		Sections 17 and 18.
		Section 20.
		Section 22.
		In section 24A(3), the words "divorce or".
		In section 25(2)(h), the words "in the case of proceedings for divorce or nullity of marriage,".
		In section 28(1), the words from "in", in the first place where it occurs, to "nullity of marriage" in the first place where those words occur.

Chapter	Short title	Extent of repeal
		In section 29(2), the words from "may begin" to "but".
		In section 30, the words "divorce" and "or judicial separation".
		In section 31, in subsection (2)(a), the words "order for maintenance pending suit and any".
		In section 41, in subsection (1) the words "divorce or" and "or a decree of judicial separation" and in subsection (2) the words "divorce or" and "or that the decree of judicial separation is not to be granted."
		Section 49.
		In section 52(2)(b), the words "to orders for maintenance pending suit and", "respectively" and "section 22 and".
		In Schedule 1, paragraph 8.
1973 c. 45.	The Domicile and Matrimonial Proceedings Act 1973.	In section 5, in subsection (1), the words "subject to section 6(3) and (4) of this Act" and, in paragraph (a), "divorce, judicial separation or" and subsection (2).
		Section 6(3) and (4).
		In Schedule 1, in paragraph 11, in sub-paragraph (2)(a), in sub-paragraph (2)(c), in the first place where they occur, and in sub-paragraph (3)(b) and (c), the words "in connection with the stayed proceedings".
1976 c. 50.	The Domestic Violence and Matrimonial Proceedings Act 1976.	The whole Act.

Chapter	Short title	Extent of repeal
1978 c. 22.	The Domestic Proceedings and Magistrates' Courts Act 1978	In section 1, paragraphs (c) and (d) and the word "or" preceding paragraph (c).
		In section 7(1), the words "neither party having deserted the other".
		Sections 16 to 18.
		Section 28(2).
		Section 63(3).
		In Schedule 2, paragraphs 38 and 53.
1980 c. 43.	The Magistrates' Courts Act 1980.	In Schedule 7, paragraph 159.
1981 c. 54.	The Supreme Court Act 1981.	In section 18(1)(d), the words "divorce or".
1982 c. 53.	The Administration of Justice Act 1982.	Section 16.
1983 c. 19.	The Matrimonial Homes Act 1983.	The whole Act.
1984 c. 42.	The Matrimonial and Family Proceedings Act 1984	Section 1.
		In section 21(f) the words "except subsection (2)(e) and subsection (4)".
		In section 27, the definition of "secured periodical payments order".
		In Schedule 1, paragraph 10.
1985 c. 61.	The Administration of Justice Act 1985.	In section 34(2), paragraph (f) and the word "and" immediately preceding it.
		In Schedule 2, in paragraph 37, paragraph (e) and the word "and" immediately preceding it.
1985 c. 71	The Housing (Consequential Provisions) Act 1985	In Schedule 2, paragraph 56.

Chapter	Short title	Extent of repeal
1986 c. 53.	The Building Societies Act 1986.	In Schedule 21, paragraph 9(f).
1986 c. 55.	The Family Law Act 1986.	In Schedule 1, paragraph 27.
1988 c. 34.	The Legal Aid Act 1988.	In section 16(9), the word "and" at the end of paragraph (a).
1988 c. 50.	The Housing Act 1988.	In Schedule 17, paragraphs 33 and 34.
1989 c. 41.	The Children Act 1989.	Section 8(4)(c) and (f).
		In Schedule 11, paragraph 6(b).
		In Schedule 13, paragraphs 33(1) and 65(1).
1990 c. 41.	The Courts and Legal Services Act 1990.	Section 58(10)(b) and (e).
		In Schedule 18, paragraph 21.
1995 c. 42.	The Private International Law (Miscellaneous Provisions) Act 1995.	In the Schedule, paragraph 3.

Children Act 1989

The Children Act 1989 appears as amended by the Family Law Act 1996. These amendments are not, at the date of writing yet in force and the reader is advised to check the date of their implementation.

PART I

INTRODUCTORY

Welfare of the child

D–62   1.—(1) When a court determines any question with respect to—

(a)   the upbringing of a child; or

(b)   the administration of a child's property or the application of any income arising from it, the child's welfare shall be the court's paramount consideration.

(2) In any proceedings in which any question with respect to the upbringing of a child arises, the court shall have regard to the general principle that any delay in determining the question is likely to prejudice the welfare of the child.

(3) In the circumstances mentioned in subsection (4), a court shall have regard in particular to—

(a)   the ascertainable wishes and feelings of the child concerned (considered in the light of his age and understanding);
(b)   his physical, emotional and educational needs;
(c)   the likely effect on him of any change in his circumstances;
(d)   his age, sex, background and any characteristics of his which the court considers relevant;
(e)   any harm which he has suffered or is at risk of suffering;
(f)   how capable each of his parents, and any other person in relation to whom the court considers the question to be relevant, is of meeting his needs;
(g)   the range of powers available to the court under this Act in the proceedings in question.

(4) The circumstances are that—

(a)   the court is considering whether to make, vary or discharge a section 8 order, and the making, variation or discharge of the order is opposed by any party to the proceedings; or
(b)   the court is considering whether to make, vary or discharge an order under Part IV.

(5) Where a court is considering whether or not to make one or more orders under this Act with respect to a child, it shall not make the order or any of the orders unless it considers that doing so would be better for the child than making no order at all.

Parental responsibility for children

2.—(1) Where a child's father and mother were married to each other at the time D–63 of his birth, they shall each have parental responsibility for the child.

(2) Where a child's father and mother were not married to each other at the time of his birth—

(a)   the mother shall have parental responsibility for the child;
(b)   the father shall not have parental responsibility for the child, unless he acquires it in accordance with the provisions of this Act.

(3) References in this Act to a child whose father and mother were, or (as the case may be) were not, married to each other at the time of his birth must be read with section 1 of the Family Law Reform Act 1987 (which extends their meaning).

(4) The rule of law that a father is the natural guardian of his legitimate child is abolished.

(5) More than one person may have parental responsibility for the same child at the same time.

(6) A person who has parental responsibility for a child at any time shall not cease to have that responsibility solely because some other person subsequently acquires parental responsibility for the child.

(7) Where more than one person has parental responsibility for a child, each of them may act alone and without the other (or others) in meeting that responsibility; but nothing in this Part shall be taken to affect the operation of any enactment which requires the consent of more than one person in a matter affecting the child.

(8) The fact that a person has parental responsibility for a child shall not entitle him to act in any way which would be incompatible with any order made with respect to the child under this Act.

(9) A person who has parental responsibility for a child may not surrender or transfer any part of that responsibility to another but may arrange for some or all of it to be met by one or more persons acting on his behalf.

(10) The person with whom any such arrangement is made may himself be a person who already has parental responsibility for the child concerned.

(11) The making of any such arrangement shall not affect any liability of the person making it which may arise from any failure to meet any part of his parental responsibility for the child concerned.

Meaning of "parental responsibility"

D–64   3.—(1) In this Act "parental responsibility" means all the rights, duties, powers, responsibilities and authority which by law a parent of a child has in relation to the child and his property.

(2) It also includes the rights, powers and duties which a guardian of the child's estate (appointed, before the commencement of section 5, to act generally) would have had in relation to the child and his property.

(3) The rights referred to in subsection (2) include, in particular, the right of the guardian to receive or recover in his own name, for the benefit of the child, property of whatever description and wherever situated which the child is entitled to receive or recover.

(4) The fact that a person has, or does not have, parental responsibility for a child shall not affect—

(a)   any obligation which he may have in relation to the child (such as a statutory duty to maintain the child); or

(b)   any rights which, in the event of the child's death, he (or any other person) may have in relation to the child's property.

(5) A person who—

(a)   does not have parental responsibility for a particular child; but

(b)   has care of the child,

may (subject to the provisions of this Act) do what is reasonable in all the circumstances of the case for the purpose of safeguarding or promoting the child's welfare.

Acquisition of parental responsibility by father

4.—(1)Where a child's father and mother were not married to each other at the **D–65** time of his birth—

(a)   the court may, on the application of the father, order that he shall have parental responsibility for the child; or

(b)   the father and mother may by agreement ("a parental responsibility agreement") provide for the father to have parental responsibility for the child.

(2) No parental responsibility agreement shall have effect for the purposes of this Act unless—

(a)   it is made in the form prescribed by regulations made by the Lord Chancellor; and

(b)   where regulations are made by the Lord Chancellor prescribing the manner in which such agreements must be recorded, it is recorded in the prescribed manner.

(3) Subject to section 12(4), an order under subsection (1)(a), or a parental responsibility agreement, may only be brought to an end by an order of the court made on the application—

(a)   of any person who has parental responsibility for the child; or

(b)   with leave of the court, of the child himself.

(4) The court may only grant leave under subsection (3)(b) if it is satisfied that the child has sufficient understanding to make the proposed application.

PART II

ORDERS WITH RESPECT TO CHILDREN IN FAMILY PROCEEDINGS

General

Residence, contact and other orders with respect to children

8.—(1) In this Act—   **D–66**

"a contact order" means an order requiring the person with whom a child lives, or is to live, to allow the child to visit or stay with the person named in the order, or for that person and the child otherwise to have contact with each other;

"a prohibited steps order" means an order that no step which could be taken by a parent in meeting his parental responsibility for a child, and which is of a kind specified in the order, shall be taken by any person without the consent of the court;

"a residence order" means an order settling the arrangements to be made as to the person with whom a child is to live; and

"a specific issue order" means an order giving directions for the purpose of determining a specific question which has arisen, or which may arise, in connection with any aspect of parental responsibility for a child.

(2) In this Act "a section 8 order" means any of the orders mentioned in subsection (1) and any order varying or discharging such an order.

(3) For the purposes of this Act "family proceedings" means (subject to subsection (5)) any proceedings—

(a)   under the inherent jurisdiction of the High Court in relation to children; and

(b)   under the enactments mentioned in subsection (4),
but does not include proceedings on an application for leave under section 100(3).

(4) The enactments are—

(a)   Parts I, II and IV of this Act;

(b)   the Matrimonial Causes Act 1973;

(c)   [repealed]

(d)   the Adoption Act 1976;

(e)   the Domestic Proceedings and Magistrates' Courts Act 1978;

(f)   [repealed]

(g)   Part III of the Matrimonial and Family Proceedings Act 1984.

(h)   the Family Law Act 1996.

D–67   [(5) For the purposes of any reference in this Act to family proceedings, powers which under this Act are exercisable in family proceedings shall also be exercisable in relation to a child, without any such proceedings having been commenced or any application having been made to the court under this Act, if—

(a)   a statement of marital breakdown under section 5 of the Family Law Act 1996 with respect to the marriage in relation to which that child is a child of the family has been received by the court; and

(b)   it may, in due course, become possible for an application for a divorce order or for a separation order to be made by reference to that statement.]

(as amended by the Family Law Act 1996.)

Restrictions on making section 8 orders

D–68   9.—(1) No court shall make any section 8 order, other than a residence order, with respect to a child who is in the care of a local authority.

(2) No application may be made by a local authority for a residence order or contact order and no court shall make such an order in favour of a local authority.

(3) A person who is, or was at any time within the last six months, a local authority foster parent of a child may not apply for leave to apply for a section 8 order with respect to the child unless—

(a)   he has the consent of the authority;

(b)   he is a relative of the child; or

(c)   the child has lived with him for at least three years preceding the application.

(4) The period of three years mentioned in subsection (3) (c) need not be continuous but must have begun not more than five years before the making of the application.

(5) No court shall exercise its powers to make a specific issue order or prohibited steps order—

(a)   with a view to achieving a result which could be achieved by making a residence or contact order; or

(b)   in any way which is denied to the High Court (by section 100(2)) in the exercise of its inherent jurisdiction with respect to children.

(6) No court shall make any section 8 order which is to have effect for a period which will end after the child has reached the age of sixteen unless it is satisfied that the circumstances of the case are exceptional.

(7) No court shall make any section 8 order, other than one varying or discharging such an order, with respect to a child who has reached the age of sixteen unless it is satisfied that the circumstances of the case are exceptional.

Power of court to make section 8 orders

10.—(1) In any family proceedings in which a question arises with respect to the D–69 welfare of any child, the court may make a section 8 order with respect to the child if—

(a)   an application for the order has been made by a person who—

(i) is entitled to apply for a section 8 order with respect to the child; or

(ii) has obtained the leave of the court to make the application; or

(b)   the court considers that the order should be made even though no such application has been made.

(2) The court may also make a section 8 order with respect to any child on the application of a person who—

(a)   is entitled to apply for a section 8 order with respect to the child; or

(b)   has obtained the leave of the court to make the application.

(3) This section is subject to the restrictions imposed by section 9.

(4) The following persons are entitled to apply to the court for any section 8 order with respect to a child—

(a)   any parent or guardian of the child;

(b)   any person in whose favour a residence order is in force with respect to the child.

(5) The following persons are entitled to apply for a residence or contact order with respect to a child—

241

(a)   any party to a marriage (whether or not subsisting) in relation to whom the child is a child of the family;

(b)   any person with whom the child has lived for a period of at least three years;

(c)   any person who—

(i) in any case where a residence order is in force with respect to the child, has the consent of each of the persons in whose favour the order was made;

(ii) in any case where the child is in the care of a local authority, has the consent of that authority; or

(iii) in any other case, has the consent of each of those (if any) who have parental responsibility for the child.

(6) A person who would not otherwise be entitled (under the previous provisions of this section) to apply for the variation or discharge of a section 8 order shall be entitled to do so if—

(a)   the order was made on his application; or

(b)   in the case of a contact order, he is named in the order.

(7)Any person who falls within a category of person prescribed by rules of court is entitled to apply for any such section 8 order as may be prescribed in relation to that category of person.

(8) Where the person applying for leave to make an application for a section 8 order is the child concerned, the court may only grant leave if it is satisfied that he has sufficient understanding to make the proposed application for the section 8 order.

(9) Where the person applying for leave to make an application for a section 8 order is not the child concerned, the court shall, in deciding whether or not to grant leave, have particular regard to—

(a)   the nature of the proposed application for the section 8 order;

(b)   the applicant's connection with the child;

(c)   any risk there might be of that proposed application disrupting the child's life to such an extent that he would be harmed by it; and

(d)   where the child is being looked after by a local authority—

(i) the authority's plans for the child's future; and

(ii) the wishes and feelings of the child's parents

(10) The period of three years mentioned in subsection (5) (b) need not be continuous but must not have begun more than five years before, or ended more than three months before, the making of the application.

General principles and supplementary provisions

D–70   11.—(7) A section 8 order may—

(a)   contain directions about how it is to be carried into effect;

(b) impose conditions which must be complied with by any person—

   (i) in whose favour the order is made;
   (ii) who is a parent of the child concerned;
   (iii) who is not a parent of his but who has parental responsibility for him; or
   (iv) with whom the child is living,

and to whom the conditions are expressed to apply;

(c) be made to have effect for a specified period, or contain provisions which are to have effect for a specified period;

(d) make such incidental, supplemental or consequential provision as the court thinks fit.

Change of child's name or removal from jurisdiction

13.—(1) Where a residence order is in force with respect to a child, no person may—

(a) cause the child to be known by a new surname; or

(b) remove him from the United Kingdom;

without either the written consent of every person who has parental responsibility for the child or the leave of the court.

(2) Subsection (1)(b) does not prevent the removal of a child, for a period of less than one month, by the person in whose favour the residence order is made.

(3) In making a residence order with respect to a child the court may grant the leave required by subsection (1)(b), either generally or for specified purposes.

Enforcement of residence orders

14.—(1) Where—   D–71

(a) a residence order is in force with respect to a child in favour of any person; and

(b) any other person (including one in whose favour the order is also in force) is in breach of the arrangements settled by that order,

the person mentioned in paragraph (a) may, as soon as the requirement in subsection (2) is complied with, enforce the order under section 63(3) of the Magistrates' Courts Act 1980 as if it were an order requiring the other person to produce the child to him.

(2) The requirement is that a copy of the residence order has been served on the other person.

(3) Subsection (1) is without prejudice to any other remedy open to the person in whose favour the residence order is in force.

FINANCIAL RELIEF

(amended by Courts and Legal Services Act 1990, s. 116, Sched. 16, para. 10(1)).

Orders for financial relief with respect to children

15.—(1) Schedule 1 (which consists primarily of the re-enactment, with consequential amendments and minor modifications, of provisions of [section 6 of the Family Law Reform Act 1969] the Guardianship of Minors Acts 1971 and 1973, the Children Act 1975 and of sections 15 and 16 of the Family Law Reform Act 1987) makes provision in relation to financial relief for children.

(2) The powers of a magistrates' court under section 60 of the Magistrates' Courts Act 1980 to revoke, revive or vary an order for the periodical payment of money [and the power of the clerk of a magistrates' court to vary such an order] shall not apply in relation to an order made under Schedule 1.

PART IV

CARE AND SUPERVISION

General

Care and supervision orders

D–72   31.—(1) On the application of any local authority or authorised person, the court may make an order—

(a)   placing the child with respect to whom the application is made in the care of a designated local authority; or

(b)   putting him under the supervision of a designated local authority or of a probation officer.

(2) A court may only make a care order or supervision order if it is satisfied—

(a)   that the child concerned is suffering, or is likely to suffer, significant harm; and

(b)   that the harm, or likelihood of harm, is attributable to—

(i) the care given to the child, or likely to be given to him if the order were not made, not being what it would be reasonable to expect a parent to give to him; or

(ii) the child's being beyond parental control.

(3) No care order or supervision order may be made with respect to a child who has reached the age of 17 (or 16, in the case of a child who is married).

(4) An application under this section may be made on its own or in any other family proceedings.

(5) The court may—

(a)   on the application for a care order, make a supervision order;

(b)   on an application for a supervision order, make a care order.

(6) Where an authorised person proposes to make an application under this section he shall—

(a)   if it is reasonably practicable to do so; and

(b)   before making the application,

consult the local authority appearing to him to be the authority in whose area the child concerned is ordinarily resident.

(7) An application made by an authorised person shall not be entertained by the D–73 court if, at the time when it is made, the child concerned is—

(a)   the subject of an earlier application for a care order, or supervision order, which has not been disposed of; or

(b)   subject to—

    (i) a care order or supervision order;

    (ii) an order under section 7(7)(b) of the Children and Young Persons Act 1969; or

    (iii) a supervision requirement within the meaning of the Part II of the Children (Scotland) Act 1995*

(8) The local authority designated in a care order must be—

(a)   the authority within whose area the child is ordinarily resident; or

(b)   where the child does not reside in the area of a local authority, the authority within whose area any circumstances arose in consequence of which the order is being made.

(9) In this section—

"authorised person" means—

(a)   the National Society for the Prevention of Cruelty to Children and any of its officers; and

(b)   any person authorised by order of the Secretary of State to bring proceedings under this section and any officer of a body which is so authorised;

"harm" means ill-treatment or the impairment of health or development; "development" means physical, intellectual, emotional, social or behavioural development; "health" means physical or mental health; and "ill-treatment" includes sexual abuse and forms of ill-treatment which are not physical.

(10) Where the question of whether harm suffered by a child is significant turns on the child's health or development, his health or development shall be compared with that which could reasonably be expected of a similar child.

* Amended by the Children (Scotland) Act 1995, Sched. 4, para. 48(2).

(11) In this Act—

"a care order" means (subject to section 105(1)) an order under subsection (1)(a) and (except where express provision to the contrary is made) includes an interim care order made under section 38; and

"a supervision order" means an order under subsection (1)(b) and (except where express provision to the contrary is made) includes an interim supervision order made under section 38.

Effect of a care order

D–74   33.—(7) While a care order is in force with respect to a child, no person may—

(a)   cause the child to be known by a new surname; or

(b)   remove him from the United Kingdom,

without either the written consent of every person who has parental responsibility for the child or the leave of the court.

(8) Subsection (7)(b) does not—

(a)   prevent the removal of such a child, for a period of less than one month, by the authority in whose care he is; or

(b)   apply to arrangements for such a child to live outside England and Wales (which are governed by paragraph 19 of Schedule 2).

Interim orders

D–75   38.—(1) Where—

(a)   in any proceedings on an application for a care order or supervision order, the proceedings are adjourned; or

(b)   the court gives a direction under section 37(1),

the court may make an interim care order or an interim supervision order with respect to the child concerned.

(2) A court shall not make an interim care order or interim supervision order under this section unless it is satisfied that there are reasonable grounds for believing that the circumstances with respect to the child are as mentioned in section 31(2).

(3) Where, in any proceedings on an application for a care order or supervision order, a court makes a residence order with respect to the child concerned, it shall also make an interim supervision order with respect to him unless satisfied that his welfare will be satisfactorily safeguarded without an interim order being made.

(4) An interim order made under or by virtue of this section shall have effect for such period as may be specified in the order, but shall in any event cease to have effect on whichever of the following events first occurs—

(a)   the expiry of the period of eight weeks beginning with the date on which the order is made;

(b)   if the order is the second or subsequent such order made with respect to the same child in the same proceedings, the expiry of the relevant period;

(c)   in a case which falls within subsection (1)(a), the disposal of the application;

(d)   in a case which falls within subsection (1)(b), the disposal of an application for a care order or supervision order made by the authority with respect to the child;

(e)   in a case which falls within subsection (1)(b) and in which—

(i) the court has given a direction under section 37(4), but

(ii) no application for a care order or supervision order has been made with respect to the child,

the expiry of the period fixed by that direction.

(5) In subsection (4)(b) "the relevant period" means—

(a)   the period of four weeks beginning with the date on which the order in question is made; or

(b)   the period of eight weeks beginning with the date on which the first order was made if that period ends later than the period mentioned in paragraph (a).

(6) Where the court makes an interim care order, or interim supervision order, it may give such directions (if any) as it considers appropriate with regard to the medical or psychiatric examination or other assessment of the child; but if the child is of sufficient understanding to make an informed decision he may refuse to submit to the examination or other assessment.

(7) A direction under subsection (6) may be to the effect that there is to be—

(a)   no such examination or assessment; or

(b)   no such examination or assessment unless the court directs otherwise.

(8) A direction under subsection (6) may be—

(a)   given when the interim order is made or at any time while it is in force; and

(b)   varied at any time on the application of any person falling within any class of person prescribed by rules of court for the purposes of this subsection.

(9) Paragraphs 4 and 5 of Schedule 3 shall not apply in relation to an interim supervision order.

(10) Where a court makes an order under or by virtue of this section it shall, in determining the period for which the order is to be in force, consider whether any party who was, or might have been, opposed to the making of the order was in a position to argue his case against the order in full.

38A.—(1) Where—   D–76

(a)   on being satisfied that there are reasonable grounds for believing that the circumstances with respect to a child are as mentioned in section 31(2)(a) and (b)(i), the court makes an interim care order with respect to a child, and

(b)   the conditions mentioned in subsection (2) are satisfied,

the court may include an exclusion requirement in the interim care order.

(2) The conditions are—

(a)   that there is reasonable cause to believe that, if a person ("the relevant person") is excluded from a dwelling-house in which the child lives, the child will cease to suffer, or cease to be likely to suffer, significant harm, and

(b)   that another person living in the dwelling-house (whether a parent of the child or some other person)—

(i) is able and willing to give to the child the care which it would be reasonable to expect a parent to give him, and

(ii) consents to the inclusion of the exclusion requirement.

(3) For the purposes of this section an exclusion requirement is any one or more of the following—

(a)   a provision requiring the relevant person to leave a dwelling-house in which he is living with the child,

(b)   a provision prohibiting the relevant person from entering a dwelling-house in which the child lives, and

(c)   a provision excluding the relevant person from a defined area in which a dwelling-house in which the child lives is situated.

(4) The court may provide that the exclusion requirement is to have effect for a shorter period than the other provisions of the interim care order.

(5) Where the court makes an interim care order containing an exclusion requirement, the court may attach a power of arrest to the exclusion requirement.

(6) Where the court attaches a power of arrest to an exclusion requirement of an interim care order, it may provide that the power of arrest is to have effect for a shorter period than the exclusion requirement.

(7) Any period specified for the purposes of subsection (4) or (6) may be extended by the court (on one or more occasions) on an application to vary or discharge the interim care order.

(8) Where a power of arrest is attached to an exclusion requirement of an interim care order by virtue of subsection (5), a constable may arrest without warrant any person whom he has reasonable cause to believe to be in breach of the requirement.

(9) Sections 47(7), (11) and (12) and 48 of, and Schedule 5 to, the Family Law Act 1996 shall have effect in relation to a person arrested under subsection (8) of this section as they have effect in relation to a person arrested under section 47(6) of that Act.

(10) If, while an interim care order containing an exclusion requirement is in force, the local authority have removed the child from the dwelling-house from which the relevant person is excluded to other accommodation for a continuous period of more than 24 hours, the interim care order shall cease to have effect in so far as it imposes the exclusion requirement.

D–77   38B.—(1) In any case where the court has power to include an exclusion requirement in an interim care order, the court may accept an undertaking from the relevant person.

(2) No power of arrest may be attached to any undertaking given under subsection (1).

(3) An undertaking given to a court under subsection (1)—

(a)   shall be enforceable as if it were an order of the court, and

(b)   shall cease to have effect if, while it is in force, the local authority have removed the child from the dwelling-house from which the relevant person is excluded to other accommodation for a continuous period of more than 24 hours.

(4) This section has effect without prejudice to the powers of the High Court and county court apart from this section.

(5) In this section "exclusion requirement" and "relevant person" have the same meaning as in section 38A.

(Sections 38A & 38B added by the Family Law Act 1996)

Orders for emergency protection of children

44.—(1) Where any person ("the applicant") applies to the court for an order to D–78 be made under this section with respect to a child, the court may make the order if, but only if, it is satisfied that—

(a)   there is reasonable cause to believe that the child is likely to suffer significant harm if—

    (i)   he is not removed to accommodation provided by or on behalf of the applicant; or

    (ii)   he does not remain in the place in which he is then being accommodated;

(b)   in the case of an application made by a local authority—

    (i)   enquiries are being made with respect to the child under section 47(1)(b); and

    (ii)   those enquiries are being frustrated by access to the child being unreasonably refused to a person authorised to seek access and that the applicant has reasonable cause to believe that access to the child is required as a matter of urgency; or

(c)   in the case of an application made by an authorised person—

    (i)   the applicant has reasonable cause to suspect that a child is suffering, or is likely to suffer, significant harm;

    (ii)   the applicant is making enquiries with respect to the child's welfare; and

    (iii)   those enquiries are being frustrated by access to the child being unreasonably refused to a person authorised to seek access and the applicant has reasonable cause to believe that access to the child is required as a matter of urgency.

(2) In this section—

(a)   "authorised person" means a person who is an authorised person for the purposes of section 31; and

249

(b) "a person authorised to seek access", means—

    (i) in the case of an application by a local authority, an officer of the local authority or a person authorised by the authority to act on their behalf in connection with the enquiries; or

    (ii) in the case of an application by an authorised person, that person.

(3) Any person—

(a) seeking access to a child in connection with enquiries of a kind mentioned in subsection (1); and

(b) purporting to be a person authorised to do so,

shall, on being asked to do so, produce some duly authenticated document as evidence that he is such a person.

(4) While an order under this section ("an emergency protection order") is in force it—

(a) operates as a direction to any person who is in a position to do so to comply with any request to produce the child to the applicant;

(b) authorises—

    (i) the removal of the child at any time to accommodation provided by or on behalf of the applicant and his being kept there; or

    (ii) the prevention of the child's removal from any hospital, or other place, in which he was being accommodated immediately before the making of the order; and

(c) gives the applicant parental responsibility for the child.

D–79   (5) Where an emergency protection order is in force with respect to a child, the applicant—

(a) shall only exercise the power given by virtue of subsection (4)(b) in order to safeguard the welfare of the child;

(b) shall take, and shall only take, such action in meeting his parental responsibility for the child as is reasonably required to safeguard or promote the welfare of the child (having regard in particular to the duration of the order); and

(c) shall comply with the requirements of any regulations made by the Secretary of State for the purposes of this subsection.

(6) Where the court makes an emergency protection order, it may give such directions (if any) as it considers appropriate with respect to—

(a) the contact which is, or is not, to be allowed between the child and any named person;

(b) the medical or psychiatric examination or other assessment of the child.

(7) Where any direction is given under subsection (6)(b), the child may, if he is of sufficient understanding to make an informed decision, refuse to submit to the examination or other assessment.

(8) A direction under subsection (6)(a) may impose conditions and one under subsection (6)(b) may be to the effect that there is to be—

(a)   no such examination or assessment; or

(b)   no such examination or assessment unless the court directs otherwise.

(9) A direction under subsection (6) may be—

(a)   given when the emergency protection order is made or at any time while it is in force; and

(b)   varied at any time on the application of any person falling within any class of person prescribed by rules of court for the purposes of this subsection.

(10) Where an emergency protection order is in force with respect to a child and—

(a)   the applicant has exercised the power given by subsection (4)(b)(i) but it appears to him that it is safe for the child to be returned; or

(b)   the applicant has exercised the power given by subsection (4)(b)(ii) but it appears to him that it is safe for the child to be allowed to be removed from the place in question,

he shall return the child or (as the case may be) allow him to be removed.

(11) Where he is required by subsection (10) to return the child the applicant **D–80** shall—

(a)   return him to the care of the person from whose care he was removed; or

(b)   if that is not reasonably practicable, return him to the care of—

   (i) a parent of his;

   (ii) any person who is not a parent of his but who has parental responsibility for him; or

   (iii) such other person as the applicant (with the agreement of the court) considers appropriate.

(12) Where the applicant has been required by subsection (10) to return the child, or to allow him to be removed, he may again exercise his powers with respect to the child (at any time while the emergency protection order remains in force) if it appears to him that a change in the circumstances of the case makes it necessary for him to do so.

(13) Where an emergency protection order has been made with respect to a child, the applicant shall, subject to any direction given under subsection (6), allow the child reasonable contact with—

(a)   his parents;

(b)   any person who is not a parent of his but who has parental responsibility for him;

(c)   any person with whom he was living immediately before the making of the order;

(d)   any person in whose favour a contact order is in force with respect to him;

(e)   any person who is allowed to have contact with the child by virtue of an order under section 34; and

(f)   any person acting on behalf of any of those persons.

(14) Wherever it is reasonably practicable to do so, an emergency protection order shall name the child; and where it does not name him it shall describe him as clearly as possible.

(15) A person shall be guilty of an offence if he intentionally obstructs any person exercising the power under subsection (4)(b) to remove, or prevent the removal of, a child.

(16) A person guilty of an offence under subsection (15) shall be liable on summary conviction to a fine not exceeding level 3 on the standard scale.

D–81   44A.—(1) Where—

(a)   on being satisfied as mentioned in section 44(1)(a), (b) or (c), the court makes an emergency protection order with respect to a child, and

(b)   the conditions mentioned in subsection (2) are satisfied,

the court may include an exclusion requirement in the emergency protection order.

(2) The conditions are—

(a)   that there is reasonable cause to believe that, if a person ("the relevant person") is excluded from a dwelling-house in which the child lives, then—

    (i) in the case of an order made on the ground mentioned in section 44(1)(a), the child will not be likely to suffer significant harm, even though the child is not removed as mentioned in section 44(1)(a)(i) or does not remain as mentioned in section 44(1)(a)(ii), or

    (ii) in the case of an order made on the ground mentioned in paragraph (b) or (c) of section 44(1), the enquiries referred to in that paragraph will cease to be frustrated, and

(b)   that another person living in the dwelling-house (whether a parent of the child or some other person)—

    (i) is able and willing to give to the child the care which it would be reasonable to expect a parent to give him, and

    (ii) consents to the inclusion of the exclusion requirement.

(3) For the purposes of this section an exclusion requirement is any one or more of the following—

(a)   a provision requiring the relevant person to leave a dwelling-house in which he is living with the child,

(b)   a provision prohibiting the relevant person from entering a dwelling-house in which the child lives, and

(c)   a provision excluding the relevant person from a defined area in which a dwelling-house in which the child lives is situated.

(4) The court may provide that the exclusion requirement is to have effect for a shorter period than the other provisions of the order.

(5) Where the court makes an emergency protection order containing an exclusion requirement, the court may attach a power of arrest to the exclusion requirement.

(6) Where the court attaches a power of arrest to an exclusion requirement of an emergency protection order, it may provide that the power of arrest is to have effect for a shorter period than the exclusion requirement.

(7) Any period specified for the purposes of subsection (4) or (6) may be extended by the court (on one or more occasions) on an application to vary or discharge the emergency protection order.

(8) Where a power of arrest is attached to an exclusion requirement of an emergency protection order by virtue of subsection (5), a constable may arrest without warrant any person whom he has reasonable cause to believe to be in breach of the requirement.

(9) Sections 47(7), (11) and (12) and 48 of, and Schedule 5 to, the Family Law Act 1996 shall have effect in relation to a person arrested under subsection (8) of this section as they have effect in relation to a person arrested under section 47(6) of that Act.

(10) If, while an emergency protection order containing an exclusion requirement is in force, the applicant has removed the child from the dwelling-house from which the relevant person is excluded to other accommodation for a continuous period of more than 24 hours, the order shall cease to have effect in so far as it imposes the exclusion requirement.

44B.—(1) In any case where the court has power to include an exclusion **D–82** requirement in an emergency protection order, the court may accept an undertaking from the relevant person.

(2) No power of arrest may be attached to any undertaking given under subsection (1).

(3) An undertaking given to a court under subsection (1)—

(a)   shall be enforceable as if it were an order of the court, and

(b)   shall cease to have effect if, while it is in force, the applicant has removed the child from the dwelling-house from which the relevant person is excluded to other accommodation for a continuous period of more than 24 hours.

(4) This section has effect without prejudice to the powers of the High Court and county court apart from this section.

(5) In this section "exclusion requirement" and "relevant person" have the same meaning as in section 44A.

(Sections 44A & 44B added by the Family Law Act 1996)

SCHEDULE 1

FINANCIAL PROVISION FOR CHILDREN

Orders for financial relief against parents

1.—(1) On an application made by a parent or guardian of a child, or by any **D–83** person in whose favour a residence order is in force with respect to a child, the court may—

(a)   in the case of an application to the High Court or a county court, make one or more of the orders mentioned in sub-paragraph (2);

(b)   in the case of an application to a magistrates' court, make one or both of the orders mentioned in paragraphs (a) and (c) of that sub-paragraph.

(2) The orders referred to in sub-paragraph (1) are—

(a)   an order requiring either or both parents of a child—

(i) to make to the applicant for the benefit of the child; or
(ii) to make to the child himself,

such periodical payments, for such term, as may be specified in the order;

(b)   an order requiring either or both parents of a child—

(i) to secure to the applicant for the benefit of the child; or
(ii) to secure to the child himself,

such periodical payments, for such term, as may be so specified;

(c)   an order requiring either or both parents of a child—

(i) to pay to the applicant for the benefit of the child; or
(ii) to pay to the child himself,

such lump sum as may be so specified;

(d)   an order requiring a settlement to be made for the benefit of the child, and to the satisfaction of the court, of property—

(i) to which either parent is entitled (either in possession or in reversion); and
(ii) which is specified in the order;

(e)   an order requiring either or both parents of a child—

(i) to transfer to the applicant, for the benefit of the child; or
(ii) to transfer to the child himself,

such property to which the parent is, or the parents are, entitled (either in possession or in reversion) as may be specified in the order.

(3) The powers conferred by this paragraph may be exercised at any time.

(4) An order under sub-paragraph (2)(a) or (b) may be varied or discharged by a subsequent order made on the application of any person by or to whom payments were required to be made under the previous order.

(5) Where a court makes an order under this paragraph—

(a)   it may at any time make a further such order under sub-paragraph (2)(a), (b) or (c) with respect to the child concerned if he has not reached the age of eighteen;

(b)   it may not make more than one order under sub-paragraph (2)(d) or (e) against the same person in respect of the same child.

(6) On making, varying or discharging a residence order the court may exercise any of its powers under this Schedule even though no application has been made to it under this Schedule.

[(7) Where a child is a ward of court, the court may exercise any of its powers under this Schedule even though no application has been made to it.] [1990 c. 41 s.116, Sched. 16, para. 10(2).]

Orders for financial relief for persons over eighteen

2.—(1) If, on an application by a person who has reached the age of eighteen, it **D–84** appears to the court—

(a)   that the applicant is, will be or (if an order were made under this paragraph) would be receiving instruction at an educational establishment or undergoing training for a trade, profession or vocation, whether or not while in gainful employment; or

(b)   that there are special circumstances which justify the making of an order under this paragraph,

the court may make one or both of the orders mentioned in sub-paragraph (2).

(2) The orders are—

(a)   an order requiring either or both of the applicant's parents to pay to the applicant such periodical payments, for such term, as may be specified in the order;

(b)   an order requiring either or both of the applicant's parents to pay to the applicant such lump sum as may be so specified.

(3) An application may not be made under this paragraph by any person if, immediately before he reached the age of sixteen, a periodical payments order was in force with respect to him.

(4) No order shall be made under this paragraph at a time when the parents of the applicant are living with each other in the same household.

(5) An order under sub-paragraph (2) (a) may be varied or discharged by a subsequent order made on the application of any person by or to whom payments were required to be made under the previous order.

(6) In sub-paragraph (3) "periodical payments order" means an order made under—

(a)   this Schedule;

(b)   [*Repealed by the Child Support Act 1991, s.58(14).*]

(c)   section 23 or 27 of the Matrimonial Causes Act 1973;

(d)   Part I of the Domestic Proceedings and Magistrates' Courts Act 1978, for the making or securing of periodical payments.

(7) The powers conferred by this paragraph shall be exercisable at any time.

(8) Where the court makes an order under this paragraph it may from time to time while that order remains in force make a further such order.

Duration of orders for financial relief

3.—(1) The term to be specified in an order for periodical payments made under **D–85** paragraph 1 (2) (a) or (b) in favour of a child may begin with the date of the making of an application for the order in question or any later date or a date ascertained in accordance with subparagraph (5) or (6) but—

(a)   shall not in the first instance extend beyond the child's seventeenth birthday unless the court thinks it right in the circumstances of the case to specify a later date; and

(b)   shall not in any event extend beyond the child's eighteenth birthday.

(2) Paragraph (b) of sub-paragraph (1) shall not apply in the case of a child if it appears to the court that—

(a)   the child is, or will be or (if an order were made without complying with that paragraph) would be receiving instruction at an educational establishment or undergoing training for a trade, profession or vocation, whether or not while in gainful employment; or

(b)   there are special circumstances which justify the making of an order without complying with that paragraph.

(3) An order for periodical payments made under paragraph 1(2)(a) or 2(2)(a) shall, notwithstanding anything in the order, cease to have effect on the death of the person liable to make payments under the order.

(4) Where an order is made under paragraph 1(2)(a) or (b) requiring periodical payments to be made or secured to the parent of a child, the order shall cease to have effect if—

(a)   any parent making or securing the payments; and

(b)   any parent to whom the payments are made or secured,

live together for a period of more than six months.

(5) Where—

(a)   a maintenance assessment ("the current assessment") is in force with respect to a child; and

(b)   an application is made for an order under paragraph 1(2)(a) or (b) of this Schedule for periodical payments in favour of that child—

(i) in accordance with section 8 of the Child Support Act 1991; and

(ii) before the end of the period of 6 months beginning with the making of the current assessment,

the term to be specified in any such order made on that application may be expressed to begin on, or at any time after, the earliest permitted date.

(6) For the purposes of subsection (5) above, "the earliest permitted date" is whichever is the later of—

(a)   the date 6 months before the application is made; or

(b)   the date on which the current assessment took effect or, where successive maintenance assessments have been continuously in force with respect to a child, on which the first of those assessments took effect.

(7) Where—

(a)   a maintenance assessment ceases to have effect or is cancelled by or under any provision of the Child Support Act 1991, and

(b)   an application is made, before the end of the period of 6 months beginning with the relevant date, for an order for periodical payments under paragraph 1(2)(a) or (b) in favour of a child with respect to whom that maintenance assessment was in force immediately before it ceased to have effect or was cancelled, the term to be specified in any such order, or in any interim order under paragraph 9, made on that application may begin with the date on which that maintenance assessment ceased to have effect or, as the case may be, the date with effect from which it was cancelled, or any later date.

(8) In sub-paragraph (7)(b)—

(a)   where the maintenance assessment ceased to have effect, the relevant date is the date on which it so ceased; and

(b)   where the maintenance assessment was cancelled, the relevant date is the later of—

(i) the date on which the person who cancelled it did so, and
(ii) the date from which the cancellation first had effect.

Amended by, and subparagraphs (5) and (6) added by, Maintenance Orders (Backdating) Order 1993 (S.I. 1993 No.623).

Matters to which court is to have regard in making Orders for financial relief

4.—(1) In deciding whether to exercise its powers under paragraph 1 or 2, and if **D–86** so in what manner, the court shall have regard to all the circumstances including—

(a)   the income, earning capacity, property and other financial resources which each person mentioned in sub-paragraph (3) has or is likely to have in the foreseeable future;

(b)   the financial needs, obligations and responsibilities which each person mentioned in sub-paragraph (3) has or is likely to have in the foreseeable future;

(c)   the financial needs of the child;

(d)   the income, earning capacity (if any), property and other financial resources of the child;

(e)   any physical or mental disability of the child;

(f)   the manner in which the child was being, or was expected to be, educated or trained.

(2) In deciding whether to exercise its powers under paragraph 1 against a person who is not the mother or father of the child, and if so in what manner, the court shall in addition have regard to—

(a)   whether that person had assumed responsibility for the maintenance of the child and, if so, the extent to which and basis on which he assumed that responsibility and the length of the period during which he met that responsibility;

(b)   whether he did so knowing that the child was not his child;

(c)   the liability of any other person to maintain the child.

(3) Where the court makes an order under paragraph 1 against a person who is not the father of the child, it shall record in the order that the order is made on the basis that the person against whom the order is made is not the child's father.

(4) The persons mentioned in sub-paragraph (1) are—

(a)   in relation to a decision whether to exercise its powers under paragraph 1, any parent of the child;

(b)   in relation to a decision whether to exercise its powers under paragraph 2, the mother and father of the child;

(c)   the applicant for the order;

(d)   any other person in whose favour the court proposes to make the order.

SCHEDULE 14

Parental responsibility of parents

D–87   6.—(2) Where—

(a)   a child's father and mother were not married to each other at the time of his birth; and

(b)   there is an existing order with respect to the child,

section 2 shall apply as modified by sup-paragraphs (3) and (4).

(3)   [*Not printed*].

(4)   The modifications are that—

(a)   for the purposes of section 2(2), where the father has custody or care and control of the child by virtue of any existing order, the court shall be deemed to have made (at the commencement of that section) an order under section 4(1) giving him parental responsibility for the child; and

(b)   Where by virtue of paragraph (a) a court is deemed to have made an order under section 4(1) in favour of a father who has care and control of a child by virtue of an existing order, the court shall not bring the order under section 4(1) to an end at any time while he has care and control of the child by virtue of the order.

Persons who are not parents but who have custody or care and control

7.—(1) Where a person who is not the parent or guardian of a child has custody or care and control of him by virtue of an existing order, that person shall have parental responsibility for him so long as he continues to have that custody or care and control by virtue of the order.

(2) Where sub-paragraph (1) applies, Parts I and II and paragraph 15 of Schedule 1 shall have effect as modified by this paragraph.

(3) The modifications are that—

(a)   for section 2(8) there shall be substituted—

"(8) the fact that a person has parental responsibility for a child does not entitle him to act in a way which would be incompatible with any existing order or with any order made under this Act with respect to the child";

(b)   at the end of section 10(4) there shall be inserted—

"(c) any person who has custody or care and control of a child by virtue of any existing order"; and

(c) at the end of section 34(1)(c) there shall be inserted—

"(cc) where immediately before the care order was made there was an existing order by virtue of which a person had custody or care and control of the child, that person";

(d) for paragraph 15 of Schedule 1 there shall be substituted—

"15. Where a child lives with a person as the result of a custodianship order within the meaning of section 33 of the Children Act 1975, a local authority may make contributions to that person towards the cost of the accommodation and maintenance of the child so long as that person continues to have legal custody of that child by virtue of the order."

Supreme Court Act 1981

Powers of High Court with respect to injunctions and receivers

37.—(1) The High Court may by order (whether interlocutory or final) grant an **D–88** injunction or appoint a receiver in all cases in which it appears to the court to be just and convenient to do so.

(2) Any such order may be made either unconditionally or on such terms and conditions as the court thinks just.

(3) The power of the High Court under subsection (1) to grant an interlocutory injunction restraining a party to any proceedings from removing from the jurisdiction of the High Court, or otherwise dealing with, assets located within that jurisdiction shall be exercisable in cases where that party is, as well as in cases where he is not, domiciled, resident or present within that jurisdiction.

(4) The power of the High Court to appoint a receiver by way of equitable execution shall operate in relation to all legal estate and interests in land, and that power—

(a) may be exercised in relation to an estate or interest in land whether or not a charge has been imposed on that land under section 1 of the Charging Orders Act 1979 for the purpose of enforcing the judgment, order or award in question; and

(b) shall be in addition to, and not in derogation of, any power of any court to appoint a receiver in proceedings for enforcing such a charge.

(5) Where an order under the said section 1 imposing a charge for the purpose of enforcing a judgment, order or award has been, or has effect as if, registered under section 6 of the Land Charges Act 1972, subsection (4) of the said section 6 (effect of non-registration of writs and orders registrable under that section) shall not apply to an order appointing a receiver made either—

(a) in proceedings for enforcing the charge; or

(b) by way of equitable execution of the judgment, order or award or, as the case may be, of so much of it as requires payment of moneys secured by the charge.

Distribution of business between civil and criminal divisions

D–89 53.—(1) Rules of court may provide for the distribution of business in the Court of Appeal between the civil and criminal divisions, but subject to any such rules business shall be distributed in accordance with the following provisions of this section.

(2) The criminal division of the Court of Appeal shall exercise—

(a) all jurisdiction of the Court of Appeal under Parts I and II of the Criminal Appeal Act 1968;

(b) the jurisdiction of the Court of Appeal under section 13 of the Administration of Justice Act 1960 (appeals in cases of contempt of court) in relation to appeals from orders and decisions of the Crown Court;

(c) all other jurisdiction expressly conferred on that division by this or any other Act; and

(d) the jurisdiction to order the issue of venire de novo.

(3) The civil division of the Court of Appeal shall exercise the whole of the jurisdiction of that court not exercisable by the criminal division.

(4) Where any class of proceedings in the Court of Appeal is by any statutory provision assigned to the criminal division of that court, rules of court may provide for any enactment relating to—

(a) appeals to the Court of Appeal under Part I of the Criminal Appeals Act 1968; or

(b) any matter connected with or arising out of such appeals,

to apply in relation to proceedings of that class or, as the case may be, to any corresponding matter connected with or arising out of such proceedings, as it applies in relation to such appeals or, as the case may be, to the relevant matter within paragraph (b), with or without prescribed modifications in either case.

County Courts Act 1984

Remedies available in county courts

D–90 38.—(1) Subject to what follows, in any proceedings in a county court the court may make any order which could be made by the High Court if the proceedings were in the High Court.

(2) Any order made by a county court may be—

(a) absolute or conditional;
(b) final or interlocutory.

(3) A county court shall not have power—

(a) to order mandamus, certiorari or prohibition; or
(b) to make any order of a prescribed kind.

(4) Regulations under subsection (3)—

(a) may provide for any of their provisions not to apply in such circumstances or descriptions of case as may be specified in the regulations;
(b) may provide for the transfer of the proceedings to the High Court for the purpose of enabling an order of a kind prescribed under subsection (3) to be made;
(c) may make such provision with respect to matters of procedure as the Lord Chancellor considers expedient; and
(d) may make provision amending or repealing any provision made by or under any enactment, so far as may be necessary or expedient in consequence of the regulations.

(5) In this section "prescribed" means prescribed by regulations made by the Lord Chancellor under this section.

(6) The power to make regulations under this section shall be exercised by statutory instrument.

(7) No such statutory instrument shall be made unless a draft of the instrument has been approved by both Houses of Parliament.

Application of practice of High Court

76. In any case not expressly provided for by or in pursuance of this Act, the general principles of practice in the High Court may be adopted and applied to proceedings in a county court.

Magistrates Court Act 1980

Orders other than for payment of money

Orders other than for payment of money

63.—(1) Where under any Act passed after 31st December 1879 a magistrates' D–91 court has power to require the doing of anything other than the payment of money, or to prohibit the doing of anything, any order of the court for the purpose of exercising that power may contain such provisions for the manner in which anything is to be done, for the time within which anything is to be done, or during which anything is not to be done, and generally for giving effect to the order, as the court thinks fit.

(2) The court may by order made on complaint suspend or rescind any such order as aforesaid.

D–92 (3) Where any person disobeys an order of a magistrates' court made under an Act passed after 31st December 1879 to do anything other than the payment of money or to abstain from doing anything the court may—

(a) order him to pay a sum not exceeding £50 for every day during which he is in default or a sum not exceeding [£5,000];* or

(b) commit him to custody until he has remedied his default or for a period not exceeding 2 months;

but a person who is ordered to pay a sum for every day during which he is in default or who is committed to custody until he has remedied his default shall not by virtue of this section be ordered to pay more than £1,000 or be committed for more than 2 months in all for doing or abstaining from doing the same thing contrary to the order (without prejudice to the operation of this section in relation to any subsequent default).

(4) Any sum ordered to be paid under subsection (3) above shall for the purposes of this Act be treated as adjudged to be paid by a conviction of a magistrates' court.

(5) The preceding provisions of this section shall not apply to any order for the enforcement of which provision is made by any other enactment.

Family proceedings

Meaning of family proceedings

D–93 65.—(1)In this Act "[family proceedings]"ᵃ means proceedings under any of the following enactments, that is to say—

(a) the Maintenance Orders (Facilitation for Enforcement) Act 1920;

(b) section 43 [. . .]ᵇ of the National Assistance Act 1948;

(c) section 3 of the Marriage Act 1949;

(d) [. . .]ᶜ

(e) [. . .]ᵈ

[(ee) section 35 of the Matrimonial Causes Act 1973;]ᵉ

(f) Part I of the Maintenance Orders (Reciprocal Enforcement) Act 1972;

---

* N.B. The material in square brackets was substituted by the Criminal Justice Act 1991, s.17(3), Sched. 4. In light of this amendment the purported maximum figure of £1,000 in section 63(3) above appears to be an error.

ᵃ Words substituted by the Children Act 1989, s.92(11), Sched. 11, para. 8.

ᵇ Words repealed by the Family Law Reform Act 1987, s.33(4), Sched. 4.

ᶜ Paragraph repealed by the Family Law Reform Act 1987, s.33(4), Sched. 4.

ᵈ Paragraph repealed by the Children Act 1989, s.108(7), Sched. 15.

ᵉ Paragraph inserted by the Matrimonial and Family Proceedings Act 1984, s.44.

(g)   [. . .]ᶠ

(h)   the Adoption Act 1976, except proceedings under section 34 of that Act;

(i)   section 18 [. . .]ᵍ of the Supplementary Benefits Act 1976;

(j)   Part I of the Domestic Proceedings and Magistrates' Courts Act 1978;

(k)   [. . .]ʰ

(l)   section 60 of this Act; [. . .]ⁱ

(m)   Part I of the Civil Jurisdiction and Judgments Act 1982, so far as that Part relates to the recognition or enforcement of maintenance orders;]ʲ

[(m)   [. . .]

[(m)   [. . .]

[(n)   the Children Act 1989]ᵏ;

[(n)   section 106 of the Social Security Administration Act 1992;

[(o)   section 20 (so far as it provides, by virtue of an order under section 45(b), for appeals to be made to a court) or section 27 of the Child Support Act 1991;]ˡ

[(p)   Part IV of the Family Law Act 1996]ᵐ

except that, subject to subsection (2) below, it does not include—

(i)   proceedings for the enforcement of any order made, confirmed or registered under any of those enactments;

(ii)   proceedings for the variation of any provision for the periodical payment of money contained in an order made, confirmed or registered under any of those enactments; or

(iii)   proceedings on an information in respect of the commission of an offence under any of those enactments.

(2) The court before which there fall to be heard any of the following proceedings, **D–94** that is to say—

(a)   proceedings (whether under this Act or any other enactment) for the enforcement of any order made, confirmed or registered under any of the enactments specified in paragraphs (a) to (k) [(m) and (n)]ⁿ of subsection (1) above;

(b)   proceedings (whether under this Act or any other enactment) for the variation of any provision for the making of periodical payments contained in an order made, confirmed or registered under any of those enactments;

(c)   proceedings for an attachment of earnings order to secure maintenance payments within the meaning of the Attachment of Earnings Act 1971 or for the discharge or variation of such an order; or

---

ᶠ Paragraph repealed by the Children Act 1989, s.108(7), Sched. 15.

ᵍ Words repealed by the Family Law Reform Act 1987, s.33(4), Sched. 4.

ʰ Paragraph repealed by the Courts and Legal Services Act 1990, s.116(2), 125(7), Sched. 16, para. 40, Sched. 20.

ⁱ Paragraph (added by the Family Law Reform Act 1987, s.33(1), Sched. 2, para. 82) repealed by the Children Act 1989, s.108(7), Sched. 15.

ʲ Paragraph added by the Civil Jurisdiction and Judgments Act 1982, s.15(4), Sched. 12, Pt. I, para. 7(a).

ᵏ Paragraph added by the Children Act 1989, s.92(11), Sched. 11, para. 8(a).

ˡ Inserted by S.I. 1993 No. 1698, Sched. 2.

ᵐ Paragraph added by FLA 1996, Sched. 8, Pt. III.

ⁿ Words substituted (for the words added by the Civil Jurisdiction and Judgments Act 1982, s.15(4), Sched. 12, Pt. I, para. 7(b)) by the Children Act 1989, s.92(11), Sched. 11, para. 8(b).

(d)   proceedings for the enforcement of a maintenance order which is registered in a magistrates' court under Part II of the Maintenance Orders Act 1950 or Part I of the Maintenance Orders Act 1958 or for the variation of the rate of payments specified by such an order,

[(e)   section 20 (so far as it provides, by virtue of an order under section 45, for appeals to be made to a court) or section 27 of the Child Support Act 1991,][0]

may if it thinks fit order that those proceedings and any other proceedings being heard therewith shall, notwithstanding anything in subsection (1) above, be treated as [family proceedings][p] for the purposes of this Act.

(3) Where the same parties are parties—

(a)   to proceedings which are [family proceedings][p] by virtue of subsection (1) above, and

(b)   to proceedings which the court has power to treat as [family proceedings][p] by virtue of subsection (2) above,

and the proceedings are heard together by a magistrates' court, the whole of those proceedings shall be treated as [family proceedings][p] for the purposes of this Act.

(4) No appeal shall lie from the making of, or refusal to make, an order under subsection (2) above.

Sittings of magistrates' courts for family proceedings

D–95   69.—(1) The business of magistrates' courts shall, so far as is consistent with the due dispatch of business, be arranged in such manner as may be requisite for separating the hearing and determination of *[family proceedings] from other business.

(2) In the case of *[family proceedings] in a magistrates' court other than proceedings under the Adoption Act 1976, no person shall be present during the hearing and determination by the court of the proceedings except—

(a)   officers of the court;

(b)   parties to the case before the court, their [†legal representatives], witnesses and other persons directly concerned in the case;

(c)   representatives of newspapers or news agencies;

(d)   any other person whom the court may in its discretion permit to be present, so, however, that permission shall not be withheld from a person who appears to the court to have adequate grounds for attendance.

(3) In relation to any *[family proceedings] under the Adoption Act 1976, subsection (2) above shall apply with the omission of paragraphs (c) and (d).

(4) When hearing *[family proceedings], a magistrates' court may, if it thinks it necessary in the interest of the administration of justice or of public decency, direct

[0] Inserted by S.I. 1993 No. 1698, Sched. 2.
[m] Paragraph added by FLA 1996, Sched. 8, Pt. III.
[p] Words substituted by the Children Act 1989, s.92(11), Sched. 11, para. 8.
[*] 1989 c.41 Sched. 11, Pt. II. para. 8(c).
[†] 1990 c.41 Sched. 18, para. 25.

that any persons, not being officers of the court or parties to the case, the parties' [†legal representatives], or other persons directly concerned in the case, be excluded during the taking of any indecent evidence.

(5) The powers conferred on a magistrates' court by this section shall be in addition and without prejudice to any other powers of the court to hear proceedings in camera.

(6) Nothing in this section shall affect the exercise by a magistrates' court of the power to direct that witnesses shall be excluded until they are called for examination.

(7) Until the coming into operation of the Adoption Act 1976 this section shall have effect as if for any reference to that Act there were substituted a reference to the Adoption Act 1958, the Adoption Act 1960 and Part I of the Children Act 1975.

REMAND

Remand in custody or on bail

128.—(1) Where a magistrates' court has power to remand any person, then, D–96 subject to section 4 of the Bail Act 1976 and to any other enactment modifying that power, the court may—

(a) remand him in custody, that is to say, commit him to custody to be brought before the court [subject to subsection (3A) below], at the end of the period of remand or at such earlier time as the court may require; or

(b) where it is [proceeding with a view to transferring the proceedings against that person for trial or is] trying an offence alleged to have been committed by that person or has convicted him of an offence, remand him on bail in accordance with the Bail Act 1976, that is to say, by directing him to appear as provided in subsection (4) below; or

(c) except in a case falling within paragraph (b) above, remand him on bail by taking from him a recognizance (with or without sureties) conditioned as provided in that subsection;

and may, in a case falling within paragraph (c) above, instead of taking recognizances in accordance with that paragraph, fix the amount of the recognizances with a view to their being taken subsequently in accordance with section 119 above.

[(1A) Where—

(a) on adjourning a case under [section 4(4)], 10(1), 17C or 18(4) above the court proposes to remand or further remand a person in custody; and

(b) he is before the court: and

(c) [. . .]*

(d) he is legally represented in that court,

---

† 1990 c.41 Sched. 18, para. 25.
* Repealed: Criminal Procedure & Investigations Act 1996.

it shall be the duty of the court—

    (i) to explain the effect of subsections (3A) and (3B) below to him in ordinary language; and

    (ii) to inform him in ordinary language that, notwithstanding the procedure for a remand without his being brought before a court, he would be brought before a court for the hearing and determination of at least every fourth application for his remand, and of every application for his remand heard at a time when it appeared to the court that he had no †[legal representative] acting for him in the case.

(1B) for the purposes of subsection (1A) above a person is to be treated as legally represented in a court if, but only if, he has the assistance of †[legal advisors] to represent him in the proceedings in that court.

(1C) After explaining to an accused as provided by subsection (1A) above the court shall ask him whether he consents to the hearing and determination of such applications in his absence.]

(2) Where the court fixes the amount of a recognizance under subsection (1) above or section 8 (3) of the Bail Act 1976 with a view to its being taken subsequently the court shall in the meantime commit the person so remanded to custody in accordance with paragraph (*a*) of the said subsection (1).

(3) Where a person is brought before the court after remand, the court may further remand him.

[(3A) Subject to subsection (3B) below, where a person has been remanded in custody, [and the remand was not a remand under section 128A below for a period exceeding 8 clear days,] the court may further remand him [(otherwise than in the exercise of the power conferred by that section)] on an adjournment under [section 4(4)], 10(1), 17C or 18(4) above without his being brought before it if it is satisfied—

(a)   that he gave his consent, either in response to a question under subsection (1C) above or otherwise, to the hearing and determination in his absence of any application for his remand on an adjournment of the case under any of those provisions; and

(b)   that he has not by virtue of this subsection been remanded without being brought before the court on more than two such applications immediately preceding the application which the court is hearing; and

(*c*)   [. . .]*

(d)   that he has not withdrawn his consent to their being so heard and determined.

(3B) The court may not exercise the power conferred by subsection (3A) above if it appears to the court, on an application for a further remand being made to it, that the person to whom the application relates has no †[legal representative] acting for him in the case (whether present in court or not).

† Repealed by Criminal Procedure and Investigations Act 1996.
* 1990 (c.41), Sched. 18, para. 25.

(3C) Where— **D–97**

(a) a person has been remanded in custody on an adjournment of a case under [section 4(4)], 10(1), 17C or 18(4) above; and

(b) an application is subsequently made for his further remand on such an adjournment; and

(c) he is not brought before the court which hears and determines the application; and

(d) that court is not satisfied as mentioned in subsection (3A) above,

the court shall adjourn the case and remand him in custody for the period for which it stands adjourned.

(3D) an adjournment under subsection (3C) above shall be for the shortest period that appears to the court to make it possible for the accused to be brought before it.

(3E) Where—

(a) on an adjournment of a case under [section 4(4)], 10(1), 17C or 18(4) above a person has been remanded in custody without being brought before the court; and

(b) it subsequently appears—

(i) to the court which remanded him in custody; or

(ii) to an alternate magistrates' court to which he is remanded under section 130 below,

that he ought not to have been remanded in custody in his absence, the court shall require him to be brought before it at the earliest time that appears to the court to be possible.]

(4) Where a person is remanded on bail under subsection (1) above the court may, where it remands him on bail in accordance with the Bail Act 1976 direct him to appear or, in any other case, direct that his recognizance be conditioned for his appearance—

(a) before that court at the end of the period of remand; or

(b) at every time and place to which during the course of the proceedings the hearing may be from time to time adjourned;

and, where it remands him on bail conditionally on his providing a surety [when it is proceeding with a view to transfer for trial] may direct that the recognizance of the surety be conditioned to secure that the person so bailed appears—

(c) at every time and place to which during the course of the proceedings the [proceedings] may be from time to time adjourned and also before the Crown Court in the event of the [proceedings against the person so bailed being transferred] for trial there.

(5) Where a person is directed to appear or a recognizance is conditioned for a **D–98** person's appearance in accordance with paragraph (b) or (c) of subsection (4) above, the fixing at any time of the time for him next to appear shall be deemed to be a remand; but nothing in this subsection or subsection (4) above shall deprive the court of power at any subsequent hearing to remand him afresh.

(6) Subject to the provisions of [sections 128A and] 129 below, a magistrates' court shall not remand a person for a period exceeding 8 clear days, except that—

(a)   if the court remands him on bail, it may remand him for a longer period if he and the other party consent;

(b)   where the court adjourns a trial under section 10(3) or 30 above, the court may remand him for the period of the adjournment;

(c)   where a person is charged with an offence triable either way, then, if it falls to the court to try the case summarily but the court is not at the time so constituted, and sitting in such a place, as will enable it to proceed with the trial, the court may remand him until the next occasion on which it will be practicable for the court to be so constituted, and to sit in such a place, as aforesaid, notwithstanding that the remand is for a period exceeding 8 clear days.

(7) A magistrates' court having power to remand a person in custody may, if the remand is for a period not exceeding 3 clear days, commit him to [detention at a police station]

[(8) Where a person is committed to detention at a police station under subsection (7) above—

(a)   he shall not be kept in such detention unless there is a need for him to be so detained for the purposes of inquiries into other offences;

(b)   if kept in such detention, he shall be brought back before the magistrates' court which committed him as soon as that need ceases;

(c)   he shall be treated as a person in police detention to whom the duties under section 39 of the Police and Criminal Evidence Act 1984 (responsibilities in relation to persons detained) relate;

(d)   his detention shall be subject to periodic review at the times set out in section 40 of that Act (review of police detention).]

Remands in custody for more than eight days

D–99   [128A.—(1) The Secretary of State may by order made by statutory instrument provide that this section shall have effect—

(a)   in an area specified in the order; or

(b)   in proceedings of a description so specified,

in relation to any accused person ("the accused") who has attained the age of 17.

(2) A magistrates' court may remand the accused in custody for a period exceeding 8 clear days if—

(a)   it has previously remanded him in custody for the same offence; and

(b)   he is before the court,

but only if, after affording the parties an opportunity to make representations, it has set a date on which it expects that it will be possible for the next stage in the proceedings, other than a hearing relating to a further remand in custody or on bail, to take place, and only—

(i)   for a period ending not later than that date; or

(ii) for a period of 28 clear days,

whichever is the less.

(3) Nothing in this section affects the right of the accused to apply for bail during the period of the remand.

(4) A statutory instrument containing an order under this section shall not be made unless a draft of the instrument has been laid before Parliament and been approved by a resolution of each House.]

This section has been in force since 1991 (order 91/2667).

Further remand

129.—(1) If a magistrates' court is satisfied that any person who has been D–100 remanded is unable by reason of illness or accident to appear or be brought before the court at the expiration of the period for which he was remanded, the court may, in his absence, remand him for a further time; and section 128(6) above shall not apply.

(2) Notwithstanding anything in section 128(1) above, the power of a court under subsection (1) above to remand a person on bail for a further time—

(a)   where he was granted bail in criminal proceedings, includes power to enlarge the recognizance of any surety for him to a later time;

(b)   where he was granted bail otherwise than in criminal proceedings, may be exercised by enlarging his recognizance and those of any sureties for him to a later time.

(3) Where a person remanded on bail is bound to appear before a magistrates' court at any time and the court has no power to remand him under subsection (1) above, the court may in his absence—

(a)   where he was granted bail in criminal proceedings appoint a later time as the time at which he is to appear and enlarge the recognizances of any sureties for him to that time;

(b)   where he was granted bail otherwise than in criminal proceedings, enlarge his recognizance and those of any sureties for him to a later time;

and the appointment of the time or the enlargement of his recognizance shall be deemed to be a further remand.

(4) Where a magistrates' court [transfers for trial proceedings against a person who has been remanded on bail] and the recognizance of any surety for him has been conditioned in accordance with paragraph (a) of subsection (4) of section 128 above the court may, in the absence of the surety, enlarge his recognizance so that he is bound to secure that the person [in respect of whom proceedings have been transferred] for trial appears also before the Crown Court.

Law Reform (Husband and Wife) Act 1962

Actions in tort between husband and wife

1.—(1) Subject to the provisions of this section, each of the parties to a marriage D–101 shall have the like right of action in tort against the other as if they were not married.

(2) Where an action in tort is brought by one of the parties to a marriage against the other during the subsistence of the marriage, the court may stay the action if it appears—

(a)   that no substantial benefit would accrue to either party from the continuation of the proceedings; or

(b)   that the question or questions in issue could more conveniently be disposed of on an application made under section seventeen of the Married Women's Property Act, 1882 (determination of questions between husband and wife as to the title to or possession of property);

and without prejudice to paragraph (b) of this subsection the court may, in such an action, either exercise any power which could be exercised on an application under the said section seventeen, or give such directions as it thinks fit for the disposal under that section of any question arising in the proceedings.

(3) Provision shall be made by rules of court for requiring the court to consider at an early stage of the proceedings whether the power to stay an action under subsection (2) of this section should or should not be exercised; [. . .]

(4) This section does not extend to Scotland.

Family Law Act 1986

Orders to which Part 1 applies

D–102   1.—(1) Subject to the following provisions of this section, in this Part "[Part 1 order]¹" means—

[(a) a section 8 order made by a court in England and Wales under the Children Act 1989, other than an order varying or discharging such an order]²;

(b) [not printed]

(c) [not printed]

[(d) an order made by a Court in England and Wales in the exercise of the inherent jurisdiction of the High Court with respect to children—

(i) so far as it gives care of a child to any person or provides for contact with, or the education of, a child; but

(ii) excluding an order varying or revoking such an order]³

Power to order recovery of child

D–103   34.—(1) Where—

(a)   a person is required by a [Part I order]¹, or an order for the enforcement of a [Part I order]¹, to give up a child to another person ("the person concerned"), and

¹ Words substituted by the Children Act 1989, s.108(5), Sched. 13, para. 62(1), (2)(a).
² Paragraph substituted by the Children Act 1989, s.108(5), Sched. 13, para. 63(1)(a).
³ Paragraph substituted by the Children Act 1989, s.108(5), Sched. 13, para. 63(1)(b).

(b)   the court which made the order imposing the requirement is satisfied that the child has not been given up in accordance with the order,

the court may make an order authorising an officer of the court or a constable to take charge of the child and deliver him to the person concerned.

(2) The authority conferred by subsection (1) above includes authority—

(a)   to enter and search any premises where the person acting in pursuance of the order has reason to believe the child may be found, and

(b)   to use such force as may be necessary to give effect to the purpose of the order.

(3) Where by virtue of—

[(a)   section 14 of the Children Act 1989],[4] or

(b)   Article 37 of the Domestic Proceedings (Northern Ireland) Order 1980,

a [Part I order][1] (or a provision of a [Part I Order][1]) may be enforced as if it were an order requiring a person to give up a child to another person, subsection (1) above shall apply as if the [Part I order][1] had included such a requirement.

(4) This section is without prejudice to any power conferred on a court by or under any other enactment or rule of law.

Criminal Justice Act 1982

Detention of persons aged [18] to 20 for default or contempt (as amended by CJA 1991, s.63(1), (5)).

9.—(1) In any case where, but for section 1(1) above, a court would have D–104 power—

(a)   to commit a person under 21 but not less than [18] years of age to prison for default in payment of a fine or any other sum of money; or

(b)   to make an order fixing a term of imprisonment in the event of such a default by such a person; or

(c)   to commit such a person to prison for contempt of court or any kindred offence,

the court shall have power, subject to section 1(5) above, to commit him to be detained under this section or, as the case may be, to make an order fixing a term of detention under this section in the event of default, for a term not exceeding the term of imprisonment.

(2) For the purposes of subsection (1) above, the power of a court to order a person to be imprisoned under section 23 of the Attachment of Earnings Act 1971 shall be taken to be a power to commit him to prison.

[4] Paragraph substituted by the Children Act 1989, s.108(5), Sched. 13, para. 70.

Contempt of Court Act 1981

Penalties for contempt and kindred offences

Proceedings in England and Wales

D–105   14.—(1) In any case where a court has power to commit a person to prison for contempt of court and (apart from this provision) no limitation applies to the period of committal, the committal shall (without prejudice to the power of the court to order his earlier discharge) be for a fixed term, and that term shall not on any occasion exceed two years in the case of committal by a superior court, or one month in the case of committal by an inferior court.

(2) In any case where an inferior court has power to fine a person for contempt of court and (apart from this provision) no limit applies to the amount of the fine, the fine shall not on any occasion exceed [£2,500].

[(2A) In the exercise of jurisdiction to commit for contempt of court or any kindred offence the court shall not deal with the offender by making an order under section 17 of the Criminal Justice Act 1982 (an attendance centre order) if it appears to the court, after considering any available evidence, that he is under 17 years of age.]

[(2A) A fine imposed under subsection (2) above shall be deemed, for the purposes of any enactment, to be a sum adjudged to be paid by a conviction.]

(3) [*Repealed by Criminal Justice Act 1982, Sched. 16.*]

(4) Each of the superior courts shall have the like power to make a hospital order or guardianship order under [section 37 of the Mental Health Act 1983] [or an interim hospital order under [section 38 of that Act]] in the case of a person suffering from mental illness or [severe mental impairment] who could otherwise be committed to prison for contempt of court as the Crown Court has under that section in the case of a person convicted of an offence.

[(4A) Each of the superior courts shall have the like power to make an order under [section 35 of the said Act of 1983] (remand for report on accused's mental condition) where there is reason to suspect that a person who could be committed to prison for contempt of court is suffering from mental illness or severe mental impairment as the Crown Court has under that section in the case of an accused person within the meaning of that section.]

[(4A) For the purposes of the preceding provisions of this section a county court shall be treated as a superior court and not as an inferior court.]

(5) The enactments specified in Part II of Schedule 2 shall have effect subject to the amendments set out in that Part, being amendments relating to the penalties and procedure in respect of certain offences of contempt in coroners' courts, county courts and magistrates' courts.

Amended by Mental Health (Amendment) Act 1982, s.65(1) and Sched. 3, Mental Health Act 1983, s.148 and Sched. 4, County Court (Penalties for Contempt Act 1983, Criminal Justice Act 1982, Scheds. 12 and 16 and S.I. 1984 No. 447 and the Criminal Justice Act 1993, s.65(3), (4) and Sched. 3. There are two subss. (2A) and (4A).

Administration of Justice Act 1960

Appeal to House of Lords in criminal cases

Right of appeal

1.—(1) Subject to the provisions of this section, an appeal shall lie to the House D–106 of Lords, at the instance of the defendant or the prosecutor,—

(a)   from any decision of a Divisional Court of the Queen's Bench Division in a criminal cause or matter;

(b)   [. . .]

(2) No appeal shall lie under this section except with the leave of the court below or of the House of Lords; and such leave shall not be granted unless it is certified by the court below that a point of law of general public importance is involved in the decision and it appears to that court or to the House of Lords, as the case may be, that the point is one which ought to be considered by that House.

(3) Section five of the Appellate Jurisdiction Act, 1876 (which regulates the composition of the House of Lords for the hearing and determination of appeals) shall apply to the hearing and determination of an appeal or application for leave to appeal under this section as it applies to the hearing and determination of an appeal under that Act; and any order of that House which provides for the hearing of such applications by a committee constituted in accordance with the said section five may direct that the decision of that committee shall be taken on behalf of the House.

(4) For the purpose of disposing of an appeal under this section the House of Lords may exercise any powers of the court below or may remit the case to that court.

(5) In this Act, unless the context otherwise requires, "leave to appeal" means leave to appeal to the House of Lords under this section.

(S.1(1)(b) repealed by the Criminal Appeal Act 1968, s.54, Sched. 7.)

Application for leave to appeal

2.—(1) Subject to the provisions of this section, an application to the court below for leave to appeal shall be made within the period of fourteen days beginning with the date of the decision of that court; and an application to the House of Lords for such leave shall be made within the period of fourteen days beginning with the date on which the application is refused by the court below.

(2) [. . .]

(3) Except in a case involving sentence of death, the House of Lords or the court below may, upon application made at any time by the defendant, extend the time within which an application may be made by him to that House or that court under subsection (1) of this section.

(S.2(2) repealed by the Criminal Appeal Act 1968, s.54, Sched. 7.)

Appeal in cases of contempt of court

D–107 13.—(1) Subject to the provisions of this section, an appeal shall lie under this section from any order or decision of a court in the exercise of jurisdiction to punish for contempt of court (including criminal contempt); and in relation to any such order or decision the provisions of this section shall have effect in substitution for any other enactment relating to appeals in civil or criminal proceedings.

(2) An appeal under this section shall lie in any case at the instance of the defendant and, in the case of an application for committal or attachment, at the instance of the applicant; and the appeal shall lie—

(a) from an order or decision of any inferior court not referred to in the next following paragraph, to a Divisional Court of the High Court;

(b) from an order or decision of a county court or any other inferior court from which appeals generally lie to the Court of Appeal, and from an order or decision of a single judge of the High Court, or of any court having the powers of the High Court or of a judge of that court, to the Court of Appeal;

(bb) from an order or decision of the Crown Court to the Court of Appeal;

(c) from an order or decision of a Divisional Court or the Court of Appeal (including a decision of either of those courts on an appeal under this section) and from an order or decision of the Court of Criminal Appeal or the Courts-Martial Appeal Court, to the House of Lords.

(3) The court to which an appeal is brought under this section may reverse or vary the order or decision of the court below, and make such other order as may be just; and without prejudice to the inherent powers of any court referred to in subsection (2) of this section, provision may be made by rules of court for authorising the release on bail of an appellant under this section.

(4) Subsections (2) to (4) of section one and section two of this Act shall apply to an appeal to the House of Lords under this section as they apply to an appeal to that House under the said section one, except that so much of the said subsection (2) as restricts the grant of leave to appeal shall apply only where the decision of the court below is a decision on appeal to that court under this section.

(5) In this section "court" includes any tribunal or person having power to punish for contempt; and references in this section to an order or decision of a court in the exercise of jurisdiction to punish for contempt of court include references—

(a) to an order or decision of the High Court, the Crown Court or a county court under any enactment enabling that court to deal with an offence as if it were contempt of court;

(b) to an order or decision of a county court, under section 14, 92 or 118 of the County Courts Act 1984;

(c) to an order or decision of a magistrates' court under subsection (3) of section 63 of the Magistrates' Courts Act 1980,

but do not include references to orders under section five of the Debtors Act 1869, or under any provision of the Magistrates' Courts Act 1980, or the County Courts Act 1984, except those referred to in paragraphs (b) and (c) of this subsection and

274

except sections 38 and 142 of the last mentioned Act so far as those sections confer jurisdiction in respect of contempt of court.

(6) This section does not apply to a conviction or sentence in respect of which an appeal lies under Part I of the Criminal Appeal Act 1968, or to a decision of the criminal division of the Court of Appeal under that Part of that Act.

Amended by the Courts Act 1971, Sched. 8, para. 40(1) and Sched. 11, and the Criminal Appeal Act 1968, Sched. 5 and S.C.A. 1981, s.152(4) and Sched. 7 and the County Courts Act 1984, Sched. 2.

Protection from Harassment Act 1997

At the time of writing sections 1, 2, 4, 5 and 7–12 are in force. Readers are advised to consult *Current Law* for the implementation dates of the remaining sections.

ARRANGEMENT OF SECTIONS

ENGLAND AND WALES

Section   D–108

SCOTLAND

GENERAL

An Act to make provision for protecting persons from harassment and similar conduct.
[21 st March 1997]

BE IT ENACTED by the Queen's most Excellent Majesty, by and with the advice and consent of the Lords Spiritual and Temporal, and Commons, in this present Parliament assembled, and by the authority of the same, as follows:—

ENGLAND AND WALES

D–109   1.—(1) A person must not pursue a course of conduct—

(a)   which amounts to harassment of another, and

(b)   which he knows or ought to know amounts to harassment of the other.

(2) For the purposes of this section, the person whose course of conduct is in question ought to know that it amounts to harassment of another if a reasonable person in possession of the same information would think the course of conduct amounted to harassment of the other.

(3) Subsection (1) does not apply to a course of conduct if the person who pursued it shows—

(a)   that it was pursued for the purpose of preventing or detecting crime,

(b)   that it was pursued under any enactment or rule of law or to comply with any condition or requirement imposed by any person under any enactment, or

(c)   that in the particular circumstances the pursuit of the course of conduct was reasonable.

D–110   2.—(1) A person who pursues a course of conduct in breach of section 1 is guilty of an offence.

(2) A person guilty of an offence under this section is liable on summary conviction to imprisonment for a term not exceeding six months, or a fine not exceeding level 5 on the standard scale, or both.

(3) In section 24(2) of the Police and Criminal Evidence Act 1984 (arrestable offences), after paragraph (m) there is inserted—

"(n) an offence under section 2 of the Protection from Harassment Act 1997 (harassment).".

D–111   3.—(1) An actual or apprehended breach of section 1 may be the subject of a claim in civil proceedings by the person who is or may be the victim of the course of conduct in question.

(2) On such a claim, damages may be awarded for (among other things) any anxiety caused by the harassment and any financial loss resulting from the harassment.

(3) Where—

(a)   in such proceedings the High Court or a county court grants an injunction for the purpose of restraining the defendant from pursuing any conduct which amounts to harassment, and

(b)   the plaintiff considers that the defendant has done anything which he is prohibited from doing by the injunction, the plaintiff may apply for the issue of a warrant for the arrest of the defendant.

(4) An application under subsection (3) may be made—

(a) where the injunction was granted by the High Court, to a judge of that court, and

(b) where the injunction was granted by a county court, to a judge or district judge of that or any other county court.

(5) The judge or district judge to whom an application under subsection (3) is made may only issue a warrant if—

(a) the application is substantiated on oath, and

(b) the judge or district judge has reasonable grounds for believing that the defendant has done anything which he is prohibited from doing by the injunction.

(6) Where—

(a) the High Court or a county court grants an injunction for the purpose mentioned in subsection (3)(a), and

(b) without reasonable excuse the defendant does anything which he is prohibited from doing by the injunction,

he is guilty of an offence.

(7) Where a person is convicted of an offence under subsection (6) in respect of any conduct, that conduct is not punishable as a contempt of court.

(8) A person cannot be convicted of an offence under subsection (6) in respect of any conduct which has been punished as a contempt of court.

(9) A person guilty of an offence under subsection (6) is liable—

(a) on conviction on indictment, to imprisonment for a term not exceeding five years, or a fine, or both, or

(b) on summary conviction, to imprisonment for a term not exceeding six months, or a fine not exceeding the statutory maximum, or both.

4.—(1) A person whose course of conduct causes another to fear, on at least two **D–112** occasions, that violence will be used against him is guilty of an offence if he knows or ought to know that his course of conduct will cause the other so to fear on each of those occasions.

(2) For the purposes of this section, the person whose course of conduct is in question ought to know that it will cause another to fear that violence will be used against him on any occasion if a reasonable person in possession of the same information would think the course of conduct would cause the other so to fear on that occasion.

(3) It is a defence for a person charged with an offence under this section to show that—

(a) his course of conduct was pursued for the purpose of preventing or detecting crime,

(b) his course of conduct was pursued under any enactment or rule of law or to comply with any condition or requirement imposed by any person under any enactment, or

(c)   the pursuit of his course of conduct was reasonable for the protection of himself or another or for the protection of his or another's property.

(4) A person guilty of an offence under this section is liable—

(a)   on conviction on indictment, to imprisonment for a term not exceeding five years, or a fine, or both, or

(b)   on summary conviction, to imprisonment for a term not exceeding six months, or a fine not exceeding the statutory maximum, or both.

(5) If on the trial on indictment of a person charged with an offence under this section the jury find him not guilty of the offence charged, they may find him guilty of an offence under section 2.

(6) The Crown Court has the same powers and duties in relation to a person who is by virtue of subsection (5) convicted before it of an offence under section 2 as a magistrates' court would have on convicting him of the offence.

D–113   5.—(1) A court sentencing or otherwise dealing with a person ("the defendant") convicted of an offence under section 2 or 4 may (as well as sentencing him or dealing with him in any other way) make an order under this section.

(2) The order may, for the purpose of protecting the victim of the offence, or any other person mentioned in the order, from further conduct which—

(a)   amounts to harassment, or

(b)   will cause a fear of violence,

prohibit the defendant from doing anything described in the order.

(3) The order may have effect for a specified period or until further order.

(4) The prosecutor, the defendant or any other person mentioned in the order may apply to the court which made the order for it to be varied or discharged by a further order.

(5) If without reasonable excuse the defendant does anything which he is prohibited from doing by an order under this section, he is guilty of an offence.

(6) A person guilty of an offence under this section is liable—

(a)   on conviction on indictment, to imprisonment for a term not exceeding five years, or a fine, or both, or

(b)   on summary conviction, to imprisonment for a term not exceeding six months, or a fine not exceeding the statutory maximum, or both.

D–114   6. In section 11 of the Limitation Act 1980 (special time limit for actions in respect of personal injuries), after subsection (1) there is inserted—

"(1A) This section does not apply to any action brought for damages under section 3 of the Protection from Harassment Act 1997."

D–115   7.—(1) This section applies for the interpretation of sections 1 to 5.

(2) References to harassing a person include alarming the person or causing the person distress.

(3) A "course of conduct" must involve conduct on at least two occasions.

(4) "Conduct" includes speech.

SCOTLAND

8.—(1)Every individual has a right to be free from harassment and, accordingly, a **D–116** person must not pursue a course of conduct which amounts to harassment of another and—

(a)   is intended to amount to harassment of that person; or

(b)   occurs in circumstances where it would appear to a reasonable person that it would amount to harassment of that person.

(2) An actual or apprehended breach of subsection (1) may be the subject of a claim in civil proceedings by the person who is or may be the victim of the course of conduct in question; and any such claim shall be known as an action of harassment.

(3) For the purposes of this section—

"conduct" includes speech;

"harassment" of a person includes causing the person alarm or distress; and

a course of conduct must involve conduct on at least two occasions.

(4) It shall be a defence to any action of harassment to show that the course of conduct complained of—

(a)   was authorised by, under or by virtue of any enactment or rule of law;

(b)   was pursued for the purpose of preventing or detecting crime; or

(c)   was, in the particular circumstances, reasonable.

(5) In an action of harassment the court may, without prejudice to any other remedies which it may grant—

(a)   award damages;

(b)   grant—

(i) interdict or interim interdict;

(ii) if it is satisfied that it is appropriate for it to do so in order to protect the person from further harassment, an order, to be known as a "non-harassment order", requiring the defender to refrain from such conduct in relation to the pursuer as may be specified in the order for such period (which includes an indeterminate period) as may be so specified,

but a person may not be subjected to the same prohibitions in an interdict or interim interdict and a non-harassment order at the same time.

(6) The damages which may be awarded in an action of harassment include damages for any anxiety caused by the harassment and any financial loss resulting from it.

(7) Without prejudice to any right to seek review of any interlocutor, a person against whom a non-harassment order has been made, or the person for whose protection the order was made, may apply to the court by which the order was made for revocation of or a variation of the order and, on any such application, the court may revoke the order or vary it in such manner as it considers appropriate.

(8) In section 10(1) of the Damages (Scotland) Act 1976 (interpretation), in the definition of "personal injuries", after "to reputation" there is inserted ", or injury

resulting from harassment actionable under section 8 of the Protection from Harassment Act 1997".

D–117 9.—(1) Any person who is found to be in breach of a non-harassment order made under section 8 is guilty of an offence and liable—

(a) on conviction on indictment, to imprisonment for a term not exceeding five years or to a fine, or to both such imprisonment and such fine; and

(b) on summary conviction, to imprisonment for a period not exceeding six months or to a fine not exceeding the statutory maximum, or to both such imprisonment and such fine.

(2) A breach of a non-harassment order shall not be punishable other than in accordance with subsection (1).

D–118 10.—(1) After section 18A of the Prescription and Limitation (Scotland) Act 1973 there is inserted the following section—

"Actions of harassment.

18B.—(1) This section applies to actions of harassment (within the meaning of section 8 of the Protection from Harassment Act 1997) which include a claim for damages.

(2) Subject to subsection (3) below and to section 19A of this Act, no action to which this section applies shall be brought unless it is commenced within a period of 3 years after—

(a) the date on which the alleged harassment ceased; or

(b) the date, (if later than the date mentioned in paragraph (a) above) on which the pursuer in the action became, or on which, in the opinion of the court, it would have been reasonably practicable for him in all the circumstances to have become, aware, that the defender was a person responsible for the alleged harassment or the employer or principal of such a person.

(3) In the computation of the period specified in subsection (2) above there shall be disregarded any time during which the person who is alleged to have suffered the harassment was under legal disability by reason of nonage or unsoundness of mind.".

(2) In subsection (1) of section 19A of that Act (power of court to override time-limits), for "section 17 or section 18 and section 18A" there is substituted "section 17, 18, 18A or 18B".

D–119 11. After section 234 of the Criminal Procedure (Scotland) Act 1995 there is inserted the following section—

"Non-harassment orders

Non-harassment orders

234A.—(1) Where a person is convicted of an offence involving harassment of a person ("the victim"), the prosecutor may apply to the court to make a non-harassment order against the offender requiring him to refrain from such conduct in relation to the victim as may be specified in the order for such period (which includes an indeterminate period) as may be so specified, in addition to any other disposal which may be made in relation to the offence.

(2) On an application under subsection (1) above the court may, if it is satisfied on a balance of probabilities that it is appropriate to do so in order to protect the victim from further harassment, make a non-harassment order.

(3) A non-harassment order made by a criminal court shall be taken to be a sentence for the purposes of any appeal and, for the purposes of this subsection "order" includes any variation or revocation of such an order made under subsection (6) below.

(4) Any person who is found to be in breach of a non-harassment order shall be guilty of an offence and liable—

(a)   on conviction on indictment, to imprisonment for a term not exceeding 5 years or to a fine, or to both such imprisonment and such fine; and

(b)   on summary conviction, to imprisonment for a period not exceeding 6 months or to a fine not exceeding the statutory maximum, or to both such imprisonment and such fine.

(5) The Lord Advocate, in solemn proceedings, and the prosecutor, in summary proceedings, may appeal to the High Court against any decision by a court to refuse an application under subsection (1) above; and on any such appeal the High Court may make such order as it considers appropriate.

(6) The person against whom a non-harassment order is made, or the prosecutor at whose instance the order is made, may apply to the court which made the order for its revocation or variation and, in relation to any such application the court concerned may, if it is satisfied on a balance of probabilities that it is appropriate to do so, revoke the order or vary it in such manner as it thinks fit, but not so as to increase the period for which the order is to run.

(7) For the purposes of this section "harassment" shall be construed in accordance with section 8 of the Protection from Harassment Act 1997.".

GENERAL

12.—(1) If the Secretary of State certifies that in his opinion anything done by a D–120 specified person on a specified occasion related to—

(a)   national security,
(b)   the economic well-being of the United Kingdom, or
(c)   the prevention or detection of serious crime,
and was done on behalf of the Crown, the certificate is conclusive evidence that this Act does not apply to any conduct of that person on that occasion.

(2) In subsection (1), "specified" means specified in the certificate in question.

(3) A document purporting to be a certificate under subsection (1) is to be received in evidence and, unless the contrary is proved, be treated as being such a certificate.

D–121   13. An Order in Council made under paragraph 1(1)(b) of Schedule 1 to the Northern Ireland Act 1974 which contains a statement that it is made only for purposes corresponding to those of sections 1 to 7 and 12 of this Act—

(a)   shall not be subject to sub-paragraphs (4) and (5) of paragraph 1 of that Schedule (affirmative resolution of both Houses of Parliament), but

(b)   shall be subject to annulment in pursuance of a resolution of either House of Parliament.

D–122   14.—(1) Sections 1 to 7 extend to England and Wales only.

(2) Sections 8 to 11 extend to Scotland only.

(3) This Act (except section 13) does not extend to Northern Ireland.

15.—(1) Sections 1, 2, 4, 5 and 7 to 12 are to come into force on such day as the Secretary of State may by order made by statutory instrument appoint.

(2) Sections 3 and 6 are to come into force on such day as the Lord Chancellor may by order made by statutory instrument appoint.

(3) Different days may be appointed under this section for different purposes.

16. This Act may be cited as the Protection from Harassment Act 1997.

INDEX

SA

346 .
420
15
DEH